Playing with Print

Second Edition

Fun Activities and Ideas for Fostering Emergent Literacy

Carol Ann Bloom

Aligns to International Reading Association and National Council of Teachers of English Standards

A
GOOD
YEAR
BOOK™

Good Year Books
Tucson, Arizona

Dedication

*This book is dedicated to my parents, Richard and Norma Bloom,
and to my sister, Sherry, for all their love and encouragement.*

Playing with Print: Fostering Emergent Literacy contains lessons and activities that reinforce and develop skills spanning the early childhood curriculum as defined by the International Reading Association and National Council of Teachers of English as appropriate for students in preschool to Grade 1. The activities in the book include exposure to a wide range of print materials; use of spoken, written, and visual language within all areas of the classroom and dramatic play settings; experience with a wide range of print materials; recognition of the value and purpose of print as a necessary part of daily actions and communications; experience with open-ended problems; use of print and non-print resources; development of an understanding of diversity in language and print use; use of spoken, written, and visual language to accomplish purposes and goals; and participation as knowledgeable, reflective, and creative members of a literacy-friendly classroom community. See www.goodyearbooks.com for information on how lessons correlate to specific standards.

Good Year Books

Our titles are available for most basic curriculum subjects plus many enrichment areas. For information on other Good Year Books and to place orders, contact your local bookseller or educational dealer, or visit our website at www.goodyearbooks.com. For a complete catalog, please contact:

Good Year Books
P.O. Box 91858
Tucson, AZ 85752-1858
www.goodyearbooks.com

Cover Redesign: Sean O'Neill
Original Cover Design: Karen Kohn & Associates, Ltd.
Text Design: Dan Miedaner
Drawings: Yoshi Miyake

Contents

Chapter 4: The Role of the Teacher

Appendices 1–22

How to Use This Book

What Is Emergent Literacy?

Literacy is the ability to read and write. Emergent literacy refers to the beginnings of this ability in young children as they become aware of print and its many uses. Although some degree of this awareness is a natural occurrence (we have all witnessed a two-year-old recognizing the words Disney, McDonald's®, STOP, or food brand names), you can greatly enhance the development of emergent literacy in all early childhood curriculum areas by creating a more stimulating learning environment and providing a wide range of exciting play experiences.

Why Foster Emergent Literacy through Play?

Attention to print, recognition of print, and involvement with print are crucial steps along the path to conventional reading and writing. Too often, children are introduced to print in a realm outside their own experiences. Planned reading readiness experiences often consist of stencils, worksheets, flashcards, letter-match games, and other abstract activities. These activities are disconnected from the interests and endeavors of a child's world and viewed by many children as "work."

When children enjoy meaningful play experiences in a print-rich environment, they naturally attach meaning to the printed word and build positive attitudes toward activities involving written language. Through play, children can be given countless opportunities to use literacy tools. Any time an activity is child-initiated or self-selected, it immediately takes on more relevance and importance to the child. Perceived as play, these exposures to literacy will be tangible and lasting, providing a solid foundation for conventional reading and writing.

How Will This Book Help You Plan and Implement Emergent Literacy Activities?

The purpose of this book is to present a multitude of ways to incorporate the many functions of print and literacy into every aspect of the early childhood curriculum. The book is divided into four chapters. You may select, adapt, and change any of the procedures to meet the needs of your own classroom, based on environment, materials, curriculum, and developmental levels.

Chapter 1: Environment

includes suggestions and examples of adding print to the classroom with a variety of labeling techniques. This section also provides ideas for classroom organization and arrangement, including the use of furnishings as space dividers and the construction of dividers from readily available materials.

Chapter 2: Curriculum

presents a variety of ways to incorporate the many functions of print and literacy into every aspect of the classroom. Each domain of the curriculum is related to emergent literacy through activities and projects that add print and provide practice using literacy props and tools in every part of the child's day. The goal is to provide children with ordinary items from their environment that demonstrate logical reasons and purposes for letters and print. They are natural choices in the course of play, offering information and enjoyable experiences with literacy without the risk of failure. This section identifies an eclectic assortment of procedures for creating a classroom that invites, fosters, and nurtures the early gleanings of literacy.

Chapter 3: Dramatic Play

provides ideas for themes and props to enhance the role-playing areas of the classroom. This type of symbolic or pretend play allows children to actively practice literacy behaviors in the context of a pretend play setting. The prop lists for each of the themed centers include a combination of scenario props, dress-up props, and literacy-related props. While scenario and dress-up props contribute to the realism of the play setting, literacy props provide children with opportunities to practice a variety of literate behaviors to enhance their play. Suggestions for sources and construction of literacy props accompany each Dramatic Play center.

Chapter 4: The Role of the Teacher

provides suggestions for becoming a facilitator of emergent literacy in the classroom. After preparing the environment, incorporating print and other literacy props, and implementing activities, the teacher's role is that of spectator, advisor, resource, and scribe. This section addresses each role, providing examples and sample dialogue.

Perhaps there is nothing so enjoyable as watching young children on the brink of discovering the connections between the printed word and reading. The early childhood educator is in the unique and fortunate position of being able to affect beginning attitudes toward reading and writing. Children may view literacy processes and materials either as "schoolwork" or as a purposeful part of life that contributes to independence and self-satisfaction. Much of this attitude has to do with first experiences. First contacts with literacy can be formal and separate from the child's world or exploratory and connected to something children do best—play.

It is my wish that early childhood educators will elect the latter method and, with this book as a guide, allow each child to choose, from a vast assortment of literacy props and experiences, their own paths to the same destination: proficiency in the skills of literacy and an ever-growing appreciation of the written word.

—Carol Ann Bloom

Note: All measurements are in the U.S. Customary system. To convert to metric, use the chart below:

inches x 2.54 = centimeters

feet x .3048 = meters

ounces x 29.57 = milliliters

ounces x .03 = liters

1 cup = 8 oz. = 237 ml = .24 l

1 tablespoon = 1/2 oz. = 14.8 ml

1 teaspoon = 1/3 tablespoon = 4.9 ml

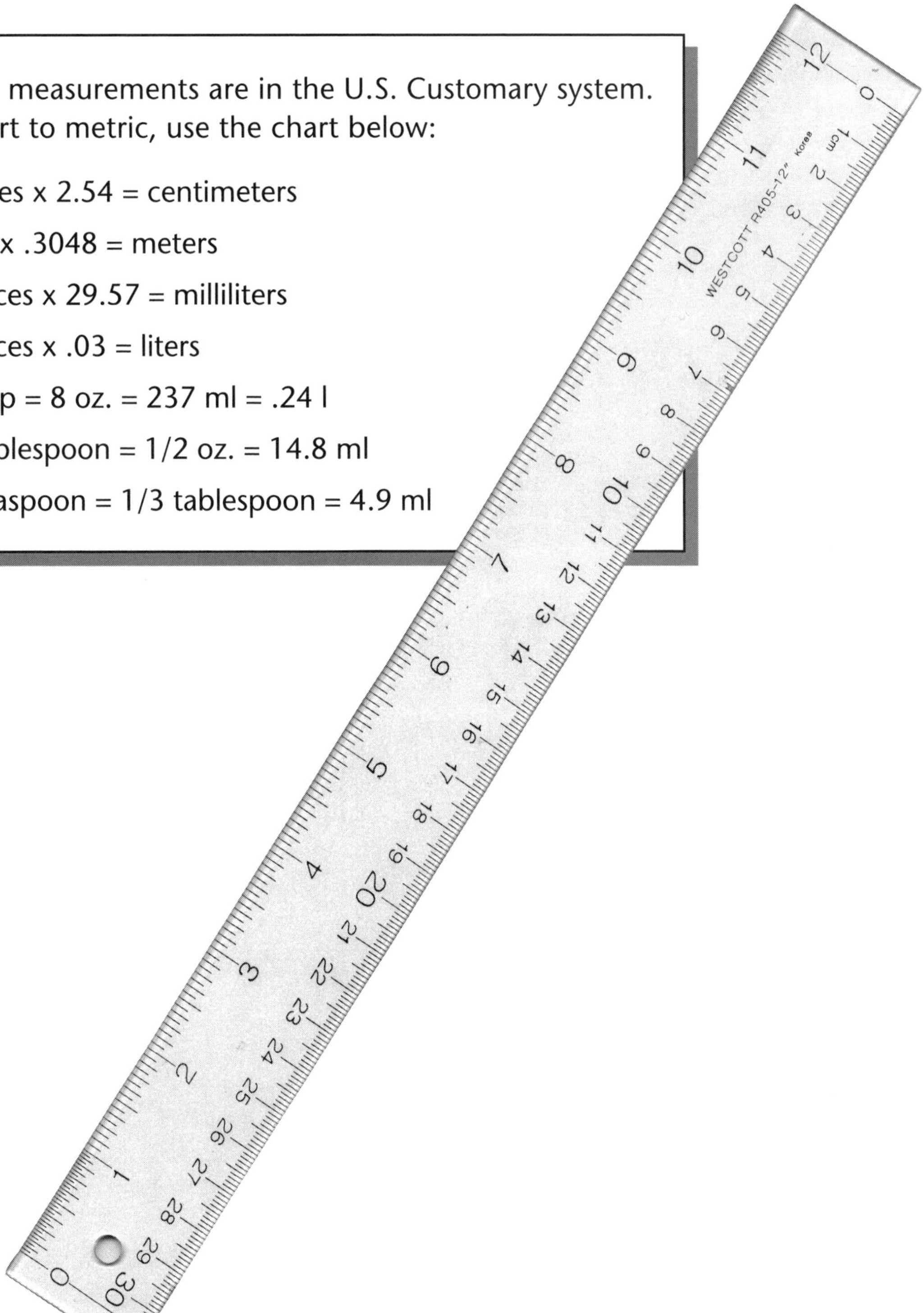

4

Environment

How to Visibly Add Print to the Classroom

One of the first ways children attach meaning to the printed word is through the print they see in their environment. Before initiating any literacy program, pay close attention to the classroom environment—both the physical setup, discussed on p. 23, and the print found in the classroom, the subject of the following discussions.

The literate classroom will make use of print in countless ways. Children's names, labels, lists, maps, directions, experience charts, word webs, titles, schedules, and labeled photos and artwork will be visible everywhere. This section provides suggestions for adding print to the classroom environment through various labeling techniques.

Types of Labels

Labeling is much more than a piece of paper saying DOOR hanging on a doorknob. This chapter provides directions for more effective labeling activities, including ways to incorporate children's names in the environment.

Labeling, as it is discussed here, is divided into two main groups: Types of Labels and the Forms of Labels each type can take. The five Types of Labels are Identification Labels, which identify or name objects and materials; Location Labels, which locate or help find them; Interest Area Labels, which name various areas and centers in the classroom; Outdoor Labels, which take print to an environment beyond the classroom; and Children's Name Labels, which include the classroom population in the environmental print. The form of labeling used will depend on the item(s) to be labeled, the purpose of the label, and the space available. Most significantly, the variety of forms fill the need for diverse and interesting uses of print. The eight forms of labeling discussed are Arrow Labels, Cube Labels, Free-standing Labels, Necklace Labels, Paper Bag Labels, Stand-up Labels, Tactile Labels, and Tent Labels.

Identification Labels

Identification Labels display the name of the object, in bold print, heightening children's awareness of the symbolic nature of print. This is the type of labeling found in most classrooms.

Label fixtures (doors, windows, sink), furnishings (table, chair, easel), toys and playthings (blocks, puzzles, beads), supplies (paper, paint, markers, tape), and personal items (coats, paint smocks, toothbrushes).

Making Identification Labels

Cut labels in various sizes from construction paper. Use a black marker to print labels. To make labels stand out, add a border of another color, but avoid overdecorating. Alternatively, back labels with a different color of (similar weight) paper cut larger to make the labels more noticeable.

Craft foam is an excellent material for label making. Write directly on craft foam with markers. This makes a colorful, sturdy label, perfect for indoor and outdoor use. You can also place craft foam labels in sand and water play areas.

Using Identification Labels

Hang Identification Labels directly on the named item, at children's eye level. This works well for labeling fixtures and furnishings. When labeling toys and supplies, put the Identification Labels directly on shelves. You can attach a second set of labels to containers holding the items. Fasten these labels to the front or top of the containers, or lay the label directly on top of the toys or supplies in the container. When children use the items, they can set aside the label and replace it when cleaning up. The touching and manipulating of the label is, in itself, an indirect experience with print and literacy. Children also have the opportunity to observe a word match between the container label and the shelf label each time they use the items.

Involving Children

Let children help hang Identification Labels. Set aside a group time for this purpose so all children can take part and observe the labels being hung. Children can also assist in the construction of the labels—for example, mounting them on larger paper.

If the labels include a foreign language (see Tips), invite a child who has experience with the language in his or her home to share the words with the class. The child's parents may also attend a group time to introduce the new words and help with pronunciations.

Rather than label an entire classroom overnight, begin with a few Identification Labels at a time. This will prevent children from becoming overwhelmed and foster a gradual awareness of each new addition to the environment. It may be advantageous to label furnishings first, the art area several days later, toy shelves next, and so on.

- When labeling shelf items, consider putting a small picture of the item in the corner of the label or directly under the word. Use catalog pictures (outdated supply and toy catalogs are a great source), draw the object, or trace around it (labels may need to be larger to accommodate traced objects). This method works especially well for toddlers.

- Use lowercase letters for the shelf labels and uppercase letters for the matching container labels. This gives children an opportunity to observe the same word written in two forms, especially good practice for older preschoolers.

- Explore a foreign language by labeling some objects twice, applying both a primary- and a secondary-language label. Set the foreign-language label apart from the English label by using a different shape of paper, such as an oval, or writing in another color, such as red.

Location Labels

In contrast to Identification Labels, which tell the child "what," Location Labels tell "where." This labeling helps children locate, find, or return objects. It shows them how helpful it can be to understand print. Label closed containers, drawers, and other storage areas where toys and supplies are kept but are not clearly visible. Location Labels require more attention than other types of labels because children must be aware of the Location Label on the outside of closed storage areas in order to obtain items within.

Making Location Labels

Follow directions for making Identification Labels. Some Location Labels may need to be smaller to fit the areas they will occupy. A small picture on the label is helpful, at least until children become accustomed to using the labels.

Using Location Labels

Attach Location Labels to easily accessed bins, cupboard doors, and other storage areas where children can find toys and supplies that they can use freely. If drawers and cupboards are in short supply, create closed storage areas using shoe boxes, egg cartons, or even paper lunch bags. Label these containers, indicating what is inside, just as you would drawers and cupboard doors; keep them on shelves mixed in with open toy baskets and art supply containers.

Involving Children

As with Identification Labels, children can help with the construction and placement of Location Labels. They can also fill and refill containers, bags, and boxes. Place all supplies on one table and labeled containers on another, allowing children to sort the supplies and fill the containers according to the label.

Though labeling helps keep a classroom tidy, expect labels to get mixed up and items to be placed in the wrong bin. If this occurs, have children sort the items into their proper places—either on the spot or during a special group time.

- When children become accustomed to Location Labels and have had ample time to use them, remove picture clues from the labels.

Interest Area Labels

Designate various interest areas, play spaces, and learning centers in the classroom with eye-catching Interest Area Labels. These labels should be distinctive, fairly large, and separate from other labeling in the area. While Free-standing Labels (p. 16) and giant Tent Labels (p. 21) work well, labels that hang from the ceiling, lights, doorways, or windows have the advantage of being as large as necessary and not block valuable floor space. Remember, as important as print is to the early childhood classroom, it must never get in the way of play. Labels that use too much space, need to be moved regularly to accommodate play, or are often found under playthings are probably not serving their purpose. Hang labels safely above children's eye level, over the space being named. Draw attention to the label with color, large letters, or unique hanging ideas.

Making Interest Area Labels

When constructing hanging Interest Area Labels, put as much thought into how to hang the label as how to make it. Often, the method used to suspend the label generates much interest and attention. In so doing, it serves one of the main purposes of labeling: giving young children a variety of opportunities to develop an awareness of print.

Experiment with a variety of sign shapes: the basic circle, square, triangle, heart, and diamond as well as animal, teddy bear, house, and car shapes. Keep shaped signs simple: Use outlines or silhouettes without a lot of details, such as facial features and windows, to avoid detracting from the lettering on the label. Shapes that relate directly to the area or center being named contribute greatly to children's recognition of the word. For example, hang the shape of a paint-brush labeled PAINT over the easel painting area, a car shape labeled CARS over the vehicle play area, or a BOOKS sign featuring a variety of book jackets over the library.

Using Interest Area Labels

Hang Interest Area Labels on yarn, string, rope, or ribbon, attaching them in the center with one piece or at each corner using two pieces. Try a paper spiral, paper chain, or lace-around label for something different. Look around your classroom for other good "hang-up" materials: a Slinky® cut shorter, a chain of old shoelaces, braids of yarn, lengths of craft foam, or strings of wooden beads. For labeling areas where more than one word is needed, try a fun and eye-catching "clothesline of labels," using clothespins to suspend letters or labels from the line.

Involving Children

One of the most enjoyable ways to include children in making Interest Area Labels is to encourage them to help with the "hanger." Children can put together paper chain links, cut spirals, and lace-up signs pre-punched with holes.

Instead of printing labels with a marker, stencil letters onto dark-colored paper, cut them out, and glue them onto a lighter background. This will enhance visibility—a distinct advantage, because these labels are often viewed from a distance.

- Use the Tent Label (p. 21) idea to make giant Tent Labels that can be placed on the floor to identify interest areas. One side names the area; the other side tells the number of children allowed or shows a picture relating to the area. To make sturdy floor-sized Tent Labels, cut two adjoining sides from any size cardboard box and set the structure vertically or horizontally.

- Other forms of labeling that can be adapted to Floor Labels for Interest Areas are Free-standing Labels (p. 16) (both detergent box and plastic jug types), Paper Bag Labels (p. 18), and Stand-up Labels (p. 18) made on a large scale. Even a large cardboard box that is covered, decorated, and labeled makes a distinctive Interest Area Label.

Outdoor Labels

Don't forget the great outdoors when labeling! This is an area where children spend some of their most pleasurable time, yet one in which they are unaccustomed to seeing print. Why not take advantage of this situation by adding Outside Labels to a playground or other outside play area? A variety of label types (Identification Labels and Location Labels) as well as label forms (Arrow Labels, Free-standing Labels, etc.) work very well here.

Making Outdoor Labels

The main things to consider when making Outdoor Labels are durability and mobility. Label many outdoor items with simple Identification Labels: TREES, FENCE, GATE, GARDEN, PICNIC TABLE, BENCH. Cut labels from construction paper and print letters with black markers. Slip labels into plastic bags and tape closed. Attach bagged labels to a large wooden block or several smaller blocks taped together. Use tape or yarn to secure labels to wood and place labels near the object being labeled.

Craft foam is an excellent material for outdoor labels. It is sturdy and fairly weatherproof. Be certain to use permanent markers on craft foam and other materials being used outdoors.

Make Location Labels for the playground or other outside areas the same way you did those for the inside. Use tape or clothespins to anchor labels to crates or bins of outdoor toys.

Construct Arrow Labels (p. 14) to indicate direction and remind children to play safely. Place labels on climbers, slides, and swing areas to show high, up, down, low, under.

Follow the instructions for Free-standing Labels (p. 16) to construct Outdoor Labels that you can move inside or easily store with playground toys at the end of the day.

Try a variation of the Necklace Label (p. 17)—using longer yarn—for hanging on playground equipment. You can remove these labels and take them inside. Be certain to tie Necklace Labels high enough so that children won't catch their feet in them when playing.

Make Tent Labels (p. 21) with giant cardboard boxes. These are sturdy enough for outdoor use and work especially well as traffic signs, bike path markers, and bases or score keepers for ball games of all kinds.

Using Outdoor Labels

Use Free-standing Labels to name designated areas, indicate the number of children permitted in an area, or create signs that will enhance play situations, such as STOP, SLOW, BENCH, GARAGE, and PARKING LOT.

Tie Necklace Labels to trees, climbers, and fences using heavy-duty yarn or rope that does not knot too easily.

Involving Children

Involve children by having them help with lacing yarn, cutting paper, putting labels in plastic bags, and taping labels to blocks.

Alternatively, label the area independently of children, letting them discover the labeling on their own. Children's awareness of print in a place not normally associated with it will make it more noticeable and thus more interesting.

Involve children in the placement of labels each time playground toys and outdoor equipment are set out and cleaned up. Regular practice with label set-up strengthens children's familiarity with the print and object names.

Whichever type and form of labeling techniques you use in the outdoor area, be prepared for labels to be moved, kicked, run over, and even "hauled off" from time to time. Readjust them when time permits and encourage children to "deliver" them back to their appropriate spots. The focus here is integrating print with outdoor fun and making children aware of its existence. As children get used to the labels, they will help to keep them at their designated spots. Do not discourage playing with the labels.

- Don't forget chalk as a tool for spontaneous, though temporary, labeling.

- If you know a carpenter or have a classroom parent who enjoys woodworking, wood plaques with raised wood letters make ideal Outdoor Labels. If climbers, sandboxes, and other pieces of outdoor equipment are wooden, nail plaques directly to the equipment, making them an interesting part of the outside area with which children can interact year after year.

- Laminate Outdoor Labels or cover with clear Contac® paper for added protection against the elements.

Children's Name Labels

Among the many examples of print that children should find in their environment is their own printed name. Few things are as powerful or appealing to a child as this. Awareness of their printed name often engenders in children an interest for other print, particularly if such print is used in conjunction with their name.

Making Children's Names Labels

Use craft foam or construction paper to make several labels for each child. Place them in a container for easy access.

All types of labels work well for children's names: Tent Labels (p. 21), Arrow Labels (p. 14), Paper Bag Labels (p. 18), and Necklace Labels (p. 17).

Include paper for Children's Name Labels in a Label-making Box (see p. 14) so that names can be made on the spot, as needed.

Using Children's Name Labels

Affix Children's Name Labels to lockers, baskets, cubbies, or bins that hold personal belongings. Label chairs, tables, and other individual work or play areas. Helper charts, birthday displays, photos, and artwork should also exhibit names.

For a further extension of classroom labeling, combine children's names with other words in the environment. Use children's names with the following activities, which you will find throughout this book:

♦ show-and-tell items
♦ an accomplishment, such as a completed puzzle, a building project, a clay project, a self-made book
♦ a news event
♦ an experience chart
♦ a rebus message
♦ graphing activities
♦ "Question of the Day" activities
♦ "Waiting Lists" for activities
♦ personal mail boxes or message boards
♦ "Child of the Week" activity
♦ name puzzles
♦ bulletin boards combining art, quotes, or ideas and children's names

Involving Children

When the need for a name label arises, encourage children to sort through the name labels and find their own.

Have children print their own name label using the supplies in the Label-making Box (see p. 14). If children cannot write their full name, encourage them to write the letters they know, and you can write their full name in the corner of the label.

Follow children's lead, supplying name labels for use with belongings, projects, and shared items.

Vary the print on the labels, selecting uppercase letters for the initial letter in each name and lowercase letters for the rest of the name.

♦ Young children do not often see their last name in print. Occasionally, include last names on the labels. Printed in conjunction with a first name, with which children will be more familiar, last names become recognizable, and eventually, reproducible.
♦ Use fun mediums for name printing, such as three-dimensional paint, felt, sandpaper, sequins, craft foam, and glitter.

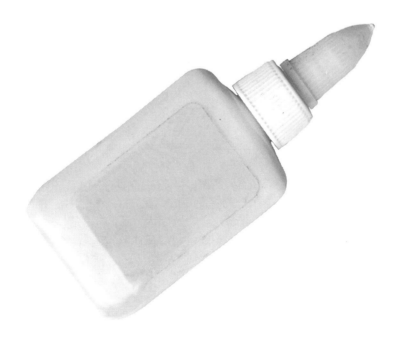

Forms of Labels

Arrow Labels

Arrow Labels work well for objects that are otherwise difficult to label, such as plants, classroom pets, sinks, and chalkboards. Use this type of label to designate where things are located and to indicate direction. Children enjoy the unique shape of this label and quickly understand its meaning.

Making Arrow Labels

Cut long and short arrows out of construction paper. Make arrows more noticeable by bordering with a black marker or mounting on a slightly larger arrow cut from black paper. Print in the center of the arrow.

Using Arrow Labels

When hanging Arrow Labels, be sure to point them directly at the object being named. In addition to item identification, use this type of label to point the way to the bathroom, playground, kitchen, or exit. When used to direct children, Arrow Labels effectively demonstrate the usefulness and function of print, such as WET BOOTS HERE or DRY PAINTINGS HERE.

Involving Children

As with most labels, children can help with cutting, adding a border, or mounting and hanging finished labels. Include children in decisions about properly positioning Arrow Labels: pointing left, right, up, or down.

Combining Labeling Techniques: Arrow Labels offer a unique opportunity to combine labeling techniques, giving children a chance to see the same word printed more than once, match words, and, perhaps, attach more meaning to print. For example, supply a bin for used dishes during a snack or lunch clean-up routine. An Arrow Label points to the bin, directing DISHES AND CUPS. Two Identification Labels in the bin or on the rim help children to sort, putting DISHES on one side and CUPS on the other.

Arrow Labels are often hung at a distance from the objects that they label or point out. For clarity, add small pictures drawn or cut from magazines.

Label-making Box: Put together a Label-making Box for on-the-spot labeling by you and the children. Any size box will do, but a shoe box works especially well. Decorate the box with paper, stickers, ribbon, and yarn. Label the box and fill it with precut paper, markers, and tape; a premade set of children's name labels is also useful.

A Label-making Box will come in handy throughout the day for labeling objects at children's request, making labels for children's work or items brought from home, and labeling other projects that require immediate attention.

Cube Labels

Durable and very mobile, Cube Labels are among the most noticeable labels in a classroom environment. Other advantages include quick construction and ease of use—they can be changed and used again and again.

Making Cube Labels

Use any cube-shaped box or container to make Cube Labels; half-gallon milk cartons work especially well. Recycling cartons this way is a practice that is good for the environment and is also good role-modeling for children.

Clean empty milk cartons with soapy water, rinse thoroughly, and dry. Let the cartons air out for a day or two. Open the spout top of the carton, and cut through the folded sides so the top can be closed and taped. Cover the carton with brightly colored construction paper or gift wrap. Lay the carton in the center of the paper and wrap it like a present, folding and tucking in the ends.

Print labels on white paper and tape them to the side of the covered carton. Remove labels and attach new ones, as needed.

Using Cube Labels

Set these labels on any table, shelf, counter, or work surface. Put Cube Labels wherever children are working and playing. Easy to move or work around, Cube Labels make print a part of any activity.

Involving Children

Include children in any and every aspect of making Cube Labels. They can help wash and rinse cartons, tape the ends closed once they are cut, and cover the carton with paper.

Make use of three sides of the Cube Label.

- Place the same label on the top and two sides, so that the print shows no matter how the cube is positioned. Keep the bottom blank.

- Add pictures corresponding to the label printed on one side. For example, for a bouquet of flowers brought to the classroom, use a Cube Label and print the word FLOWERS on one side. On the other three sides, attach pictures of flowers either cut from magazines or drawn by children. Display the Cube Label next to the bouquet.

- Use Cube Labels for any four-step activity, printing each step on a different, numbered side of the cube. Children begin at Step 1 and turn the Cube Label four times, following the steps. For example, if children are making animals for a group mural titled "The Zoo," use the cube to label the steps:

  Step 1—Trace
  Step 2—Draw a face
  Step 3—Color
  Step 4—Cut

  Add picture clues, such as a crayon or a pair of scissors, to help children understand the print, as needed.

Free-standing Labels

This type of labeling works effectively to name a play area, indicate an interest center, and divide space. Due to its size (fairly large) and placement (usually conspicuous), even toddlers attend to these labels. Move the labels anywhere, use both sides, and change the print as needed. The pleasing appearance, mobility, and durability of Free-standing Labels makes them desirable in any print-rich classroom.

Making Free-standing Labels

Detergent Box: Empty a giant, economy-size detergent box completely (bits of detergent in the eyes can be dangerous). For stability, weight with sand, pebbles, or rocks. If detergent box lids have a handle on the top, keep it intact, attaching the paper covering around it. The handle will be very useful when moving the label. Tape the lid closed. Cut paper several inches larger than the front and back surface so it can be folded and taped around the top and sides. Use one large piece of newsprint or brown craft paper, if you prefer. Cover the box with paper and tuck the ends as though wrapping a gift. Label the box directly on the paper or make separate labels and tape them to the box for easy sign changing or replacement.

Plastic Water or Milk Jug Bases: Rinse and dry thoroughly. Weight jugs with sand, pebbles, or soil and cap the top. Plastic jug bases can be decorated with stickers, colored tape, pictures attached with glue, or acrylic paints.

Sign Poles and Sign Tops: Use cardboard gift wrap tubes to make sign poles for both detergent box and plastic water jug bases. Cut the length of the tube to make it eye level for most children. Decorate the tube with paint or markers or wrap it with crêpe-paper strips.

Make sign tops for the poles by taping two pieces of colored construction paper together on three sides, creating an envelope. Use the front and back for labeling and slip the "envelope" down over the top of the tube. Secure with tape, if necessary. A large manila envelope used in the same way works equally well.

After constructing and weighting the bases following the preceding instructions, attach the cardboard tube sign poles:

- **On detergent boxes**
  Trace the end of the tube onto the top of the box and cut on the traced line to make a hole. Insert the tube in the hole and tape around the hole to secure the sign pole.
- **On plastic water/milk jugs**
  Place the tube over the capped top and secure with tape.

Using Free-standing Labels

Set labels at the entrance to interest centers and play areas or place the labels in the corners of these areas so they can be moved to more conspicuous locations when the centers are in use.

Involving Children

Children can help wrap crêpe paper diagonally around the gift wrap tube and/or decorate the paper covering on the detergent box.

Provide children with a funnel and measuring cups. Have them fill jugs and detergent boxes one-third to one-half full with sand, soil, or other material to weight them before use. Make a paper cone funnel for children to use if they are adding pebbles.

Necklace Labels

Have fun with this type of labeling! Any stuffed animal, doll, or puppet in the classroom can wear a Necklace Label. Use these labels to identify objects by noun, proper name, or both. Necklace Labels can be removed for play and even become part of the play scenario.

Making Necklace Labels

Cut desired shapes out of construction paper or craft foam and print the label with black marker. Punch two holes at the top for lacing yarn. Cut lengths of yarn long enough to fit over the heads of the stuffed animals or dolls being identified. Necklace Labels should be easy for children to remove and replace.

Using Necklace Labels

Hang these labels on any doll, puppet, or stuffed animal in the classroom. Allow children to play with the toys with the Necklace Labels on or remove them, replacing them after play. The removal and replacement of Necklace Labels draws attention to print and encourages print discrimination. Keep Necklace Labels in a shoe box or other container when they are not in use.

Involving Children

Children can help identify soft toys and dolls for labeling, name them, and lace yarn through labels.

Free-standing Labels offer a two-sided surface. Make use of both sides by:

- labeling both sides the same way
- labeling one side with the name of the play or work area and the other side with the number of children permitted in an area
- using it as a "Waiting List" for turns in the center
- writing STOP or CLOSED on it, for use when the area is not open

An added benefit of necklace labeling is that when children remove the labels, they have the opportunity to replace them. If children seek your help in doing this, encourage them to try on their own to elicit the help of a friend. If Necklace Labels become misplaced, set aside a few minutes at the beginning of any group time to rearrange them, so that all children can take part.

- Children may enjoy taking this idea home by making two or three Necklace Labels for favorite toys.

Paper Bag Labels

Recycle large, brown-paper grocery bags and newspaper or shredded paper to make various sizes of these fun puffy labels. Paper Bag Labels stand up on their own, have real "presence," and are easy for children to help make.

Making Paper Bag Labels

Begin by printing the label in the center of the grocery bag. Open the bag and stuff it half full of crumpled newspaper or shredded paper; be certain to stuff firmly. Fold the top down and tuck in the ends, similar to wrapping a gift. Tape or staple closed.

Using Paper Bag Labels

Use these labels anywhere that labels are normally found, including display tables, science centers, and book areas. This label also works well when combined with an art display: use one to title an art project, identify the artist, and/or provide information about the process.

Involving Children

Children love to crumple the newspaper and stuff Paper Bag Labels. They can help add color to the labels by gluing precut borders to the surface of the bags before stuffing.

Stand-up Labels

There are numerous ways to construct Stand-up Labels appropriately sized for table or counter use. A blank piece of posterboard or cardboard attached to the front of an easy-to-make stand, creates a hand, reusable Stand-up Label.

Making Stand-up Labels

One of the easiest ways to make Stand-up Labels is to remove the easel backing from old photograph frames and attach them with glue to a piece of cardboard or posterboard. Affix to the cardboard a piece of paper cut the same size as the cardboard and add the print. Try attaching a somewhat smaller piece of paper (of a contrasting color) to the (colored) posterboard so that the posterboard serves as a decorative border; add the print.

If old backings are not readily available, cut a piece of cardboard or posterboard of the desired size, and then follow these directions for making stands.

Triangle Easel: Cut a cardboard right triangle several inches smaller than the height of the cardboard mounting you selected. Score a line down the straight side of the triangle from one edge to the other. Use a utility knife or sharp scissors and score against a ruler, but do not cut through. This makes the cardboard easy to bend. Tape the triangle easel to the cardboard mounting and bend along the score so that the easel stands. Mount paper to the front of the cardboard, and add print.

Chapter 1: Environment

Trapezoid Easel: Cut a cardboard trapezoid several inches smaller than the cardboard mounting. Score a horizontal line 1" to 2" from the top. Tape the top to the cardboard mounting and bend at the scored line. Attach a tape "hinge" from the trapezoid to the mounting. To make a "hinge," attach one end of a piece of tape to the back of the trapezoid. Adjust the trapezoid to the desired slant, and attach the other end of the tape to the cardboard mounting, leaving an inch or two of tape like a bridge between the two pieces. This "hinge" secures the easel stand at an angle supporting the cardboard. Mount paper to the front of the cardboard; add print.

Cylinder Easel: Make a stand for use on any small table by cutting a cylindrical oatmeal box or any round container into 3"-high disks. Cut two slits—one on either side in the top of the disk— and slip labels into the slits. Reuse disk stands by simply changing the labels.

Using Stand-up Labels

Use Stand-up Labels on any table, shelf, or counter to identify materials and displays. Combine Stand-up Labels with artwork, show-and-tell items, child-built structures, or books. This type of label is well suited to a science table or sensory area. Accent dramatic play settings with Stand-up Labels: use them to label items in the Grocery Store Center, to designate the waiting area in the Doctor's Office Center, or as menus in the Restaurant Center (read more about Centers in Chapter 3).

Involving Children

Children will enjoy choosing pictures from calendars or magazines to place on easel-back stands. Label pictures after they are mounted.

Give children an opportunity to choose a piece of their own artwork and make a paper frame for it. Mount framed art on an easel-back stand and use a second easel-back stand to provide information about the artist: name, age, favorite food, color, and activities.

After you've cut disks, let children paint or decorate them with paper. They may enjoy using them to display their art projects.

Try using small lunch bags in smaller areas. Look for printed and colored bags. Any size will work as long as the bottoms will sit flat. Write labels on plain paper and tape or glue to the bag.

- Stuff bags with other materials: Try dried beans, wood chips, shredded paper, or anything similar that is available in large quantity.

- This is an excellent recycling activity, something you will want to stress with children.

Find easel backs on old picture frames at flea markets or garage sales.

- Use a ready-made easel back as a pattern for constructing cardboard backs.

- Use paper clips, not glue, to mount labels and pictures on cardboard. This makes it easy to change items.

Tactile Labels

Tactile Labels present lots of sensory fun as they help children understand the purpose of print. Just as adding color words to labels and writing the word in the color it names makes words more "readable," you can help children recognize words by making the words relate more directly to the item or material being named. Tactile Labels, made with materials that children can both see and touch, help them "read" and recognize print.

Making Tactile Labels

Using the object or material named to do the actual lettering, make Tactile Labels for supplies such as COTTON and SAND. First, use a dark-colored marker to clearly print the object's or material's name. Use all upper- or lowercase letters, allowing a little extra space between each letter. Next, apply white glue on the marker lines, making the letters. Place, pour, or sprinkle the appropriate material over the glue. Allow the material to set before shaking off the excess.

The following materials make great Tactile Labels:

- ♦ glitter
- ♦ cotton
- ♦ sand
- ♦ soil
- ♦ sawdust
- ♦ Velcro®
- ♦ crayons (shaved pieces)
- ♦ glue
- ♦ tape
- ♦ rice
- ♦ sandpaper
- ♦ oatmeal

Using Tactile Labels

Hang Tactile Labels naming frequently used materials/objects near the items they describe, such as in the Art Areas or at the sand table. If children will be using sawdust, rice, or other materials at the sand table, change the label accordingly. Hang labels at eye level, making them accessible to children and inviting their investigation. Display labels naming items reserved for special projects, such as glitter, only when the material is in use. Keep such labels on shelves with the supplies so they can be pulled out easily and placed on the table during the project. Children will enjoy seeing them at these special times. Tent Labels (described next) work well as Tactile Labels. Look for items in the Science Area to label this way. Cooking activities also lend themselves to Tactile labeling. For example, when making "Rebus Recipes" (p. 50), use Tactile Labels for ingredients such as flour or oatmeal.

Involving Children

Present children with pre-printed labels, letting them help to apply glue and other materials needed to make the labels.

Tent Labels

Tent Labels can quickly increase the abundance of print in any classroom. Perhaps the easiest of the labeling techniques, Tent Labels can be made in minutes and used anywhere. Tuck Tent Labels into small places where children will see them. Tent Labels require little space and can be easily worked around, making them suitable for any work space.

Making Tent Labels

Cut rectangles out of bright-colored construction paper. Fold paper in half to make a tent. Write labels in black marker.

Adjust the size of Tent Labels to suit the areas in which they will be used. Larger Tent Labels may need a base to keep them standing. To make a base, fold paper in thirds and tape sides together, making a pyramid structure.

Using Tent Labels

Place Tent Labels on art shelves, display tables, or children's work areas. Use the labels to identify supplies and toys, name found objects, label art displays, and draw attention to specific items.

Write children's names on Tent Labels and use them as snack and lunch place cards, to designate a specific play area, or to identify seating at activity tables. Adding Tent Labels to art display tables, book areas, building areas, and items brought from home (for example, ANNIE'S XYLOPHONE) is an excellent way to combine children's names with Identification Labels. Personalizing Identification Labels in this way directs more attention to the labeling. Children feel a sense of pride when they see their name exhibited in conjunction with other words.

Involving Children

Children will enjoy choosing colors for Tent Labels and may also help in the (straight line) cutting and folding of the paper. Allow those who express an interest to write their own names on labels.

In a toddler or preschool classroom that is abundant with print and labeling, children will often find new places for labels or recognize a need for labels in an area overlooked by adults. Easy-to-make Tent Labels let you respond to children's labeling requests almost immediately.

For lengthy words or scarce materials, use the tactile material for the first letter of the word only. Write the rest of the word in marker, or make a border around the word with the tactile material.

- Put glitter, sand, salt, and other small-grained materials in a spice jar and allow children to sprinkle it onto letters. Children will have fun shaking on the substance and you will have less mess and waste.

Keep precut paper for Tent Labels on hand for on-the-spot labeling. Print the labels and/or children's names in the presence of the children. This serves as an excellent example of the purpose and function of print.

- Use Tent Labels to recognize achievements, contributions, and efforts of individual children throughout the day. Even in the middle of a busy day, take a minute to use Tent Labels to acknowledge a bouquet of flowers brought to school by one child; a clay creature made by another; a structure put together by two friends; or acts of kindness, politeness, and cooperation.

More about Labels

Other Uses of Labeling

Having labeled key items in the classroom using some of the preceding ideas, try some experimental, inventive labels in unusual places in the classroom. Children will have fun discovering these and may have ideas for creating others.

- To a mirror, affix the word MIRROR on the bottom; place an Arrow Label with the word ME in the middle.
- Try small Arrow Labels strategically placed on a mirror at EYE, NOSE, and MOUTH level. Children have fun moving their heads and facial features to line up with corresponding labels. Using a full-length mirror, try the same concept with labels such as HEAD, BODY, ARM, HAND, LEG, and FOOT.
- Add color words to labels, such as RED CHAIR, GREEN PLANT. Write color words in the appropriate color or write words in black on appropriately colored paper.
- Make labels that help identify the object named. For a CORNER, try a label that actually wraps around the corner itself.
- Hang an Identification Label on the CEILING.
- Place a label on the outside of the window reading OUTSIDE and one on the inside of the window that says INSIDE.
- Use permanent markers to print labels directly on objects used for activities that involve water and other liquids or sand, snow, clay, and other substances.
- Print PAINT on paint containers, including color words as desired.
- Print labels directly on ordinary objects, such as boxes of crayons, toys, and glue containers.
- Use a stencil to outline and cut letters for labels from magazines or catalogs. Find pictures that correspond to the object being labeled and trace stencils directly onto the pictures. Cut out the letters, arrange them to name the object and glue on plain paper. Hang the label on or near the object. Use this lettering method with a variety of types of labels:

- Cut the word BEAR from real bear or toy bear pictures. Glue the letters on a Necklace Label for classroom teddy bears.
- Cut the word FLOWERS from seed catalogs or magazine pictures. Glue the letters on a Tent Label and place on a table near fresh flowers.
- Cut the word BOOKS from book flyers or magazines. Glue the letters on an Arrow Label that points to the library or bookshelf area.
- Cut food words, such as cereal and various fruits and vegetables, from grocery store circulars, seed catalogs, and empty food boxes. Use them to label Dramatic Play Grocery Store shelves.

Guidelines for Labeling

- Use clear and correctly formed letters. Avoid fancy writing, personal touches, or excessive border decoration that may be confused with the letters. Follow a manuscript chart to ensure uniformity of classroom labeling.
- Use dark-colored markers on light backgrounds so that labels are visible from various areas of the classroom.
- Cut paper or craft foam to a size that fits the object being labeled and the placement of the label. Labels on shelves and tables can be small, those on walls and furnishings can be medium-sized, and hanging or interest area labels can be much larger.
- Change labels at least once a month if not more often. Changes need not be dramatic but are essential to maintaining interest and continued attention to labeling. Change classroom labels in any of the following ways:
  - a different background color
  - a different background shape
  - a new display position or hanging method
  - a different letter size, such as all uppercase or all lowercase letters
  - an eye-catching border, such as glitter, ribbon, yarn, or a chenille stem

Classroom Organization

Defining Space

The physical environment can greatly affect children's play behaviors and learning experiences. Part of establishing a literacy-rich environment means paying close attention to classroom organization, arrangement of furnishings, use of space, and the like. This section provides important guidelines, including floor plans and schematics, for setting up a classroom that facilitates and supports the acquisition of literacy skills. Some of these guidelines will be familiar; they are typical of those underlying many early childhood programs. Others provide new opportunities to incorporate literacy tools and props into the environment.

Classroom Arrangements

The literate classroom has clearly defined work and play areas.

- Smaller partitioned spaces work better than large open areas.
- Similar areas or those likely to be used in more than one play scenario should be adjacent.
- Quiet areas should be kept separate from more active or noisy areas.
- Interest areas should be arranged so that needed resources are close to the area.
- A traffic pattern that minimizes interruptions is desirable.

Within these clearly defined areas, place materials at the height and eye level of children. Arrange storage that is generally open and accessible, but allow some closed storage to facilitate use of Location Labels.

The salient features of the literate classroom environment will be the print, materials, and props within the well-defined areas. Uses and tools of literacy will abound. Reading and writing materials will be present in all areas of the classroom.

Consult the floor plans and schematics provided in Appendix 22 for specific ideas. Of course, the size of the classroom, furnishings, available materials, and interest-area preferences will dictate the actual setup. Notice that many areas of the classroom are interest centers that will change on a regular basis, depending on season, curriculum, theme, or choice. Other areas are permanent interest centers that will change only as materials and supplies are added and removed. The literate classroom should include these permanent interest areas:

- soft space or quiet area
- block-building and gross-motor area
- Home and Family dramatic play area. Other themed dramatic play areas should change frequently. The Home and Family Center should always be available for play.
- library
- art area
- book-making area. Separate from the library or art area, this section of the classroom will be equipped with teacher-made blank "books" and materials for use in putting together child-made books.

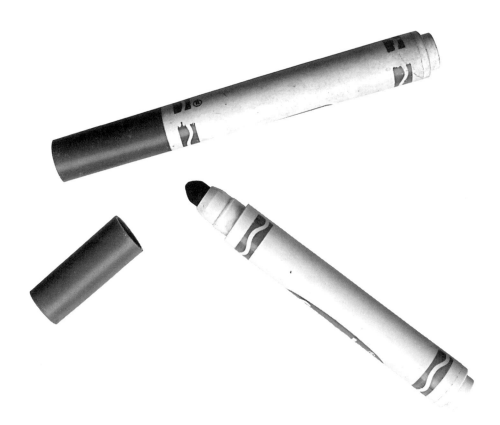

Chapter 1: Environment

Room Dividers

The schematics and floor plans provided in Appendix 22 present room arrangements that accommodate a number of interest areas, thereby offering a variety of literacy opportunities. They all make use of movable shelving and other furniture as room dividers, creating many smaller spaces within one large area. If adequate shelving and movable furniture are not available, construct room dividers using an assortment of boxes and other materials (see below). While not as sturdy as furniture, the dividers can be made to look quite attractive and will lend a unique charm and personality to any classroom as they serve a variety of purposes. Involve children in the construction of the dividers. Not only will they enjoy the process, but they will better understand the use of the final product.

Computer Paper Box Dividers

Stack computer paper boxes, with lids on, two or three high for multi-purpose dividers. Arrange the stacks side by side in any formation. Cover or decorate as desired. Removable lids provide storage for props and supplies in the centers. For extra display and counter space, place plastic trays on top of the stacks. If used to store small games or puzzles, the trays can be taken right to the floor or tables for use as additional work or play spaces.

Alternatively, stack boxes on their sides, lids off, so the openings face one way. Fasten the boxes together with wide tape placed along open edges where boxes meet. Colored masking tape, cloth tape, or printed Contac® paper cut into strips all work well. Stacked three high and five long, this will create a group of fifteen "box shelves" as well as a divider. Secure the back of the box grouping (the bottoms of the boxes) with tape placed along the seams where boxes meet, creating a grid look. Paint, cover with Contac® paper, or decorate the boxes with gift wrap before taping together, or keep the boxes plain and tape children's artwork to the sides and back. Use the open side of the unit for toys, books, or supplies. If the divider is part of a dramatic play setting, use the openings for things that relate to play. For example, in a Grocery Store setting, fill the boxes with play food and empty food boxes; in a Pet Store setting, place stuffed animals and empty pet food containers in the boxes.

Use the flat back of the computer paper box unit for children's art, a photo board, a helper chart with a "job" and child's name in each grid, or pictures relating to the adjacent play area. For example, in a block play area, hang construction and vehicle pictures; next to a library or reading corner, hang book jackets. Covered with Contac® paper, the back of the unit becomes a reusable area for quick and easy picture changing or learning games.

- Don't forget to use the flat box tops as a counter, for added storage or display.

- The lids from the computer paper boxes have a number of uses too. Place three side by side on the top of the box unit for use as removable trays for puzzles and small manipulatives, which children can carry to tables or to the floor. Use remaining lids for storage, art supplies, and other projects. Plastic crates and other types of boxes can be stacked in the same way.

Display artwork or center-related pictures on Large Appliance Box Dividers by attaching them with tape.

- Make a working learning center on two sides of the box by applying self-stick Velcro® strips to the box and to game pieces, for a shape-match, number count, or other activity.

- Cut holes in the top of the box to let in more light. This makes a fun reading area or quiet space for one or two children at a time.

- Large appliance boxes can also be used to make divider screens. Remove the top and bottom of the box. Cut down the length of one fold. The four sides (with natural bends) create the screen. Simply fan-fold in opposite directions so that the screen stands on its own. For a three-paneled screen, remove one side of the box. Make the screens sturdier and more stationary by placing slotted cardboard supports at the bottom. Use paint, Contac® paper, gift wrap, pictures, photos, or children's art to decorate the screens.

Large Appliance Box Dividers

Remove one end of a large appliance box, leaving the other end intact for added support. Reinforce the box by pressing masking tape firmly along the folds, both inside and outside of the box. Used as a divider, the box can serve a number of other functions as well:

- ◆ Paint the box and use as a bus, car, cave, or other large structure that children can climb inside to play.

- ◆ Decorate the side of the box facing a particular interest center to relate more directly to the center. For example, draw or paste flowers on the box in a Florist Shop Center. Attach pictures of breads and desserts to the box in a Bakery Center. Used in this way, dividers become an extension of dramatic play.

Natural Boundaries

If the classroom contains large floor plants, line them up in a row to create a Natural Boundary. If this is not possible, make a Tree Divider. Paint three to five sturdy cardboard boxes green or cover with green paper to create Tree Divider bases. Weight each box with several rocks or a brick. Paint three to five gift wrap tubes brown, gray, and tan to create Tree Divider "trunks." Use sponges and a dabbing motion to give them a mottled bark look. Cut a hole the size of the end of a tube in the top of each base. Insert the trunks into the bases and tape around the hole if necessary.

Cut 3"-high green paper strips to fit each box side. Fringe the strips and attach them to the top edges of the box to look like grass.

- ◆ Invite children to make paper flowers that can be glued on among the grass.

- ◆ To make the tree tops, cut several large single leaves or many smaller six-pointed leaves from green construction paper for each tree. Bunch the leaves together at one end, brush with glue, and push into the top of the tree trunk.

- ◆ Set the box bases side by side, creating a "homemade" palm tree divider.

Hanging Dividers

Hang a clothesline, rope, or heavy yarn across a designated area at a height of 3' to 4', and then try one or more of these ideas:

♦ Make paper chains out of colored construction paper and hang them side by side along the clothesline. This creates an airy, open divider that serves as an effective and colorful boundary.

♦ Decorate cardboard gift wrap tubes by painting or wrapping diagonally with crêpe paper or ribbon. Punch two holes parallel to each other in the top of each tube and thread tubes vertically across rope. Like a paper chain divider, this creates a boundary that has some movement and is fun to look at.

♦ For an interesting and more stable boundary, "weave" crêpe paper, paper strips, craft foam strips, and yarn directly onto a gift wrap tube divider. First, construct a hanging tube divider. Plain, undecorated tubes work best. Tie or tape one end of the weaving material to the first tube of the hanging divider and work the material in an over-under pattern to the last tube. Continue this procedure back and forth from top to bottom on the row of tubes, changing textures and colors by simply taping or tieing.

♦ Tie plastic six-pack rings (from canned beverages) together, end to end, until they form a boundary of a desirable size. Hang by threading top holes along rope or yarn. Or, hang on hooks across a corner or from the ceiling. Weave crêpe paper, paper strips, craft foam, or even torn strips of fabric in and out of the holes to create a more solid divider.

Fabric Dividers

Make two anchor poles for a movable fabric divider out of plastic water jugs and gift wrap tubes. Fill jugs one-half to one-third full of sand and fit a gift wrap tube over the capped opening. Secure the tube with tape. Decorate the tube if desired. Tie a sturdy rope or clothesline between the two anchor posts and hang fabric over the rope. Alternatively, use spring clothespins to attach pillowcases to the line. Or tie strips of crêpe paper or pieces of felt along the line.

Try art instead of fabric on dividers. Use spring clothespins to hang large pieces of artwork on the line. Easel paintings work well. Hang two in one spot, back to back, so they can be seen from either side. This makes a "Clothesline Art Show" that serves as a divider for a large area.

Curriculum

Activities That Incorporate Print into Every Part of the Day

Because children learn from everything they do and they learn best from active participation, the functions and uses of literacy should be linked to every aspect of the curriculum. From art to block play and from music to science, every element of a preschool program can be enhanced with literacy in a variety of ways. Provide print anywhere and everywhere. Make it a natural part of every aspect of the early childhood curriculum so that children have many opportunities handling and manipulating print as they play. As children interact with print in play, they become familiar with it naturally and associate it with enjoyment and pleasure.

Start of the Day

Children's interactions with print or literacy props may be extensive or minimal; the connections to literacy may be utilized or ignored. The key is providing opportunities for children to make use of literacy materials in work and play, not insisting that they do so.

This section focuses on making and using forms of literacy in many areas of the curriculum. It provides suggestions and specific examples for each domain. Attention is given to the preparation of materials for on-the-spot child-initiated print and literacy props. Because concepts of literacy frequently come up during gatherings, circle times, and group times—whether teacher-planned or child-initiated—the section offers traditional and new ways to look at this important part of the preschool day. "Our Day" descriptives, rebus charts, show and tell, "Question of the Day," list making, brainstorming, and "What We Know" word webs are among the new cores for group times presented here. Samples and illustrations further guide the way. See Appendix 21 for a list of early childhood literacy Web sites with more ideas for literacy activities.

An Invitation to Fun

An invitation is a fun (and effective) way to begin any day. Not only does it instill in children a sense of anticipation, but it offers an excellent opportunity to attach meaning to the printed word. Pass out individual invitations or hang up a group invitation. Read the invitation(s) at a group time at the beginning of the day.

Use the same or similar format for subsequent invitations, so that children begin to know what to expect and start to recognize frequently used words.

Hi Sarah 😊 Today we will paint a picture.

Chapter 2: Curriculum

List the Day's Events

At the first circle time or group time of the day, list, in order, the events for that day. Use chart paper or paper of a similar size (lined paper is preferable, but plain paper will also work). Attach paper to an easel or similar surface so children can watch as you write the words. Print the day's events in large block letters, upper- and lowercase, punctuating as needed. Make letters as neat and uniform as possible, but don't be overly concerned with the end product. Remember, this is a list. Write several words at a time, sitting back and making eye contact with the group frequently. Talk while writing, calling children's attention to the letters that words begin with, spelling out words, and commenting on events—for example, "Oh, this sounds like fun!" and "Remember last week, we did another kind of art printing." Keep lists brief, stopping every three words or so to reread the whole list, pointing to each item you read. When the list is complete, read it over once again, inviting children to help. Display the list prominently or lay it on a table for closer inspection. The main goal of this activity is to give children an opportunity to see words being written and to relate words to real events.

Use the same format each time, such as:

Today is _____.

Today we will:
1. paint
2. make muffins
3. take a walk
4. read a new book
5. play a drum

List the Week's Events

If a daily activities list does not suit the classroom schedule or age group, try a list of weekly events. Follow the preceding guidelines, except substitute weekly highlights for daily events. Be certain the list does not get too long—ten items (two per day) works well. Again, follow a similar format each time, such as:

This week will be fun for us.

On Monday we will:
1. cook
2. paint

On Tuesday we will:
1. make clay
2. dance

For a shorter easier-to-make "invitation," give children Welcome Hands as they arrive in class each day. Messages should include the child's name and be no more than a few words in length. Cut hand shapes from construction paper and use colorful markers or crayons to print Welcome Messages.

Individual Goal Setting

In lieu of a classroom event list, have children set their own daily goals with "What I Would Like to Do Today" cards. Write each child's name on a piece of paper and number from 1 to 3. At the start of the day, let children know they can choose three things they would like to accomplish during the school day. You may wish to leave choices open to any classroom activity or limit choices in some way. Encourage children to choose a book, do an art project, try an outdoor activity, or spend time with a toy or in an interest center. Record children's goals on the cards. As children achieve goals, have them document their progress by checking off goals or marking them with a rubber stamp or sticker. Place cards on a table or hang from a bulletin board titled "Today's Plans." A clothesline tied across a classroom corner with goal cards attached by clothespins works well, as does a "Tree Display." For the latter, anchor an actual tree branch in a bucket of sand, clay, pebbles, or plaster of Paris, and use clothespins to hang cards from the tree branch.

Review of Individual Goal Setting

You can also review Goal Setting cards from the start of the day at an End of Day group time. Remove cards from clothesline or other hanging areas and take to the group time rug. If you have opted for a tree display, move the entire tree to the rug. Look over each child's list of three goals and check off those accomplished. Encourage the child to do the checking off, using a sticker or an ink stamp to mark accomplishments. If it is not possible to look over all cards every day, do several cards each day and send the others home at the end of the day for the children to show and discuss with parents. Alternatively, limit goal setting to three or four children each day and look over their accomplishments at the end of the day, making sure all children have a turn during the week. This activity also works well if done weekly.

Changeable Newspaper

Increase children's exposure to newsprint by bringing in an assortment of local newspapers. Ask parents to contribute to the collection. Examine newspapers at a group time, pointing out the name of the newspaper, date, weather, headlines, column format, and photographs. Circle key parts of the front page with colored markers or crayons. Keep a bin of newspapers in the reading area at all times, changing them often.

Create a class newspaper that you can change each morning to accommodate children's news and classroom events. Use 20" by 24" colored posterboard or something similar. Begin by choosing a name for the newspaper. Children may wish to help with this. Use a black marker or stencil letters (and glue) to write the name of the newspaper across the top. Divide the posterboard into several parts, or columns. Precut white paper strips to fit the columns. Cover the entire posterboard with clear Contac® paper. Tape on individual precut columns (you can remove these easily when you put together a new newspaper). Note that you will probably want to do much of the prep work in advance.

During group time, invite children to help put together the class newspaper. Write the date and a weather report. Depending on class size, give three to five children per session an opportunity to contribute their news. Encourage and accept all contributions: news about visitors, a new house, a special day, a birthday, the weekend. Add classroom news and teacher news. Include children's photos and drawings as appropriate. Write "articles" for the newspaper over several days. Hang the newspaper in a central location, where children and parents can read it. Display for two weeks, then put together a new issue.

Classroom Helpers

Establish a system of classroom helpers. In addition to encouraging a sense of responsibility and belonging and establishing a routine, a classroom helper system makes use of children's names in meaningful ways. By observing their own name combined with a classroom job, each child gains an awareness of the functionality of print.

It is very important that the "job" be recognizable to the child to whom it is assigned or by whom it is chosen. There are a number of ways to accomplish this:

♦ Cut pictures from magazines that correspond or relate to the job, such as a broom and a dustpan for "Clean-up Helper" or a fish for "Pet Helper." Glue pictures next to the job title.

♦ Draw a symbol representing the job beside the job title. Draw a flag for "Flag Holder," a cup and plate for "Lunch Helper" and a door for "Door Holder."

♦ Invite children to draw the pictures themselves or color in outlined drawings. Including children in the preparations helps make the activity more meaningful and understandable to them.

Try creating two sets of labels—a set of children's names and a set of classroom jobs—for use on a Helper Chart. Or, attach permanent job labels to the Chart and let children pair name labels with jobs accordingly. Hang the chart in a central location. Use one chart throughout the year or change charts on a regular basis, according to themes, seasons, or holiday. Laminating the chart or covering it with clear Contac® paper makes it more practical and usable for children, letting them move and replace tags and labels as often as needed.

Assign Classroom Helper jobs yourself or involve children in the selection and assignment of Classroom Helper jobs. The latter may be accomplished in a number of ways:

♦ Choose helpers' names from a box or bag and match to a job already posted on a Helper Chart. In this method children choose the jobs they want.

♦ Both a name and a helper job can be chosen from separate containers and hung together; pictures accompanying job titles are very helpful for this method.

How Does It End?

Read the beginning of a short story at the start of the day. Stop about halfway through, posing the questions: "What will happen? How will it end?" Ask children to think about it and share their ideas at the end of the day. Keep the book out of children's reach, but in sight, the rest of the day. Choose stories that might end in several different ways.

Here's How It Ends

Reread the story begun at the start of the day at an End of Day group time, stopping at the same point. Encourage children to tell their versions of the story's ending. Record several of these on paper. Read the actual story ending and discuss how to compare to those offered by the children. Keep children's story endings clipped to the book, if possible. The next time you read the story, add one of the children's endings and credit the child-author. Let children request their endings or those made up by friends at the story reading.

Illustrate invented story endings during an art activity or a drawing time, and hang on a bulletin board or display on a table along with the book.

Word of the Day

Start the morning by presenting a "Word of the Day." Print the word in large letters with markers or use stenciled letters. Another fun and eye-catching way to "fly" the Word of the Day is to make a Word Flag. Cut a triangular piece of paper, print the Word of the Day on the triangle, and tape the triangle to the end of a yardstick or tree branch. Display the Word Flag or banner prominently in the classroom.

Introduce the Word of the Day at the beginning of the day. Spell the word and discuss its meaning with children. Try to use the word as frequently as possible throughout the day. Be aware of children's use of the word and acknowledge it immediately. Support and encourage children who choose to copy the word.

Story Starters

As the beginning of the day, encourage children to write their own short stories sometime during the day. Supply paper that has a smaller amount of space available for drawing or coloring and a larger lined area for print. Use plain paper (9" x 12" or larger) and line at least two-thirds of the paper before putting it out for children to use. Story Starter papers may be seasonal, theme-related, or a general assortment of topics children find fun and interesting. Theme the Story Starter paper by drawing an outline of a large pumpkin, flower, or birthday cake on the top or outer edge of the paper before lining a portion of the paper. Add new Story Starter paper anytime during the busy school day: an activity period, free art time, free play, or book time.

Most children will readily understand the purpose for the lines and dictate something to write. Other children will use the lines for their name, random letters, or even coloring. Still others may put their own inventive "writing" on the lines, composing an imaginary tale as they "write." Often the story writing of a few children will spark the interest of others to write their own stories. Whichever way children choose to use the Story Starter paper, encourage them with comments such as:

♦ "Tell me your story."

♦ "Read your words to me."

♦ "Would you like me to write what you are saying?"

TRICKY TURKEY

A tricky tom turkey did not want to be eaten for Thanksgiving dinner. This is how he kept from being served that day.

Add Words of the Day to a box on the art shelf or book-making center when the day is over. Or, make the words into Word Puzzles: Cut each word into five or six pieces and store puzzles in individual envelopes or plastic bags.

• Choose words that relate to a particular theme, occur in a book to be read that day, or are unusual and special to children, such as: birthday, dictionary, dinosaur, endangered, exercise, recipe, vacation.

• Qualities that are useful in the classroom also make excellent choices, for example:

cooperation

courtesy

friendship

helpfulness

manners

patience

politeness

responsibility

sharing

teamwork

Hang Story Starters at eye level in the classroom or group several with the same theme in a book of collected short stories. Put the collection with other books in the classroom for children to look at and read during scheduled reading times.

End of the Day

What Will Tomorrow Bring?

An excellent part of any End of Day group time is a look ahead at what is to come. This builds anticipation and teaches patience and time comprehension. Putting future plans in print, linking print to action, makes this an excellent emergent literacy activity.

Similar to the List Accomplishments activity (p. 37), head a piece of paper with the word TOMORROW. List three or four things planned for the following day. A chalkboard also works well for this activity.

Give children a fun take-home look at the next day by highlighting one planned activity. Using a set of lowercase alphabet stencils, trace the title of the activity onto sandpaper or craft foam and cut out (one-word activities work best). Glue the sandpaper or craft foam word on a piece of paper. Provide children with lightweight paper with the words "Tomorrow we will" written on the top. Show children how to place their paper on top of the raised word and rub with a crayon, transferring the word to their own paper. This is something that children can share with parents. It also helps them look ahead to the next day's events. You can introduce this "word rubbing" activity at one of the first group times of the day and make it available for children's use during activity time, free play, art time, or other periods of the day. An excellent way to make this activity available is to set up a small desk or table with a Tent Label that reads WHAT WILL WE DO TOMORROW? Next to the sign, place the raised word fastened to a clipboard, a supply of paper, and a container of crayons without wrappers. (Crayons without wrappers work best for rubbing pictures and a clipboard helps hold paper still while children rub.) This way, children can work on the activity independently. Most children love to take something home to share, and what better "gift" than words? News of the next school day offers information to parents, builds excitement in children, and serves as a conversation starter for families.

My Day Rebus

A sense of closure is important to any schedule, especially one involving young children. Gathering together to sing an End of Day song and say good-bye is a part of many early childhood classrooms. Try a rebus read-along for another good End of Day activity. This is a list of children's accomplishments, composed of children's names and pictures of classroom activities. Follow the same format each time you use the chart so children become familiar with the action words.

This activity requires advance preparation. Begin with a few materials and add to them, as needed. Make four sets of cards:

Set 1. Children's names—print them yourself or have children print them

Set 2. Classroom activities—cut pictures from magazines and catalogs to represent the many activities in the classroom; make several of each activity

Set 3. Action words—describe the many movements performed in a school day:

- played (with)
- built (with)
- made
- wrote
- painted
- drew
- colored
- dug
- poured
- read
- looked (at)
- worked (on) (with)
- put (together)

Set 4. Blank cards

Prepare chart paper, covering it with clear Contac® paper for repeated use. Title the chart "Our Day." At the end of the day, encourage children to tell about something they did. Have each pick out his or her name and a representative picture. Supply the verbs as needed. Use blank cards for activities not already printed. Tape cards to the chart as children make their choices. Read each child's accomplishment, pointing to names, action words, and pictures as you do. Encourage children to join you in this Read-Along. Give all children a turn or limit to several each day, making sure all have had a turn by the week's end.

List Accomplishments

A list that begins with the words "Today we _____" is one way to bring closure to a school day. This group list tells what the group accomplished over the course of the day. Fill in the list at an End of Day group time, encouraging four or five children per session to offer ideas.

A premade, laminated chart works well and can save time, because you can use it again and again. Write the words "Today we _____" across the top of the paper. To make a reusable chart, cover the paper or posterboard with clear Contac® paper or laminate it.

You may wish to prepare a set of action words in advance. These might include: PLAYED, WORKED, BUILT, FIXED, CLIMBED, RODE, READ, HUNG, FOUND, DREW, MADE, PAINTED, BAKED.

As children offer suggestions, tape them to (or write them on) the chart. For example, use a premade word such as PLAYED and write WITH A DOLLHOUSE on the spot. Keep blank paper and markers on hand for recording accomplishments for which there no premade words.

Child-written Stories

Use the Story Starter activity (p. 35) at the close of the day to share children's thoughts with the group. This is an excellent way to call attention to the importance and usefulness of words. As they hear their own stories and those of their friends being read, children become aware of the value and importance of words. This activity serves as a source of pride for children who have written a story and an encouragement to those who have not.

Display children's pictures or illustrations as you read their words. If children have used "invented writing" to create a story, invite them to "read" the story in their own words.

Art

In the early childhood classroom, art should be an uninterrupted, creative activity. The process is more meaningful than the product. Include print and other literacy experiences in art projects or free art activities carefully and informally, so as not to interfere with the art process.

Adding Words to Art

Supply the comics pages from newspapers for cutting, book-making, and any other use children may have for them. Add a box of comic strip "Balloons," precut from paper or traceable from heavier paper stencils. Children can glue or trace "balloons" on their drawings and then dictate words for the balloons to you or write the words themselves.

Have premade "strip labels" available at all times. Cut paper strips to fit various sizes of paper. The strip should be wide enough to include the child's name and dictated words. After you and/or the child fill in the label, attach it to the artwork with tape or glue. Remember this is available as a child-initiated choice and should not be viewed as something that must be included on all artwork.

Sign-making

Sign-making is a purposeful, useful, goal-oriented activity that fills a mutual need: providing information you want to give parents or children and involving children more directly. As the creation of something written, for a specific reason, sign-making gives real meaning to the printed word. Employ signs for any number of purposes:

1. To announce events:
   Show-and-Tell
   Field Trip
   Birthday Party
2. To inform:
   Days Off, Holidays, Vacation
   Parent Meetings
   We are out for a walk.
3. To invite:
   Open House
   Sing-Along
   Classroom Play
4. To draw attention to something:
   Look at Our Rock Museum
   See the Sun Catchers We Made
   Wet Paint
5. To make requests:
   We need some shoe boxes.
   We need ribbon for an art project.
   Food packages welcome.

Add-to Murals and Bulletin Boards

Encourage children to add their art to a pre-titled mural or bulletin board. On strips of paper, have children write their name and dictate a few words to hang with the finished art. Relate add-to murals and bulletin boards to curriculum themes or choose any title that children might find fun and interesting, such as:

- Foods We Like
- My Family
- If I Could Fly, I Would Go to _____
- I Like to Play with _____
- If I Were a King or Queen

Consider using signs to welcome new children, say farewell to departing children, or announce a new baby brother or sister.

- While it is easier to make signs ahead of time and hang them when needed, the benefits of making them with children are immeasurable. Whenever possible, print signs in the presence of children, inviting them to decorate the edges of the sign. Those children who show an interest in printing may also help letter signs.

- Designate one spot where children can hang finished signs and bring them to parents' attention. Try to make at least one sign a week, several if possible. Vary the shapes of the signs to enhance interest.

Create an "I am the Artist" bulletin board on which children can hang their own art, accompanied by words of their choosing. Provide lined white paper or large index cards to record the words children choose to include with their art. Children may wish to tell a little bit about themselves (favorites or family information), a story relating to their artwork, or how the art was created.

Choose a Title

Provide a section of premade titles designed to inspire children to draw pictures about a specific subject. Keep a shoe box lid full of titles with the drawing materials. Include titles you have made, titles from newspapers and magazines, and blank strips for on-the-spot title-making. Vary the titles, making them realistic, pretend, specific, general, and so on. Include children's names on some, and reference the class as a whole on others:

- A Trip in My Car
- My Birthday Party
- A Dinosaur for a Pet
- Swimming with Dolphins
- A Most Unusual Animal
- The Farm
- The Zoo
- Our Field Trip
- Jackson's Boat Ride
- Neeraj's Birthday
- Ethan's New House
- Ryan's New Pet

Labeled Stencils

A very effective way to bring art and print together is to label art items, such as stencils and templates, that children frequently use and to which they pay a lot of attention. Use a permanent marker to write directly on the stencil or use a white adhesive label applied to the stencils. Label stencils of all kinds: geometric shapes, animals, and seasonal items. Tracing patterns cut from craft foam can be labeled directly on the foam.

For a fun way to incorporate a child's name into environmental print, make use of favorite toys or show-and-tell items brought to class by tracing around such items, creating stencils, and labeling them with the child's name and name of the object. For example, trace around a stuffed animal, catcher's mitt, or toy car, and label the stencils:

- Stevie's Bird
- Mick's Mitt
- Christine's Car
- Brad's Wallet
- Laura's Key
- Alok's Coins

This increases the classroom supply of stencils and brings recognition to individual children, making them feel part of the classroom. Moreover, children have the opportunity, each time a stencil is used, to assign a name to both the object being stenciled and the owner of that object. Hand, foot, mitten, glove, shoe, and boot stencils are also fun to do this way:

- Kim's Mitten
- Jae Yun's Boot
- José's Hand

Read and Draw Activities

To inspire free drawing periods, stock art shelves with familiar children's stories. Incorporate recently read books by suggesting a part of the story that children may wish to illustrate differently or in their own way. Titles work especially well. After reading a book, call attention to the cover, pointing out the words, and discussing the cover illustration and its relation to the title. Tell children you will be placing the book in or near the Art Area so that they can look at it again and perhaps come up with their own ideas for a new title and cover illustration. Share your own idea for a title and illustration. Often, knowing a teacher has engaged in the same project is an incentive for children to try it. When children complete their pictures, offer to write the new title on their illustration, write it for them to copy on their picture, or dictate the letters to children who have writing skills.

Children can re-title known books with a word change or two and then rewrite and illustrate the book with the new theme. For example, consider Judi Barrett's *Cloudy with a Chance of Meatballs*. A child might change it to "Cloudy with a Chance of Strawberries," if this is what he or she wishes to see raining from the sky, and label it accordingly. *I Took My Frog to the Library* by Eric A. Kimmel might become "I Took My Cat to the Library." Other books to re-title and re-illustrate are listed in Appendix 1.

Clay and Dough Print Play

A collection of print signs combined with clay or dough activities can move these art experiences in many new directions. Make signs on small square or rectangular pieces of colored construction paper or craft foam. Use tape to attach each sign to the top of a craft stick. Provide polystyrene foam food trays, with the ends of some of the craft stick signs pushed into them. Let children stick others directly in the clay or dough. Provide vinyl placemats. Add more print to play by labeling directly on the mats: PIZZAS, DOUGHNUTS, and SPAGHETTI or BEADS, NECKLACES, and RINGS. Using vinyl placemats allows you to change label themes for each play experience. Read the signs to children before the clay activity—for example: "Today we have a bakery (or zoo) set up at the clay table, and here are some of the signs you will find there." Children may place their clay models with the corresponding signs on the polystyrene foam tray, on the vinyl mats, or with signs placed directly in clay. Be prepared to print additional signs at children's requests. Be sure to provide space for children who do not want to use print signs with their clay.

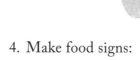

1. Make animal signs:
    SNAKES
    TURTLES
    CATS
    DOGS
    RABBITS
2. Make bakery signs:
    CAKES
    COOKIES
    MUFFINS
    BREAD
    ROLLS
    PIE
3. Make construction signs:
    CEMENT, WET CEMENT
    BRICKS
    STONE
    CONSTRUCTION SITE
    DIGGING SITE

4. Make food signs:
    APPLES
    ORANGES
    GRAPES
    PEAS
    HOT DOGS
    EGGS

If you have made clay (with or without children), add a Stand-up Label titled WHAT IS IN OUR CLAY? Under this title, list the ingredients used to make the clay, with pictures next to each word.

Polystyrene Foam Word Trays

This activity brings print and words to even the youngest learner. Collect polystyrene foam food trays, plates, egg carton lids, and fast-food containers. Use a blunt instrument, such as a craft stick, unsharpened pencil, or end of a paintbrush, and, pressing lightly, "carve" a word (see suggestions that follow) into the polystyrene foam. Press hard enough to create an indentation, but not hard enough to crack the polystyrene foam.

You can also carve small pictures into Word Trays. Word Trays might relate to class themes, special events, field trips, or any words that are fun and interesting to the class, such as:

- food words
- color words
- seasonal words
- new and unusual words
- children's names
- animals
- Happy Birthday
- stop and go
- dinosaur
- Mom
- Dad
- home
- car

Cut pieces of thin-weight paper such as newsprint or typing paper, to fit the tray. Provide these and a container of unwrapped crayons near the Word Trays.

To use the trays, children place the paper on the Word Tray and rub with a crayon to reproduce the word. Help children identify the words on their own by taping or gluing a picture representing the word on the bottom of the tray.

Provide small tables or rug-covered corners equipped with Tray Projects. Each tray can hold a different activity: a chalkboard and chalk, colored pencils and paper, craft sticks and glue, or a special set of markers and a unique piece of paper. Label the tray with the names of the art materials on each or the type of project. This allows children to find a quiet space to be alone and create.

Set up a Framing Area with Box Lid Frames for completed art projects. Gather an assortment of box lids of all sizes (jewelry box lids to shirt box lids) and paper cut to fit the lids. Include glue so children can attach their artwork inside the box lid. Offer to print dictated titles and glue them on the bottom of the picture or on the side of the box lid.

Include ample space for art displays—bulletin boards, wall space, and tabletop scrapbooks. A clothes drying rack with clothespins creates a fun display area.

Construct an Artist Box Display by covering several different-sized cartons with plain paper, gift wrap, or wallpaper. Children can also paint boxes. Use double-stick tape or glue to attach the boxes together in uneven stacks, three or four high. Display artwork on all sides of the boxes. This makes a wonderful free-standing art display. Add a Stand-up Label, LOOK AT OUR ART, on the top of the stack.

Other Print-Rich Materials for an Art Area

Stock the Art Area or Art Corner with print-related items for children to use freely. The process is child-initiated. The purpose is to give children opportunities to handle and use a variety of print materials. Children may recognize letters, copy print, be curious about what is written, use print in their artwork, or simply informally observe other children as they use print. The goal here is exposure.

1. Newsprint and store circulars:
   - cut pictures, letters, and comics
   - do folding projects
   - paint or draw with black paint, markers, or crayons
   - create collection charts for children to work on as a group: use posterboard or tape together four pieces of construction paper to form a larger piece; print the title of the collection at the top; provide glue; encourage children to add to the collection anytime (try collections of weather reports, food, baby pictures, vehicles)
2. Magazines and catalogs:
   - cut pictures and letters
   - make collages
   - create picture puzzles
   - start collection books for children to work on as a group: staple paper together and label each page with a word and picture; as children find and cut out pictures they can glue or tape them to the corresponding page in the book
3. Premade books: staple several blank pieces of paper together using a variety of textures and sizes; encourage children to use the books freely for drawing and writing
4. Maps (many children find maps fascinating):
   - cutting
   - tracing
   - using models for self-made maps
5. Outdated calendars:
   - cut pictures, letters, and numbers
   - use calendar grid for drawing and designs and letters
6. Brochures and pamphlets (all kinds, including travel, pet care, paint samples, craft):
   - cutting projects
   - folding activities
7. Greeting cards:
   - cutting
   - stencils
   - rubbings (with embossed cards)
   - models for creating verses

Chapter 2: Curriculum

Blocks and Manipulatives

Designing a print- and literacy-rich environment in an early childhood classroom should not preclude the flourishing of areas of interest that have long been an integral part of children's "school environment." Water/sand tables, blocks and building centers, vehicle play, and manipulatives of all kinds find a home in the emergent literacy classroom. In fact, including various forms of print on blocks and vehicles where children do not expect to see print may attract more attention than samples of literacy in the library, office, and other dramatic play centers, where they do expect to see it. In the powerful and natural setting of play, present children with a wide range of possibilities: large- and fine-motor activities, active and passive play, group and individual action. No matter what the individual child's preference, the literate classroom should provide exposures to literacy that are rooted in familiar and meaningful experiences.

In addition to providing labels (see following) specifically linked to various manipulatives, put supplies for sign-making in the Block-Building and Gross-Motor Area. A box holding craft foam shapes, paper, markers and crayons, tape, string, and craft sticks makes it easy for children to construct their own labels or signs or to seek your assistance in doing so. Abundant print supplies and samples are essential in the literacy-friendly classroom. They offer children an opportunity to model literate behaviors they observe and to become directly involved in the construction of print props. As children begin to realize that the labels and signs they see on familiar play items are teacher-made, they come to recognize their own print-producing abilities. And, as they eventually make their own signs, children bridge the gap between their awareness of print and the actual creation of print.

Sign Play

One way to add print to manipulative play is to include signs of all kinds with any set of blocks and manipulatives. In contrast to labels, which identify and help locate items, signs give children opportunities to incorporate print directly in their play. Children may make use of the signs every time they play, incorporate them occasionally, or rarely use the signs. Whatever the case, the key here is making print available—putting words and print among children's playthings so they can make connections to literacy if they so choose.

The concept of signs is certainly a familiar one to children. They encounter signs throughout their day, making these a natural tie-in to play activities. In most cases, introductions will not be necessary. Most children will understand the purpose of signs and know how to use them or invent their own uses.

Make the usual signs such as PARK, PLAYGROUND, BIKE PATH, NO TRUCKS, LOADING ZONE, and DEER CROSSING found in most communities and those special to the school neighborhood. Print signs on a separate piece of paper and mount them on colored construction paper cut slightly larger or write labels on craft foam. This makes the signs sturdy and more pleasing to the eye; it also facilitates the changing of signs when they become too worn.

If using paper, laminate or cover with clear Contac® paper for added durability. Craft foam labels do not need protective covering. Tape the sign onto a craft stick and anchor the stick in a square of polystyrene foam for a self-standing sign. Or, tape onto wooden blocks by attaching the bottom of the stick to the side of the block.

To airplanes, trains, and other vehicles, add signs that might be seen at an airport, a bus or train station, and so on.

For dollhouse play, provide signs that suggest a birthday party, moving day, or family vacation.

Adding Scenario signs, such as TOY SHOP, REPAIR SHOP, or FLOWER SHOP, to blocks, and other manipulatives can take building activities in new directions. Children assume a variety of roles and identities, depending on the signs in the area. Keeping sign-making supplies

on hand permits on-the-spot construction of signs as children request them. Saving premade signs in a box or folder gives children a place to look for favorite signs they wish to reuse. Help children better understand signs by adding one or several picture clues to each sign.

Other sets of signs that work well in block/manipulative play and can move such play in new directions include:

- pizza shop signs
- bakery signs
- park or playground signs
- fruit stand or vegetable market signs
- farm signs
- construction site signs
- shopping mall signs
- auto repair or garage signs

Print on Small Manipulatives

Add print to the small manipulatives in the classroom. Add it, for example, to a set of plastic animals. Cut labels and mount on colored construction paper cut slightly larger. Include a small picture of the animal in the corner of the label for younger children or for introducing the label; remove pictures when a label has been used for a time. Tape animal labels on the side of plastic berry baskets, either right side up or upside-down, for zoo or circus play. Children can put the animals in, on, or under the basket "cages."

Add a group of food names to a bead set. Cut out labels and mount on colored construction paper cut slightly larger. Again, include a small picture of the food in the corner of the label, as needed, removing pictures when appropriate. Tape food names onto a set of play dishes, bowls, and cups, such as MILK or JUICE on a cup, SOUP or PUDDING on a bowl, FRUIT or VEGETABLES on a basket, and PANCAKES or EGGS on a plate. Add the labeled dishes to a set of beads. Children may arrange the beads on dishes and in bowls, pretending to cook and prepare foods.

Follow the same procedures to add names of jewelry to a bead set. Tape jewelry labels to small jewelry boxes for children's use when stringing beads. Use names of familiar pieces of jewelry, such as NECKLACE, BRACELET, BANGLE, and CHAIN.

Print on Specialty Blocks and Building Toys

Even building toys can be a source of print. Though any paper label attached with tape will work, self-adhesive labels last longer. Cut the self-adhesive label to fit the building toy and use a marker to do the printing. A simple line border around the edge of the label sets off the print and draws attention to it; for emphasis, use a different color than the print. As with other classroom print, change labels and signs for manipulatives frequently, replace worn print, and take cues from children when creating and replacing print.

Most adhesive labels peel off easily. If you have difficulty removing them, place a dab of oil on the surface of the label. Allow the oil to penetrate and scrape off the residue. Wash thoroughly with soap and water.

House Building Sets

Make labels that name buildings, shops, and other structures found in the community. Have premade labels attached to building pieces or in containers with building sets. Introduce labels to children or wait for children to take notice and ask: "What does this say?" Be prepared to make labels on the spot if requested, such as labeling a street in a building project with the street name where a child lives. Offer to make labels for structures that children build, for example: "What did you build? Should we make a MOVIE THEATER label to hang on it?" Don't forget structures and buildings distinctive to the school community. Consider adding numbers for addresses and street names. Ideas include:

- Fire Station
- Police Station
- Hospital
- Bakery
- Hotel, Motel
- Gas Station
- Post Office
- Restaurant
- School
- Playground
- YMCA, YWCA, JCC
- Factory
- Parking Garage
- Clothing Store, Toy Store, Convenience Store
- Ball Field
- _____ Street
- _____ Avenue
- _____ Drive
- _____ Lane

Wooden Blocks

Within block sets, look for interesting and unusual shapes that suit special labels. For example, label cylinder blocks with the names of liquids: WATER, MILK, JUICE, OIL, GAS. For tall blocks consider these labels: SAND, CEMENT, FLOUR, SALT. Be imaginative. Building and pretend activities greatly multiply with the inclusion of labeled blocks. Many children are especially attentive to such print on manipulatives used in play scenarios that involve "cooking" or preparing foods, "pouring" water, "mixing" cement, "turning or twisting" knobs, driving through "tunnels," or finding the "zoo."

Puzzles and Print

By combining print with puzzles, you give children the opportunity to see and handle print each time they put together the puzzle. Use a self-adhesive label to write the title of a puzzle. Attach it on the front of the puzzle.

Hidden Puzzle Words

This works especially well with wooden-inlay puzzles. Write one word describing the puzzle in every puzzle-piece space on the puzzle board or tray and the first letter of the word on the back of every puzzle piece. This also helps to eliminate lost pieces. If, for example, the puzzle is a picture of a barn, put a "B" or "b" on the back of every puzzle piece; write the word BARN on the wooden puzzle tray where the puzzle pieces will fit (use a permanent marker for this). If the puzzle tray has divided spaces for pieces, write BARN in each space.

Labeled Structures for Manipulative Play

Use shoe boxes or similar size boxes to create structures such as garages, tunnels, parking lots, car washes, swimming pools, digging sites, and so on. Put them with car/vehicle collections and all types of block sets. Shoe boxes work best for small vehicles; use larger boxes for larger vehicles.

Label box structures with self-adhesive labels or cut paper labels and attach with tape. Cut openings in the boxes as needed. Children enjoy the new play possibilities these box structures offer. To encourage print discrimination, present several boxes together.

Combine labeled boxes with traffic and other signs. If a special theme is being discussed in the classroom, relate signs to the theme.

Cooking

Cooking activities in the early childhood classroom offer a range of hands-on, real-life experiences. While many literacy-rich activities give children the opportunity to imitate adult behaviors through role play, cooking and food preparation involve children actively in adult tasks. Don't miss this wonderful opportunity to expose children to literate behaviors and the use of print materials.

Engaging in cooking activities in the classroom does not require a kitchen or even a stove. Many kid-friendly recipes require no cooking, making them suitable for any classroom. Cooking projects offer experiences with math, language, and science; they enhance social interactions; they improve fine-motor coordination; and they promote confidence, independence, and self-assurance. Thus, cooking projects should be a regular part of any early childhood curriculum. Incorporating literacy into cooking projects is easy. When guiding cooking activities in the literate classroom, the recipe is as important as any ingredient being used in the process.

Be sure children have the opportunity to handle a variety of cookbooks, magazine recipes, and recipe cards. Choose print materials that reflect a variety of foods. Children will enjoy looking at the pictures and matching them up with the recipes.

Begin preparing materials for cooking activities by accumulating classroom cooking utensils. Parents may be a good source for cooking supplies. Prepare a letter requesting their help (see page 51).

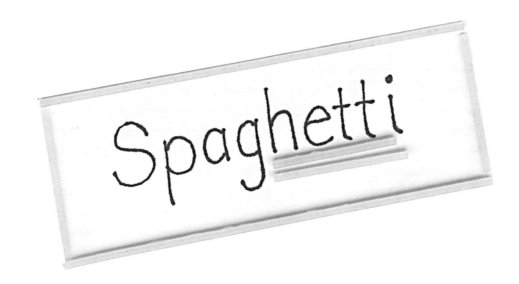

Kid Cookbooks

For an activity that children, teachers, and parents can all enjoy, create a cookbook with child-dictated recipes. Give each child an opportunity to tell how a parent makes a favorite family recipe. Tape-record recipes and transcribe later, or write recipes as children dictate. Write ingredients and directions just as children give them. Encourage children to illustrate their recipes with drawings of the ingredients, the finished dish, or parents preparing the food. Make copies of recipes and assemble them in Classroom Cookbooks. Put the cookbooks in the cooking area, on bookshelves, and in the Dramatic Play Center. Children may wish to take cookbooks home to share with friends and family. These cookbooks make fun gifts for parents and grandparents. You may want to ask parents for the actual recipes, which you can copy onto the page next to the child's recipe. This is a meaningful way to include parents in a literacy activity.

Rebus Recipes

Select a recipe and copy it on 12" x 18" paper or a large piece of newsprint. Use a combination of pictures, numbers, and words to create a Rebus-format Recipe. For example, an ingredients list might show 3 bananas (with a picture of three bananas) or 2 tablespoons (with a picture of a tablespoon and the number 2) peanut butter (with a picture of peanut butter). Number each step and use action words such as SLICE (with a picture of a knife and the bananas) and MIX (with a picture of a spoon, the bananas, and the peanut butter). As children become familiar with the Rebus Recipe format, the actions words (mix, slice pour) will become more recognizable. As children follow the recipe steps, draw their attention to the chart. Tactile Labels for FLOUR, SALT, and other ingredients, work well. To make Tactile Labels, follow the directions in Chapter 1, making the first letter of each word with the ingredient named.

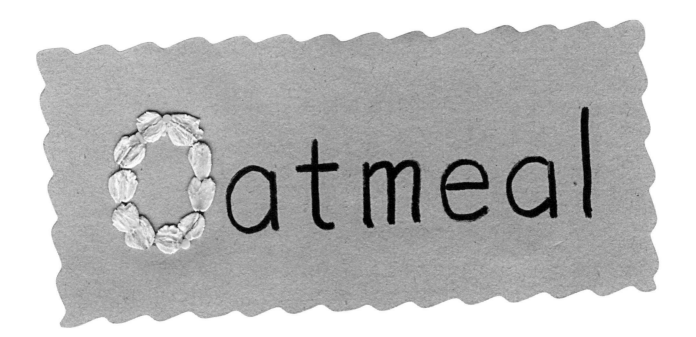

Prepare cooking materials in advance. Gather all of the necessary utensils and ingredients and assemble them on a table next to the Rebus Recipe. Group all items together or separate according to recipe steps. Use a placemat or tray for each step, displaying all the utensils and ingredients for that step on the tray. Display the corresponding recipe step number on the tray, either taped flat or as a Stand-up Tent Label. Label as many items on the tray as possible, including bags, boxes, and containers of ingredients. Though this seems to be a big task, most labels, numbers, and signs can be used again and again for other recipes, with only one or two additions. This practice results in a ready-made collection of cooking props rich in literacy connections.

Lead children through the Rebus Recipe, guiding them step by step only as needed. Many children, especially after they have experience with a rebus, will be able to follow the recipe charts independently. Your role is one of support and encouragement, allowing children to interpret and prepare the recipe step by step.

Parent Letter

Send a letter to parents before doing the cooking activity to inform them about skills that are being taught, as well as to request supplies if necessary. Appendix 2 has a sample parent letter.

There are some other things to do with Rebus Recipes.

- Share cookbooks with parents at an Open House or Parents' Night. These cookbooks also make popular and quite functional fundraisers, provided that they include actual as well as child-composed recipes.

- Reproduce the Rebus Recipes on paper and photocopy them for children to share at home.

- Rebus Recipes can also be included in parent newsletters.

- Mount each copied Rebus Recipe on slightly larger colored construction paper. Punch two holes in the left side and tie loosely together to make a Rebus Cookbook for use as a dramatic play prop. Children will enjoy incorporating it in house play, and their familiarity with the recipes from previous cooking experiences will give the cookbook more relevancy and, therefore, more meaning.

Language

Language enrichment activities in the emergent literacy classroom share much in common with language activities in traditional early childhood classrooms. In the literacy-friendly classroom, however, more language activities are put into print and recorded on paper. Language is the area of the curriculum most commonly associated with literacy. It is here that many of the early literacy concepts take root and blossom. It is also here that many attitudes toward the tools and materials of literacy develop.

Language is one of the curriculum areas in which it is easiest to incorporate print. Nearly anything presented in a language context will also have a correction to literacy. Take care, however, to present connections to print and literacy in positive and non-threatening ways. The act of "practicing" letters and rote copying is not only uninteresting to young children, but also lacks meaning or purpose. Children see no need for it, so they see no value in doing it. Viewing such practices as "work" often has a negative effect on a child's attitudes toward reading, writing, and other literacy-related activities.

Experiences with literacy need to be connected to everyday life and made functional in some way. It is more meaningful for children to compile a list, record a procedure, or make a sign than it is to copy words that begin with a B, trace the letter S connected to a squirrel's tail, or identify word and letter flashcards.

Most children love to share their thoughts and talk about themselves. As a language activity, one rich in self-expression and learning from others, verbal communications cannot be matched. Add print to these verbal communications, and the ties to literacy are multiplied and strengthened.

Message Strips

Make short messages to hand out to children as they arrive, as they go home, or anytime throughout the day. Consisting of two, three, or four words, Message Strips should have a line for the child's name and contain an illustration. You can also leave a space for a sticker, which may be used to make the message more appealing to younger children, designate a special holiday, or reward a child for something special. More importantly, a sticker can provide a picture clue helping the child "read" the message. Read the Message Strip aloud when you give it to the child. Children may want to color in the illustration before taking the message home. Use Message Strips to welcome children, compliment them, present an idea, give a reminder, provide information, or highlight an upcoming event.

List Making

One of the easiest and most effective ways to bring print to the classroom is by making lists with children—weekly, daily, or even several times a day, as the need arises. Make lists for any classroom activity:

♦ Things We Will Do This Week
♦ What We Will Do Today
♦ Special Days to Celebrate This Month
♦ What We Will Look for on Our Walk Today
♦ What We Will Do on Our Field Trip
♦ Things We Need to Cook
♦ People We Want to Thank

Use paper on an easel or stand-up display board so children can watch as you print. Begin with a title and brief discussion of the purpose of the list. Set up the scenario and invite class participation, recording responses and making verbal observations about the words as you write. For example, "Birthday begins with a letter B just like Bobby's name." "How many times did we write the word *look* on our list today?" "We will be using our eyes a lot on our walk!" Offer comments and pose questions as needed to redirect thinking and spark interest. "What will we need for mixing and pouring?" "What other things might be on the farm?" Stop every so often to read the list, pointing to each response as you read it. During some List-making sessions, number the items.

Refer to numbers as you write: "This word *book* rhymes with a word we wrote in number three, *cook*. Only the first letter is different. What letter does *book* start with? How about *cook?*" Keep the lists out and available for children: display on the easel, hang up somewhere in the classroom, or lay on a table. Use the lists during related activities, such as cooking or art projects, and review lists made for outings when you return, checking off items accomplished. The process of List Making, followed by putting lists to use during an activity or reviewing lists after an activity, gives children tangible experience with print that is both meaningful and functional.

For another effective way to note completed steps, try folding back the block when a particular step is done. Children feel a sense of accomplishment as the Time Line shortens before their eyes and the final step nears. Projects well suited to a Time Line approach include:

- party preparations
- gift making and wrapping
- group murals
- play structure constructions
- science projects
- rearranging the classroom
- setting up a new interest area or dramatic play center

Time Lines

For a variation on List Making, try making a Time Line for a day, week, or month. Time Lines also work well for more involved projects that will take several days to complete. Children like to know "what's next?" and the overview of a big project charted on a Time Line often makes individual steps more meaningful and the anticipated result more exciting.

Make a Time Line that runs horizontally from left to right, in numbered block form. Follow a procedure similar to that given for List Making when constructing the Time Line. This activity may need to be more teacher-directed because children may not be familiar with the steps necessary to complete the project.

The goal is to lay out the project step by step, in as few words as possible, before children begin. Be prepared to answer questions and respond to comments as you write; make verbal observations about the print as you go, such as you did for List Making. Reread the Time Line when it is completed. Display the Time Line so children can refer to it as they work on their project. At the completion of each step and/or at the resumption of the project, refer to the Time Line to review what has been accomplished and what comes next. Mark completed steps in some way, such as with a sticker, rubber stamp, or check mark over the number.

Photo Displays and Books

Children love to see photographs of their families, friends, teachers, and most of all, themselves. Take advantage of this attraction by combining photos with print. Assemble a collection of photographs by keeping a classroom camera on hand, asking parents to contribute family pictures, and inviting parents to play "shutterbug" when they accompany the class on field trips.

Photo Displays

Hang photos with descriptive captions throughout the classroom. For example, in the block area, display pictures of children building or posing with finished projects and add a caption that reads "Bobby and Michelle build a castle." In the Art Area, hang photos of children involved in various art projects; the caption might read, "Jessica paints flowers."

Table displays are another good way to make photos a source of print. Use large Tent Labels or easel-back Stand-up Labels to present a collection of related photos. Keep an album of captioned photos out and available for children to look at anytime. The library or book corner is a good place to keep photo albums.

Photo displays and albums can feature any event or subject:

- a field trip
- Outdoor Fun
- a special party or celebration
- a school play or musical
- classroom visitors, such as Guest Readers or parents
- Our Families

Title the collection and caption each photo with a few words. Use proper names as often as possible.

Make photo albums and displays more interesting and eye-catching by cutting photos into a variety of shapes. Long rectangles, triangles, squares, ovals, circles, diamonds, and hearts are often more appealing than uniform rectangular-shaped photos. A variety of shapes also provides more flexibility when displaying and labeling photographs.

Katie's sister

Photo Books

Create stories that use classroom photos as illustrations—children will love to see themselves featured in a story. Use any photo that fits the subject of the book; keep the text brief and the wording simple. An Alphabet Book that features photos of children engaged in classroom fun is a good place to start.

- A: Sherry is an ARTIST (with a photo of a child painting or drawing).
- B: Gregg plays with BLOCKS.
- C: Duane plays with CLAY.
- D: Gayle is a DOCTOR (with a photo of a child in a Dramatic Play Hospital setting).

Don't be concerned with filling the entire book at once. Let pages remain blank and fill them when photos are available.

Other Photo Book ideas include:

- "The Farm": a field trip to a farm provides illustrations
- "Who Are We?": a Halloween photo guessing book
- "Our Snowy Day": patterned after the Ezra Jack Keats book *The Snowy Day*
- "We Are Special": a book about likenesses and differences showing families at home and children doing favorite things

Question of the Day or Week

In a group setting, pose a question to which all children can respond; further validate their responses by recording them on paper. Use large chart paper or even the fronts and backs of large brown paper grocery bags for questions and answers. Print the question at the top of the paper and each child's name and response below. Use a dark-colored marker and position paper on an easel or clipboard so children can observe their words as you print them.

Choose questions that relate to weekly or monthly themes, special events, seasons or holidays, field trips, or books. Questions may be specific or very general and should not have right or wrong answers. Design the Question of the Day or Week to elicit personal responses, such as favorite things or experiences, informative and factual answers, imaginative replies, feelings or ideas about a given topic, or estimates and predictions.

1. Theme Questions
   Theme: Transportation/Travel
   - Name a vehicle with wheels.
   - What color is your family car?
   - Name a part of a bus.
   - Who is someone you know who lives far away?
   - Have you ever traveled on a bus, train, or airplane? Where did you go?
   - Why are wheels round?
   - Where would you like to travel?

2. Personal Questions
   - What is your favorite color?
   - What is your favorite fruit?
   - What is your favorite thing to do on a rainy day?

3. Informative Questions
   - How many children are there in your family?
   - How many windows are in your bedroom?
   - What color is your house?

4. Imaginative Questions
   - If you could be a bug, which one would you be?
   - If you had wings, where would you fly?
   - If you can have any kind of creature for a pet, which one would you choose?

5. Feeling Questions
   - How can you make a new friend feel welcome?
   - Does anything frighten (scare) you?
   - What makes you angry (mad)?

6. Idea Questions
   - What is something you eat to be healthy?
   - What happened to all of the dinosaurs that used to live on this planet?
   - Why is it important not to litter?

7. Estimate/Predict Questions
   - Do you think it will rain today?
   - What is in this small box? (Show a small box and shake it.) Taped closed, it can also be passed around for children to hold when answering.
   - What do you think lunch will be today? (This is a particularly good question if the classroom is near the kitchen.)

For more fun, try these questions:

- How many scoops of ice cream could you eat?
- Tell us something you can do very well.
- What is your favorite snack?
- What would you like to be when you grow up?
- What is something that would fit in your pocket?
- What instrument would you like to play?
- What are clouds made of?
- If you dug up a treasure chest, what would be in it?

In addition to seeing their own words printed next to their name, children will:

- hear friends' responses and see friends' words printed on the same page as their own
- be given practice at turn taking and waiting while others have a turn
- have an opportunity to hear responses that are like their own and different from their own

- begin to realize how much they have to share with others
- appreciate differences in others
- accept differences in themselves
- gain confidence speaking in front of others
- develop a sense of pride in their own words and ideas

Hang finished questions together in an area where children and parents can read them. Parents find the responses especially fun and insightful. Gather ten to twelve questions before removing them to make room for more. When you remove question lists, try cutting each child's response into a strip that he or she can take home or that you glue into each child's personal book titled "What I Think." If space is limited, collect questions (and responses) on a clipboard and display on a shelf or table, or hole-punch one corner and fasten questions together with a binder ring. Keep the most recent questions on top.

Waiting Lists

For areas of the classroom that can accommodate only a limited number of children, make a Waiting List so children can "sign up" for a turn. As children leave the area, those next on the list can take their turn. The use of Waiting Lists in interest centers and other areas of the classroom not only brings a sense of maturity and fairness to a classroom, but also offers to children numerous opportunities to write their own names. As they do so, they also observe the names of friends and practice a number of skills: rote counting, sequencing, turn taking, and time management. If children cannot write their full names, encourage them to write as much as they are able, and then fill in as needed.

"What We Know" Puzzle

For this print activity, each child contributes an idea about a topic (an animal, a vehicle, a toy, etc.), an outline of which appears on a large sheet of paper. As children tell what they know about the subject, fit their responses into the outline. Try to print responses in short-sentence form, beginning with the name of the topic each time so that children see some words written several times:

♦ Flowers grow.
♦ Flowers like sun.
♦ Flowers smell good.
♦ Flowers are many colors.
♦ Flowers have stems.

When the topic (or available space) has been exhausted, draw lines separating the responses; cut on the lines, creating the "puzzle" pieces. Reassemble the puzzle, reading "What We Know" as each piece is added. Children feel a sense of pride and accomplishment in creating a tangible picture of the many things they know about a particular topic.

To make puzzles more durable for reuse, laminate, cover with clear Contac® paper, or back with heavy cardboard before cutting. Store puzzles in an envelope or folded paper pocket with a small picture and topic word label affixed to the front.

Word Banks

Create a Word Bank in which words of special interest can be collected. Cover a round oatmeal container with brightly colored paper. Decorate the paper with markers, crayons, stickers, or small scraps of paper. Write WORD BANK on the front and cut a slot in the lid. On the back of the box, attach an envelope or a paper pocket to hold a pencil and blank paper for words. "Save" words that are new, unusual, special, or fun. Every so often, open the Bank, remove all the words, and read them. Play "Discrimination Games" with the words:

♦ sort them by beginning letter or by the number of letters in each
♦ find the longest, find the shortest
♦ use the word in a sentence
♦ arrange the words alphabetically
♦ recall where the words were found or used previously

Chapter 2: Curriculum

Find words in stories being read in class and in books that children bring from home. Introduce the Word Bank and initiate its use by suggesting that a word be added after its meaning has been discussed. For example, as a book is being read, discuss new or unfamiliar words. Take cues from children's faces and ask questions: "What does *curious* mean?" Stop to discuss confusing words immediately or discuss them at the end of the story, whichever is more comfortable. Always present the word to the group before defining it yourself: "Does anyone know what a *quarrel* is?" Often children's interpretations of words mean more to other children than an adult's explanation. If no one in the group is familiar with the word, discuss it in terms that are understandable, and present some examples of the word's usage. Then suggest: "Let's add this new word to our Word Bank." Write the word and invite a child to place it in the slot. Once you have introduced the Word Bank in this way, children will find words for it and suggest adding words being discussed in class.

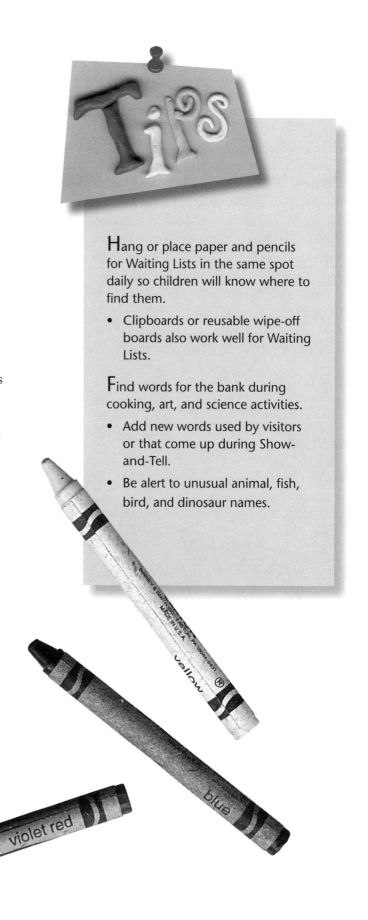

Hang or place paper and pencils for Waiting Lists in the same spot daily so children will know where to find them.

- Clipboards or reusable wipe-off boards also work well for Waiting Lists.

Find words for the bank during cooking, art, and science activities.

- Add new words used by visitors or that come up during Show-and-Tell.

- Be alert to unusual animal, fish, bird, and dinosaur names.

Word Webs

Following a theme or a topic presented in class, engage children in a brainstorming activity called Word Webbing. Write the theme or topic on a piece of paper and place it in the center of the rug during circle time; display a picture representing the topic if you choose. Be prepared with blank pieces of paper (any color or shape), markers, and yarn. Encourage children to contribute what they know about the topic using only one or two words. Write the child's name and ideas on a separate piece of paper. Allow each child to place their idea on the rug surrounding the topic. When everyone has had a turn, give each child a piece of yarn. Let them connect their words to the central theme or topic, creating a web of knowledge. Review each child's response as the yarn is connected.

Picture Word Puzzles

Make classroom puzzles that include a word for children to put together by cutting pictures into several pieces. Pictures from old calendars work especially well. Request calendars from parents and check with local bookstores or greeting card shops at the end of the year. Use a black marker to stencil the name of the object, place, or animal pictured directly onto the bottom or top of the picture. (Use a stencil rather than regular printing so letters will be bolder and more noticeable to children when assembling the puzzle.) Mount the picture on cardboard and allow to dry. Draw lines on the picture with a pencil, dividing it into several parts; cut on the lines to create a puzzle. Try to divide the picture to include one or several whole letters on each piece. As children put the puzzles together, they are handling print and experiencing informal observations of the word that names the picture.

Children enjoy making these Picture Word Puzzles. Provide a supply of pictures and invite children to choose the ones they would like to make into puzzles. Stencil on the word naming the picture, letting children help color in the stenciled letters with a black marker, if you choose. Children can also help glue the picture onto the cardboard back and cut the picture apart.

Picture Words

Children can make Picture Words similar to those made by teachers for labeling. Cover a piece of paper with pictures relating to a particular word. Do this in a random, collage-type way; glue and let dry. For example, find pictures of dogs for the word *dog;* pictures of babies, children, and adults for the word *people;* and any kind of food pictures for the word *food.* Magazines and catalogs make excellent sources of pictures for Picture Words. Use letter stencils to trace the pictured word directly onto the collage. Next, cut the necessary letters out of additional pictures of the named object and place them all in one envelope. Children can sort through the letters to find those they need to make the word. For the word *dog,* they should find the three letters all made from pictures of dogs and put them together to form the word. Providing the collage with the stenciled word will help children with letter placement. Children may form the word directly on the collage or next to it. As they become familiar with the words, they may use Picture Words without the collage.

Children will also enjoy "reading" these words, because the item being named will be visible on each individual letter.

Dictionary Making

First, introduce children to dictionaries by adding a selection of juvenile and adult dictionaries to the library or book area. Then, begin a classroom dictionary by making a blank book with a page for each letter of the alphabet. Glue several pictures on each page. Find pictures in newspapers, magazines, and catalogs or on gift wrap and children's artwork. Print child-dictated definitions next to each picture. Collect definitions during a group time or fill in the dictionary anytime during the regular classroom routine. Encourage children to add their own found pictures and definitions or begin their own dictionaries.

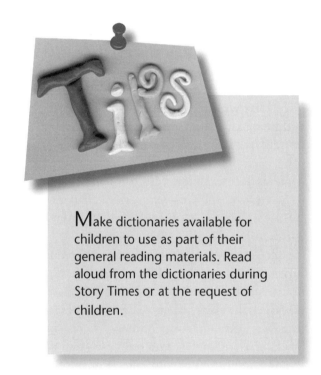

Make dictionaries available for children to use as part of their general reading materials. Read aloud from the dictionaries during Story Times or at the request of children.

Collection Books

Most children enjoy cutting pictures from magazines, newspapers, and catalogs. Take advantage of this interest and combine it with print by making Collection Books. These are scrapbooks that children can work on anytime during the day, in small groups or independently. Collection Books present one or two topics with a text of a few words and a variety of corresponding pictures. As children search for pictures, they are actively handling and experiencing a variety of print sources.

Begin Collection Books by assembling ten-page blank books of any size. On the cover, print the title of the book and glue one or two pictures relating to the title. Print the title, which also serves as the text, on every page of the book. Depending on the ages and abilities of the children, you may wish to glue several picture clues throughout the book.

Along with the books provide scissors; glue; and magazines, newspapers, catalogs, and other sources of pictures. Have crayons, pencils, and other writing instruments available as well, as some children may wish to print the title again as they work on the Collection Book. Put Collection Books and supplies on art shelves or anywhere children can use the books freely.

Collection Book topics can be anything of interest to the class, perhaps reflecting the season or an upcoming event or relating directly to weekly or monthly themes. Be prepared to accept topic suggestions from children. Topics should be broad enough and picture sources varied enough to enable children to fill Collection Books easily. If it is too difficult to find pictures, children will become frustrated and lose interest.

Collection Book topics might include:

♦ Cars and Trucks
♦ Dogs
♦ Cats
♦ Birds
♦ Flowers
♦ People
♦ Houses
♦ Families
♦ Food
♦ Tools
♦ Babies and Children

Interesting picture sources in the community might include:

♦ grocery and department store circulars
♦ seed catalogs
♦ pet store brochures
♦ car dealership booklets
♦ real estate brochures

Collection Books present a wonderful opportunity for children to work independently. Add completed Collection Books to bookshelves or the library corner. This type of book is fun to "read" together, discussing pictures and attending to the one- or two-word text (also the title).

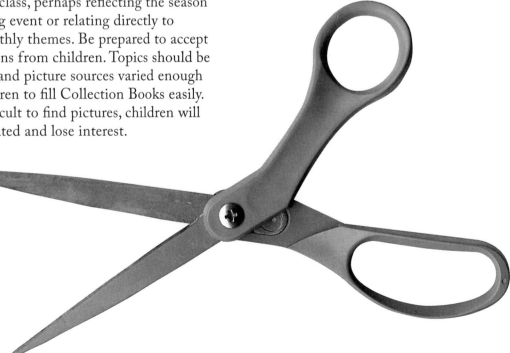

Letter Writing

Extend Letter Writing to include people other than family members. On a regular basis, compose and mail a letter to someone in the community, a classmate who has moved, or someone of interest to the class, such as a children's author or illustrator.

Set the stage for letter writing by discussing to whom the letter will be sent and for what purpose. Encourage children to contribute to the main body of the letter any information they would like to convey and questions they would like to ask. Print the letter as it is dictated or jot down several words that encompass the ideas given, composing the actual letter later. Always read the finished letter to children and allow each child to sign his or her name if possible. Follow correct letter writing procedures, including headings, return addresses, salutations, and closings. Direct children's attention to the format.

Send letters to:

- children's authors and illustrators: Direct letters to the publishing companies, addresses for which are usually found in the front of the books, or look for contact addresses on authors' Web sites.

- various local and federal governmental agencies and nonprofit organizations, such as the Forestry Department and the Wildlife Federation: These often yield return letters and posters, booklets, and so on. Obtain information about other geographic areas by writing to travel and information offices of most state capitals.

- children's magazines: These often offer opportunities for children to contribute art, ideas, and letters.

- classmates who move: Take advantage of this opportunity to correspond. Record new addresses of friends when they leave and keep in touch by mail.

- another classroom in the community or surrounding area: A wonderful way to have fun with letter writing is to begin a letter exchange. Write about classroom news and share ideas, fun, and games.

Mark all correspondences on a calendar and read return letters aloud. This is an excellent way to observe the passage of time, as well as to understand another function of print—a means of written communication between two or more people. Make both the letter and the envelope available so children can examine them more closely.

- Begin a stamp collection in a blank book or on posterboard.

- Keep track of where letters come from by placing a sticker on a map each time a letter is received.

Newsletters and Messages to Parents

Keeping parents informed through regular newsletters or take-home flyers has always been an important part of the early childhood program. Parent-teacher communications are often enhanced and strengthened through print. Traditionally, such communiqués have been prepared by teachers and administrators, with no real student involvement. Thus, two integral parts of a child's life, home and school, are communicating, and the child is no more than the messenger in this process, transporting print from one adult to another. The literacy-rich preschool program involves children in the preparation of newsletters and notes to their own parents, giving them valuable examples of the purposes and usefulness of print.

Depending on the length and nature of the communication, children can take part by:

♦ being informed of the content of the letter (highlight important words and ideas, as needed)

♦ helping to compose the actual letter or note, including short messages and reminders

♦ contributing news and information

♦ adding lettering and illustrations

Informing children of the content of letters is most effective when letters are long or not particularly interesting to children. Rather than reading the whole letter, show it and tell children what it is about, explaining that it is too long to read word for word. Highlight important words by writing them for children to see. Print days of the week and words that tell what, where, and when, such as SCHOOL, CLASSROOM, VISIT, CONFERENCE, AND MEETING. Point to these words as you discuss the letter.

Elicit children's help in composing short messages and reminders that relate most directly to their classroom experiences. Examples of the kinds of communications that children can write include invitations to visit the classroom, informative notes about classroom routines or plans (doorknob note: WE ARE ON A WALK; WE ARE AT THE LIBRARY), requests for materials or parental involvement, and reminders (SHOW-AND-TELL TOMORROW; NO SCHOOL MONDAY). Tell children the purpose of the correspondence and let them offer their own words to relate the WHAT, WHEN, WHERE, and WHY of the matter. You can help direct and encourage children's responses by writing the words WHAT, WHEN, WHERE, and WHY on a large sheet of paper and following these with children's suggested responses. Print words and ideas as children volunteer them, combine responses, and compose the letter. Some communications may be short enough for children to print the words themselves. Be sure to read the finished communication aloud before giving it to the children to deliver.

When preparing a multi-page newsletter that informs parents of events that have already happened or future classroom plans, give children an opportunity to create entire news items or short stories. Tell children the purpose of the newsletter—to inform parents of classroom news—and then ask them what they would like to include. Encourage children to dictate a few sentences about a favorite (or new) book in the classroom, a group art project, a special visitor, a recent or planned field trip, a classroom pet, or any classroom event. Record children's sentences as they dictate and combine all contributions with any items you've written into a newsletter.

Children will also enjoy decorating and illustrating notes and newsletters to parents. Provide small pieces of paper and encourage children to make pencil drawings. Tape or glue artwork on the newsletter between various news events and bits of information before copying. Or, leave spaces on the prepared newsletter where children can draw, and then copy. Another fun way to involve children is to encourage them to draw within a border the whole way around the page. A 1" or 1½" border usually provides sufficient space for children's decorations: flowers, suns, shapes of all kinds, bugs or animals, little people, and ABCs. This is a very effective way to involve even the youngest child in a print-handling experience.

Parents will enjoy reading news in their children's own words and seeing children's illustrations on these otherwise plain correspondences. Children will enjoy sharing news and demonstrating new-found skills. These literacy activities fulfill a mutual need to impart and receive information for a specific purpose. By participating, children will recognize yet another use for print—providing and sharing information.

Keep a clipboard, paper, and writing instruments handy for on-the-spot recordings. If children are reluctant to have their words written directly on artwork (or if there is little space to do so), use a separate piece of paper and invite children to tape or clip the words to the artwork in any way they choose.

- Make notebooks or blank pads of paper available throughout the classroom. Head the page with a statement or question to which children might respond. Be prepared to record children's words or elicit responses when children are in a particular area with you. Occasionally, spend a few moments at the start or end of group times to read the responses gathered. Try questions and statements like these:

  ▶ What do you see out of the window?

  ▶ It makes me think of _____. (next to a modern art picture or ink blot design)

  ▶ It feels like _____. (next to a bowl of Guessing Goop or Play Putty—see the following recipes—or next to a sealed plastic bag or dish of cold spaghetti noodles)

Dictations

Be prepared to accept and record children's words throughout the day. This is one way to emphasize that recorded dictation is actually "talk written down." When recording children's words, be a scribe, not an editor. Repeat the child's words as they are spoken, without adding your own values or correcting grammar. Children need to hear their own words read back, not your rewording. Asking questions ("Should we write your words?" or "Do you want me to write your words on your drawing?") and offering suggestions ("Let's write your words so you can take them home.") create valuable opportunities for children to see their spoken words in print. As they become accustomed to this practice, children will soon begin asking you to record their dictations. Many will model the example and begin to write their own words, requesting help with spelling only.

Making Your Own Ink or Paint Blot Designs

Fold a piece of paper in half. Open it flat. Using a spoon, craft stick, or paintbrush, put several small dabs of paint in different spots on one side of the paper near the fold. Use one color or several. Fold the unpainted side over the painted side. Rub gently with your fingers from the fold to the edges of the paper. Unfold and let dry.

Making Guessing Goop

For "goop" you can touch, hold, feel, and squeeze, mix 1 cup of cornstarch and 1 cup of water in a large bowl.

Making Play Putty

Pour 1 cup of white glue into ¾ cup of liquid starch. Add more starch (a few drops at a time) if mixture is too sticky.

Be open to other opportunities to record comments, stories, and directions. Ask children to describe how they made something or figured out something. After recording these experiences in print, ask children if they would like to illustrate the words. Read dictations back to children immediately and find opportunities to share dictations with the other children.

♦ Write a statement made by each child during Show and Tell.

♦ Write a child's directions for a pretend recipe in dramatic play.

♦ Write observations made on a walk or outing, once you return.

♦ On Friday write plans for the weekend.

Mystery Boxes

Using Mystery Boxes creates a literacy activity that involves home and parents. In this activity one child at a time is the center of attention, sharing something from home, and involving their friends in a print-rich guessing game.

Prepare a set of Mystery Boxes: Choose boxes of a variety of shapes and sizes and cover each with colored construction paper or gift wrap. Using a black marker, write a question mark on the front or lid of each box. Place a piece of string or yarn in each box.

Invite one child at a time to take a Mystery Box home, put one thing inside, tie the box closed with yarn, and bring it back. (The varied assortment of sizes and shapes will encourage children to choose items that "fit" the boxes.) Send a Mystery Box home once during the week or on Friday to be returned Monday.

When the Mystery Box is returned, invite the other children to "Guess what's inside." List each child's name on a piece of paper and print their guess next to it. Let children make guesses during a circle time or make the Mystery Box available to children throughout the day and record their guesses as they are given. (You should also make a guess.) Either way, children should have an opportunity to handle the Mystery Box: hold it, smell it, and shake it. Either at circle time or the end of the day, after everyone has had a turn to guess the contents, reread the children's names and guesses. Then let the child who filled the box untie it and reveal what's inside. Write the answer on the paper at the end of the list of names: "Jerry brought a _____."

If no one has guessed correctly, allow time for up to three clues and a few additional guesses. Once the mystery has been solved, set out the Mystery Box and its contents for further investigation, along with the list of guesses and the answer.

Consider these unusual possibilities when making different-sized Mystery Boxes:

♦ pill box

♦ tiny jewelry box

♦ square jewelry box

♦ oatmeal canister

♦ flat candy box

♦ long pencil box

♦ long flat tie box

♦ shoe box

♦ cereal box

Try a Mystery Bag, a Mystery Envelope, or a Mystery Tube (made with a paper towel tube) instead of a box.

TRAVELING TEDDY

Traveling Teddy Bear

Similar to a Mystery Box activity, this is an opportunity to involve children's families in a school activity while providing enriching languages and literacy experiences.

Choose one of the most popular stuffed animals in the classroom or buy a new one. A teddy bear works well because most children enjoy the company of a friendly bear. Assemble a backpack for this traveler with a blanket, brush, favorite book, letter of introduction, and journal. Depending on the availability of materials and the type of bear used, add other items to the backpack: a camera with film, a T-shirt, a hat, a game to play, or a small pillow. A small, lightweight backpack works best.

Each Friday, one child takes Traveling Teddy home for the weekend. While at the child's home, Teddy can take part in any weekend plans the family may have, and on Monday, Teddy returns to school with the child. When Teddy returns, talk about the weekend and record some of Teddy's adventures with the child in Teddy's journal. Bring Teddy to circle time and encourage the child to talk about the weekend, recording whatever he or she says. Add the child's words to the Bear's journal and prepare Teddy's backpack for the coming weekend's trip.

When Teddy visits the next child's house, the journal will again accompany him. The purpose of the journal is to give parents and children something to read together and to provide some ideas for things to do with Teddy. The fact that the journal entries come from classmates and friends make them more meaningful.

If you include a camera in the backpack, parents can take a picture of their child with Teddy. When the pictures are developed, add them to the appropriate journal entry.

For an example of what Traveling Teddy's first journal entry (prepared by a teacher) might look like, see Appendix 3. Traveling Teddy Bear's Introduction, also included in the backpack, might look like the one shown in Appendix 4.

Be sure to hand-print this letter of introduction. Use paper that is special in some way: actual stationery, a decorated border, or plain paper with a few bear stickers on it. Before packing the letter, fold it and put it in an envelope addressed "To My Friends."

Literature

Story time is a daily part of nearly every early childhood classroom. Regular story reading contributes greatly to the literacy development of young children. Supplement these conventional book reading experiences with a number of other book-handling and independent "reading" opportunities. One of the most important challenges the early childhood teacher faces is instilling in young children a love for books and a desire to read. A Story Time that is rich in imagination and full of the unexpected will give children many opportunities to take pleasure in books and be motivated to read. Look in Appendix 21 for more ideas for book stretching for all areas of the early childhood curriculum.

Story Reading Techniques

Vary story reading techniques so that each Story Time is a unique experience for both reader and listener. Try not to use any technique more than once a week and don't forsake the traditional, more passive reading-listening Story Time. The pleasure children experience in just listening and watching as a book is being read remains one of the best avenues to a love of books and a desire to read.

Try telling a story without the use of a book. All that is required is a comfortable familiarity with the book, an interesting storytelling style, and dramatic facial expressions. Props and visual aids can also enhance storytelling. Rather than the book as the focal point, much of the children's attention will be directed to the props. Without a visual reference, children have the opportunity to imagine characters and story events, an equally rewarding exercise.

When reading a book or telling a story, always begin with the title, author, and illustrator. Refresh children's memories of other books by the same author or illustrator and show a few of the books if possible. Often, the back cover or inside book jacket will contain a short synopsis of the story or information about any award the book may have garnered. Be attentive to the cover and first few pages of any book you read for information you can share with children: author or illustrator biographies, photos, or book dedications. Include this information in your introduction to the book. Children are fascinated to read an award-winning book, and a brief synopsis heightens interest.

Children As Storytellers

Provide opportunities for children to be Storytellers in the classroom. At the beginning or close of each Story Time, give each child a chance to tell a story either with or without a book. Or, build a special weekly Children's Story Time into the classroom schedule. Choose Storytellers at the beginning of the week, so children know in advance when they will have a turn and can plan a story, bring a prop from home, or draw an illustration for their story.

Creating a Prop Box

Use a large box, such as a computer paper box, and decorate it with gift wrap, children's artwork, or pictures of story characters. Place ten or twelve props in the box and change the selection frequently. Begin a Prop Box with some of these items: hats, musical instruments, gloves, jewelry, crowns, fans, a stuffed animal, a seashell, and so on.

Group Storytelling

Facilitate Group Storytelling with the use of pictures from magazines, newspapers, or calendars. Show the picture and encourage children to tell a story about it. Have children tell stories one at a time or let each child contribute to one group story. Record the story on tape or in print and listen to it or read it again.

Story Motivators

Add something to reading to spark interest— something to motivate both the listener and the reader. Every book or story contains numerous possibilities for motivators. Choose an integral or repetitive part of the story or something funny and unusual. Wear a hat or a piece of jewelry, carry an umbrella or a pail, ring a bell or blow a horn, or bring a stuffed animal or a jar of honey to Story Time, and children will take an immediate interest in what is about to happen. Tell children in a few words how the motivator relates to the story or simply begin, letting the group wonder how the motivator fits in.

Find a Story Motivator that can be a regular part of every Story Time. This should be something children will recognize as a signal that a special story is about to begin. Be inventive! Think of props you can make or items you can share from home.

♦ Wrap a book like a present and open it with the children before reading it.
♦ Wear a special Story Time hat.
♦ Ring a Story Time chime.
♦ Decorate a chair to use at Story Time.
♦ Use a "magic carpet" for story reading.
♦ Bring something special from your home: a music box, a childhood toy, or an unusual souvenir.

Story Tokens

As with most Story Time motivators, Story Tokens work best when used spontaneously, without children's prior knowledge. Prepare a special box or basket to hold the tokens. Decorate the box or basket with bows, shiny paper, and/or glitter to make it more appealing to children. Fill it with small tokens, and when Story Time begins, invite children to take a token from the basket to hold as you read. The token should relate to the book and evoke a feeling of connection between the listener and the story.

See Appendix 5 for some stories that work well with tokens, such as buttons, seeds, pebbles, sand, acorns, paintbrushes, beans, coins, and powder.

Chapter 2: Curriculum

Story Happenings

Create a Story Event or Happening by involving children in the preparations for a story. One way to do this is to make a Story Rug with children and use it to sit on during Story Time. Give each child a 9" x 12" piece of felt (light colors work best). Have them draw on the felt with fabric crayons or permanent markers. Sew the felt pieces together into one group story rug. If you prefer, let children decorate a plain canvas rug. Travel on the Story Rug to an Inupiaq Village in *Eskimo Boy* by Russ Kendall or *The Wump World* by Bill Peet.

Try making cone-shaped birthday hats with children and wear them while reading a story about a birthday. Sing "Happy Birthday to You" and have a special snack after stories such as *Handtalk Birthday* by Remy Charlip, *Happy Birthday Moe Dog* by Nicholas Heller, *Happy Birthday, Good Knight* by Shelley Moore Thomas, *F Is for Fiesta* by Susan Middleton Elya, or *The Birthday Fish* by Dan Yaccarino.

Provide blankets and stuffed animals so children can curl up and listen to a "bedtime story" such as *Bedtime for Frances* by Russell Hoban, *The Sleep Book* by Dr. Seuss, *Starry Safari* by Linda Ashman, *Sleepy Cadillac: A Bedtime Drive* by Thacher Hurd, or *The Practically Perfect Pajamas* by Erik Brooks.

Hang several real umbrellas from the ceiling and gather children under the umbrellas for a "rainy story" such as *Rain Drop Splash* by Alvin Tresselt, *Rain Talk* by Mary Serfozo, *I Love the Rain* by Margaret Park Bridges, *Raindrop, Plop!* by Wendy Cheyette Lewison, or *The Umbrella* by Jan Brett.

Light a Story Time candle, dim the lights, and tell or read stories with soothing, calming themes such as *Grandfather Twilight* by Barbara Berger, *Owl Moon* by Jane Yolen, *A Hug for You* by Margaret Anastas, *Three Pebbles and a Song* by Eileen Spinelli, or *The Peace Book* by Todd Parr.

Pass around an ice cube (with or without mittens) as you read a winter book such as *The Wild Toboggan Ride* by Suzan Reid, *The Winter Bear* by Ruth Craft, *The First Day of Winter* by Denise Fleming, *Hello, Snow!* by Hope Vestergaard, or *The Missing Mitten Mystery* by Steven Kellogg.

You can also use general motivators for any book or story—something that draws attention and interest, yet is not specific to the book.

- Bring an instrument, a puppet, or a bag or box containing the book to be read at Story Time.

- Tell stories with the help of a felt board. Prepare a whole set of felt props for the story or use just one or two.

- Assemble a basket of three-dimension story props. Often, a quick inventory of classroom toys will result in a basket full of props. Blocks, dollhouse furniture and dolls, small cars, and plastic animals will relate to many stories.

Choral Participation

Here's an opportunity to involve children more directly in Story Time. When reading books that contain repetition or a rhythmic, recurring verse, invite children to join in at the appropriate time.

Try these books for Choral Participation: *Alexander and the Terrible, Horrible, No Good, Very Bad Day* by Judith Viorst; *Bears in the Night* by Stan and Jan Berenstain; *Brown Bear, Brown Bear, What Do You See?* by Bill Martin, Jr.; or *There's a Hole in the Bucket* by Nadine Bernard Westcott. For more fun Choral Participation books, see Appendix 6.

Reenactments

A wonderful way to put print into action is to reenact stories with children. This works best with books that children have read several times. The more familiar children are with a story, the more comfortable and willing they will be to act it out. Assign parts or let children choose their favorite part, and then briefly run through a practice reenactment. Invite children to do the motions and facial expressions as you read the words, or act as narrator and encourage children to provide the dialogue.

Choose brief stories so that you can repeat these mini-plays as often as necessary to give all children a turn. Children will become more confident and comfortable with each repetition. A supply of props adds to the fun and often encourages children to join in; a pretend microphone will often draw even the most reluctant child into the fun.

Sound Effect Stories

Stories and books with a pattern of repetitive sounds or words present wonderful opportunities for group participation. Read a few pages, providing appropriate sounds, and then encourage children to join in the fun by repeating the sounds at the appropriate points in the story. Look for books that contain a pattern of sounds or words at regular intervals throughout the story. Try these fun Sound Effect Books: *Baby Rattlesnake* by Te Ata; *Chicka Chicka Boom Boom* by John Archambault and Bill Martin, Jr.; *Mr. Brown Says Moo, Can You?* by Dr. Seuss; or *The Very Busy Spider* by Eric Carle. For more fun Sound Effect Stories, see Appendix 7.

Add-on Stories

Read a book that involves a series of events or characters. After reading, invite children to add to the story by offering their own ideas for more events and people. List all responses on a large sheet of paper as children give them to you. Reread the story with the new additions, pointing to each as it is read. Keep the lists in case children ask to hear the add-ons at the next story reading. Books well suited to an Add-on activity include: *Hi, Pizza Man* by Virginia Walter; *Mary Wore Her Red Dress* by Merle Peek; *The Gingerbread Man* by Lucy Kincaid; *Sarah's Questions* by Harriet Ziefert; and *Here Are My Hands* by Bill Martin, Jr., and John Archambault. For more Add-on Story ideas, see Appendix 8.

Retell a Story

Choose a book to read to children several times over a period of days. After a number of story repetitions, invite children to retell the story during a group time. Move around the circle, giving each child a turn to add one more part of the story in his or her own words. If necessary, help the retelling along with questions:

- "What happened next?"
- "Then what did they do?"
- "Where did they go?"

Microphones are easy to make and come in handy for a number of language and music activities. Cover cardboard bathroom tissue tubes or a half of a paper towel tube with paper or felt. Crumple a square of aluminum foil into a ball and secure it to one end of the tube with glue. Tape a black piece of yarn to the inside of the other end, letting it dangle like a cord.

Profiling Illustrators

Introduce children to illustrators by gathering several books by the same illustrator. This focuses attention on books, but from a different perspective. Read one of the books during Story Time and show the others, looking for similar artistic techniques. Make these books available in or near the Art Area and encourage children to try some of the illustrator's techniques. If possible, show children a picture of the illustrator. Having a picture to go along with the name makes these people more real and interesting to children. Pictures can often be found on book jackets, in book club news, in children's or parents' magazines, and on the Internet. You can also write to a publishing company, requesting a picture of a particular illustrator, or find interesting facts and contact information on an illustrator's Web site. For added literacy experiences, compose letters with children's help.

Look for books by these illustrators: Jan Brett, Eric Carle, Dr. Seuss, Ezra Jack Keats, Leo Lioni, Jane Yolen, Steven Kellogg, Anthony Browne, Peter Spier, and Rosemary Wells.

Choose illustrators who use a variety of styles: intricate borders, unusual and imaginative drawings, collage, torn paper art, and rich watercolors.

Guest Readers

Nothing makes a Story Time more interesting than a new and different reader! Invite members of the community to the classroom to read books or tell stories. As children see people read whom they associate with roles such as directing traffic, helping sick people get better, or fighting fires, they develop a more positive attitude toward books and knowing how to read.

Consider the following possibilities. After a field trip to a farm, bakery, or fire station, invite the farmer, baker, or firefighter to visit the classroom and read a story. Or, simply phone the local post office, police station, or any community

facility and ask whether anyone who works there would be interested in reading a short book to a group of children. It is surprising how many people are quite excited about and accepting of these Reader Invitations. And think how exciting it will be for children to have a story about a fire truck read to them by an actual firefighter in uniform (or at least wearing an authentic hat)! A short letter of invitation (see the sample in Appendix 9) is also an effective way to locate interested community members.

Be as accommodating as possible when setting up a time for the Reader's visit. Always give Guest Readers a short time to page through the book before getting started. Provide a comfortable chair or rug area. Give a short introduction and prepare a token of thanks that the Guest Reader can take home. Try to select a book that relates in some way to the Reader. If possible, photograph the Reader as he or she reads to the children. These photos make wonderful additions to a labeled photo display or captioned album and provide a meaningful follow-up thank-you if sent to the Guest Reader.

Parents and other family members, such as grandparents or older siblings, also make wonderful Guest Readers. Invite them personally or in a short letter (see the sample in Appendix 9) and follow the same procedure you would for any Guest Reader. Select a book or let the family member share a child's favorite book from home. Book suggestions for Guest Readers are listed in Appendix 10.

One of the most enjoyable ways to enhance a Story Time is with recorded stories. Books or stories on cassettes present opportunities for independent listening and alternative Story Times. Involve family or even community members by extending an invitation to them to contribute a recorded story to the classroom collection (see a sample request letter in Appendix 11). Tape recorders, tapes, and even books can be loaned as needed. Children will enjoy sharing a parent, grandparent, or older sibling in this way. They will also find it quite rewarding and comforting to hear a familiar voice reading a favorite story in the middle of a busy day. (Appendix 12 includes guidelines for recording a story.)

Children can help make a small token of thanks to present to Guest Readers. If possible, make something to photocopy, so you can keep a supply on hand. Consider these ideas:

- a paper or craft foam bookmark decorated by children with crayon or marker

- a certificate of thanks, colored or decorated by children; children can write the words THANK YOU if they choose; a special drawing, colored in by children, with a note from you; or a photograph of the Reader in the classroom, in a "Thank You" frame. Use card stock, posterboard, craft sticks, or craft foam to make colorful frames. With children's help, write "Thank You" directly on the frame.

Rewrite a Favorite Story

Children can rewrite a familiar book or one recently read in class. The newly created story should follow the original story line but contain new key words and phrases selected by the children and substituted in appropriate places. Present children with a revised title or let children invent new titles with you. Print suggestions as children offer them.

Reread the book with children's revisions. Add the new version to the bookshelf. Children may wish to add illustrations. Many books lend themselves to this activity, including *A Snowy Day* by Ezra Jack Keats, which becomes "A Sunny Day"; *Over in the Meadow* by David Carter, which becomes "Down by the Seashore"; or *Clifford the Big Red Dog* by Norman Bridwell, which becomes "Catherine the Big Red Cat." For more book ideas, see Appendix 13.

Rhyme Time

Children enjoy the rhythm and rhyme of words. You can easily incorporate numerous children's poetry and rhyming books into Story Time. While reading a poem or rhyme before a book at Story Time provides excellent practice, using rhyme outside the framework of a book fosters a new appreciation for language.

Initiate an impromptu Rhyme Time, when everything—and everyone—in the classroom stops for a quick rhyme or poem. A Rhyme Time could come anytime throughout the day. Catch children's attention by using the same Rhyme Time signal each time. A bell, buzzer, or triangle works well, but any instrument will do. Prepare a selection of short rhymes, poems, and prose so you can choose one quickly at the sound of the signal. Print rhymes and poems on an index card and keep them in a Rhyme Time Box. A decorated shoe box works well. When the signal sounds, choose a card from the box and read the rhyme or poem aloud, from any position in the classroom. All activity in the classroom should immediately cease or "freeze" for the reading of the rhyme. Read your own rhymes, child-written verse, or any appropriate children's poetry. Read the title and author first. Read as expressively as possible. If children have become familiar with the verse or rhyme, they may join in; encourage this. Read the selection once, replace it, and go about the normal routine until the next Rhyme Time.

Rather than select from the Rhyme Time Box, choose verses beforehand to emphasize a birthday, season, special holiday, or daily happening. Try these charming sources for Rhymes and Poems: *Animals, Animals* by Eric Carle; *Bird Watch* by Jane Yolen; *Circus* by Jack Prelutsky; *Poems Children Will Sit Still For* compiled by Beatrice Schenk de Regniers, Eva Moore, and Mary Michaels White; or *Sing a Song of Popcorn* edited by Beatrice Schenk deRegniers. For more ideas, See Appendix 14.

Don't restrict selections to "children's verse." Be open to poems and prose written by renowned poets. Try Japanese haiku and even song lyrics. Children's magazines are also wonderful sources of rhymes and verse.

Books in the Classroom

Books have long been an integral part of the early childhood program, providing a variety of literacy experiences as well as an abundance of pleasure. Put books to use for regularly scheduled Story Times and independent activities; make them available in the classroom library and in a quiet area; use them as invaluable sources of language enrichment.

In a print-rich and literacy-friendly classroom, opportunities abound for book-handling experiences throughout the day. These should include opportunities for children to interact independently with printed material. The interactions should encompass the whole classroom and not be restricted to areas where children expect to find books, such as the classroom library or bookshelves.

Multiply book-handling experiences by making books available in every defined space in the classroom. Often children who do not spend time in the classroom library or visit bookshelves frequently will interact with books when they come upon them in the course of play. Display one to three related books on shelves adjacent to toys and supplies. Put a book directly into containers of toys: a book about construction vehicles in a basket of blocks, a book about travel in a box of cars, or a book about colors with a jar of beads. Change book choices frequently in these areas.

Set up one or two special Book Trays in the classroom. Choose one tray for everyday use in the Reading Area or classroom library. It should be large enough to hold most books when they are open. Label the tray A SPECIAL BOOK, using either a flat label or a Stand-up or Tent Label. Decorate the tray with a felt mat, paper doilies, a piece of shiny Mylar or foil, some ribbon glued on the edges and hanging on corners, or even holiday tinsel. Use a second Book Tray to display a new book, library book, child- or class-made book, a book shared from home, a magazine, or a book with a special theme. Put this Tray in any area that relates in some way to the book being displayed and decorate accordingly. For example, with a book about dinosaurs, add a few plastic dinosaurs to the tray, add several postcards to a book about travel, place a stuffed animal on a Book Tray with a book about a teddy bear, or add real pennies to a book about shopping. Encourage children to take the books from the trays to read and look at, replacing them when they are finished. Change the books at least weekly and move one Book Tray frequently so children will find it in different areas of the classroom.

Chapter 2: Curriculum

Books for All Areas in the Classroom

Please see Appendix 15 for a detailed list of books that are suitable for the following areas: Art, Bead/Peg Board/Mosaic Tile, Block and Building, Cooking, Dramatic Play/Home and Family, Math, Music, Science, Water/Sand Table or Sensory, and Outside Play.

Alphabet Books

One of the most natural ways to tie literacy to the early childhood curriculum is through Alphabet Books. ABC Books most commonly serve as selections for teacher-initiated Story Times and as free-reading selections on bookshelves.

The wide range of Alphabet Books available makes this type of book a natural for inclusion in any area of the curriculum. Add Alphabet Books to interest centers throughout the classroom. Use one as a focal point for a group time or create a whole theme around an ABC Book.

Appendix 15, Books for All Areas of the Classroom, identifies a number of Alphabet Books relevant to many classroom interest areas. As a focal point of a group time, an Alphabet Book can:

♦ strengthen letter recognition

♦ emphasize the distinction between lowercase and uppercase letters

♦ provide an opportunity for children to hear rhyming words and alliteration

♦ involve children in the verbal identification of individual letters and pictures

♦ motivate children to make their own ABC Books

♦ serve as a familiar example of the connection between print and language

Create a theme around an Alphabet Book by choosing a book and relating it to all the areas of the curriculum.

Remember, just because an area of the classroom has the potential to get messy does not mean that reading should be excluded there. With proper reminders, any area or center can contain books.

• Provide paper towels and visual reminders to children to help them remember that they need to have "clean hands" before they interact with the book or books in that area. Try placing the book in a plastic bag; this serves as an instant reminder to children to look at their hands before handling the book.

• Books protected by a plastic bag can also be placed directly in materials such as sand, oatmeal, gravel, and soil. The same procedure might also be adopted for the Art, Cooking, or Water/Sand Table areas.

Children's Magazines

These can be worthwhile additions to any literacy-friendly classroom. Magazines for children provide another example of the usefulness of print by offering a different teaching medium. They include resources that you can utilize for story reading or storytelling, craft activities, and information gathering. Often, these publications contain author or illustrator profiles and children's poetry. The magazines also lend themselves to student use. The illustrations and photographs tend to be large and colorful and the activities presented are usually easy to follow independently, even for nonreaders. There are book reviews to look at, letters and artwork submitted by other children, and, often, puzzles, mazes, and games to play.

Subscribing to a monthly Children's Magazine or choosing one from the newsstand each month (which provides a varied selection) will enhance the classroom in a number of ways:

♦ It involves children in a "grown-up" activity—receiving their own magazine.

♦ Children become more aware of the passage of time as they anticipate the arrival of the magazine. Expand on this by using a calendar to record the arrival and due dates of magazines.

♦ It provides numerous opportunities for children to strengthen communication and language skills. Encourage children to send their own artwork or letters to the magazine. Some may have the opportunity to see their correspondences published.

Integrate Children's Magazines into the curriculum and daily schedule by:

♦ Making them available in the library or book area of the classroom.

♦ Adding them to other classroom areas, depending on how they relate to the activities in that particular area. Put a magazine containing a special craft activity, opened to that page, in the Art Area. Display one showing pictures of animals or vehicles in a Science or Block Area.

♦ Supplementing with various examples of the types of magazines that adults may read.

♦ Devising ways to make magazine games, puzzles, and cutouts usable by everyone. For example, back cutouts with cardboard to make them sturdier and keep them together in a labeled box. Cover one-page pencil games or puzzles with clear Contac® paper. If children write on these pages with crayon and erase with a paper towel, they can use the pages again and again.

However you choose to adapt Children's Magazines to the classroom, do not overlook these valuable resources. Most Children's Magazines serve as excellent sources of good literature, information, artwork, and photographs—all meaningful examples of one of the purposes of print.

Classroom Library

Don't forget a Library as a permanent area of the classroom. Make weekly changes in the area to keep it fresh and interesting. Try some of the following:

◆ A cozy corner with pillows, a rug or mat, stuffed animals, and a basket of books

◆ A tape recorder and/or CD player with books, cassettes, CDs, and headphones

◆ A rocking chair, doll or stuffed animal, and a cloth bag of books for reading stories to an "audience"

◆ A basket of puppets and familiar books for reenactments

◆ A Book Box containing a special book and a selection of corresponding props

◆ A selection of different books and children's magazines borrowed from a community library

◆ A "Study Area" with a desk or table and a small table light, books, notebooks, and pencils

◆ A bookmark-making activity

◆ A Story Rug in the area where you and the children can meet for stories and related book games

◆ A chart for children's names and titles of their favorite books

◆ A borrowing system allowing several children to take home a book to share each week. Make a Library Card for each child and mark the cards with a hole punch, sticker, or rubber stamp each time a child borrows and returns a book.

◆ The Classroom Library is also a fun place for a classroom computer. Appendix 21 includes a list of Web sites offering a variety of books for children to read online.

Occasionally, present "Book Awards" to child-authored books. Have a selection of Newbery or Caldecott award-winning books available for children to look at. Discuss these awards with children. At the "Award Ceremony," present a special sticker, ribbon, or bookmark to all children who have made a book.

Making Books

When children make their own books, they begin to understand the connection between talking, writing, and reading. Personal and open-ended, this activity meets the needs of a wide range of developmental abilities. Child-made books can contain any number of pages, be illustrated with a child's own artwork or cutouts from a picture source, and consist of any number of words—from one to one hundred.

Make a Bookmaking Center a permanent part of any classroom. Set up the center so that children can use it either independently or with you. Stock the center with a variety of materials for Bookmaking:

♦ paper: single sheets and ready-made books; assorted colors, sizes, and weights

♦ pencils, crayons, markers

♦ tape

♦ glue

♦ scissors

♦ stencils

♦ picture sources: magazines, store circulars, catalogs, newspapers

♦ book cover materials: cardboard, heavyweight paper, craft foam, gift wrap

♦ binding materials: yarn, string, ribbon, tape, brass fasteners, binder rings, hole punch

Encourage children to choose their own topics. Record dictated words if asked. Invite children to read the books they have made to teachers, friends, and parents. Offer to read child-made books individually and at group Story Times. Hearing stories and seeing books made by peers serves as a powerful motivator for children to try making their own books.

Ways to Make Books

Certainly the traditional format, featuring a number of pages fastened together on the left and bound by a cover, will be the one most in evidence in the Bookmaking Center. There are many other ways to create books, however. Look through children's books in the classroom, public libraries, and bookstores for other possibilities. Try to stock the center with materials for more unusual bookmaking projects, and always be open to ideas from children. Following are four ways to make books. See Appendix 16 for ten more ways.

Greeting Card Book

Fold a square or rectangular piece of paper in half; fold it in half again, making a book that is one-quarter the size of the original paper. Children have four panels and one large area (when the paper is opened to its original size) for drawings and words. Greeting Card Books work especially well for very small children and beginning bookmakers; there are only five panels to fill, and children anticipate and enjoy the large picture surprise at the end. Because the book requires no fasteners, it is also well suited to independent bookmaking.

Plastic Bag Interchangeable Book

Fasten a number of resealable plastic sandwich bags together along the bottom of the bags. This creates the book's binding along the left, leaving the bag openings on the right. For each bag, cut a piece of paper a little smaller than the bag, so that is actually fits into the bag. Put the story words and illustrations on the individual pieces of paper and slide them into the bags and seal. You now have an interchangeable book. Insert a new or different story into the bags anytime to create a new book.

Fabric Book

Several pieces of fabric (pillowcases and old sheets work well) provide a different medium for children's bookmaking. Use pinking shears to cut book "pages" and minimize fraying and ragged edges. Fasten fabric with staples or use a hole punch to make holes for yarn ties. Use fabric crayons to write and draw on this kind of book.

Paper Bag Book

Cut several inches from the top of a number of paper lunch bags (white or brown), leaving 8"-long bags. Punch holes along the top (open) end of the bags; use brass fasteners, yarn, or string to fasten. Or, fasten the bags by stapling them together. Turn the bags so that the bottoms are on the right. This creates a book with flaps. Use this type of book to make Hidden Picture Books, Question-Answer Books, or Guessing Game Books. Most of the main picture, question, or riddle appears on the left side, and the rest of the picture, answer, or solution appears (hides) under the flap. Try using larger paper bags too.

Book Bindings

Bind books together in any number of ways, both traditional and unique. Fasten along the left side, at the top left corner, or across the top, using staples, a hole punch, brass fasteners, binder rings, chenille stems or pipe cleaners, yarn, string, ribbon, or shoe laces. Try punching a line of holes down the left side or across the top to lace up the entire edge.

Children love to have access to adult materials that they do not normally use. Provide loose-leaf binders, pocket folders, and clipboards for "temporary books." These books can be made, "read," and shared and then fastened together in some other way to take home, freeing binders and folder for other books by young authors.

Book Covers

To make book covers, follow the steps below. These measurements work for an 8" x 10" book. For other size books, adjust measurements and materials accordingly.

Materials:

- ☛ 2 pieces of cardboard, 8" x 10" each
- ☛ wide masking tape
- ☛ fabric, gift wrap, or any thin paper, about 14" x 21" (cut fabric with pinking shears)
- ☛ 2 pieces of fabric or gift wrap, 7" x 9" each
- ☛ glue
- ☛ scissors or pinking shears

Instructions:

1. Place a cardboard piece on either side of the masking tape, leaving a middle section of the tape open.

2. Lay the cardboard-and-tape unit on a long piece of fabric or gift wrap.

3. Fold in the top, bottom, and sides of the fabric or gift wrap, tucking corners much like you would a wrapped present. Glue the folded ends down. You now have the basic cover.

4. Glue one 7" x 9" piece of fabric or gift wrap on the cardboard piece where the cover is folded over. Repeat on the other side. This finishes the inside of the cover.

5. Place finished or blank pages (that have been stapled together) on the middle of the tape. Close cover and press down to secure the pages in place.

For an easy and colorful book cover, cut two pieces of craft foam the same size as the paper being used. Fasten the cover and pages together with yarn or brass fasteners.

Math and Numbers

Incorporating literacy in the math portion of the curriculum is accomplished as easily as adding print to any regular daily activities. If a Math Center or Math Table is a permanent part of the classroom, add print to the activities that are available there. If math activities are assembled on a shelf, attach print to the materials using tape or clips. Math activities that you put out for one activity period only, then put away, should include print that can be added on the spot. When storing these activities, include the print with them so they will be literacy-ready the next time they are used.

One-to-one matching, sorting and classifying, rote counting, measuring and comparing, and quantitative activities provide many opportunities for print inclusions.

One-to-One Matching

Provide an assortment of sectioned or divided containers and a variety of small objects for one-to-one correspondence activities. Children match one small object to each divided section. Add print to these activities by labeling the group of objects and the containers in which they will be placed.

On a tray or box lid, place two (empty) divided containers and two bowls or baskets, each containing a different small item, such as a bowl of stones and a bowl of nuts. The tray sets a boundary, helping children to discern what is to be done. Add tongs, a spoon, or a melon baller to the tray to make the math activity an exercise in dexterity and fine-motor control as well. Observing these items together, children will place the small items in each divided section of the two containers. If you have labeled both the bowls of items and the divided containers, children can move the stones from the bowl labeled STONES to the divided container with the matching label and the nuts from the bowl labeled NUTS to its divided container. To begin, children should find just enough small objects to fill each container section with one object. If

you are using egg cartons, for example, each bowl will contain twelve stones and twelve nuts. As children gain some experience with this activity, try numbering the sections in the containers such that two or three items might be placed in each section.

Here are some small objects that work well for One-to-One Activities: buttons, pennies, dried beans, pasta, small blocks, small novelty erasers, stones, and acorns.

Some good sources of divided containers include: ice cube trays, egg cartons, plastic paint palettes, muffin tins, sectioned craft boxes, desk drawer organizers, kitchen flatware trays, and fishing tackle boxes.

To make your own divided containers, try these ideas:

- Fasten small jewelry boxes together by taping along edges or glue the boxes onto a shoe box lid base.

- Attach paper cups or lids from fabric softener bottles to a shoe box lid with glue.

- Line up film canisters and glue to a polystyrene foam food tray.

- Set small plastic plant pots or any small containers on a tray or box lid.

Sorting and Classifying

Sorting activities help strengthen simple concepts to even the youngest learner. Incorporate print, and you multiply the opportunities children have to observe and interact with the written word.

Divide a 12" x 18" piece of paper into a grid of six squares measuring 6" x 6" each. Divide the paper with colored marker lines or, for a more tactile and three-dimensional division, use colored tape or attach lengths of yarn with glue. In each grid, print the name of an object, and glue or tape the actual object next to the word. Provide a container of small objects for sorting that correspond to those in the grids. As children sort and classify the objects into the six categories, they are in constant contact with the printed word. For younger children, use larger paper and/or fewer divisions.

Rote Counting

These activities give children opportunities to count an assortment of objects onto numbered mats or into numbered containers. Include print by using it both as a directive and for labels on numbered containers. Provide tongs or spoons with any of these activities to strengthen fine-motor control.

Counting Mats

Cut ten to twenty different shapes (geometric shapes, animals, common household items), one to twelve of each shape, from construction paper or craft foam. Use one color for each shape, and keep the shapes in a box that has been decorated with shapes. Cut shapes that relate to a particular theme being studied, such as Dinosaurs, Farm, or Travel. Use vinyl placements to make the Counting Mats, taping a label to each mat that instructs children to COUNT 3 HORSES, COUNT 7 CIRCLES. Write the numerals in a different color than the words and include the shape to be counted above the printed word. Children will sort through the shape box, finding and counting the appropriate number of shapes to each mat. The use of vinyl mats makes it easy to change labels as needed.

Chapter 2: Curriculum

Counting Baskets

Use plastic berry baskets as Counting Baskets in much the same way you did the Counting Mats. On a tray, place ten berry baskets and a container of plastic fruits and vegetables. Tape a numeral, a picture, and a word on the front of each berry basket—for example, 1 APPLE, 2 CARROTS, 3 ORANGES—and let the counting begin. If plastic fruits and vegetables are not available, use pictures mounted on heavier paper or cut fruit and vegetable shapes from craft foam. Seed catalogs are excellent sources of pictures.

Counting Tins

Line a muffin tin with straw or shredded paper, making little nests. Provide a container of tiny clay eggs. Label the container EGGS and, on the edge of the muffin tin, tape labels indicating how many eggs to count into each nest. Number in sequence, 1 EGG, 2 EGGS, and so on, or challenge children by mixing numbers, 7 EGGS, 4 EGGS, 12 EGGS. Add more print by making three or four different colors of eggs and including the color word over some or all of the muffin tin "nests": 4 BLUE EGGS, 6 YELLOW EGGS. Use markers to print color words in the color they name. Eggs of all colors can also be cut from craft foam or paper.

Counting Bags

Assemble a tray with four or five containers of counting objects: stones, beans, buttons, pennies, and keys. Label each container with the name of the object, and glue one of the objects next to the word. Place four or five plastic sandwich bags on the tray. Label the front of each bag with a numeral and an object word: 10 STONES, 18 BEANS, 20 BUTTONS. Use a piece of masking tape for this label and write directly on the tape with a marker; you can easily remove the tape and change the number or object to be counted. This activity requires the child to match the word on the bag to the word on the container and count the required number.

Box Lid Games

Use shirt box or boot box lids to make an activity similar to a board game. Cover the inside playing area of the lid with construction paper. Use stickers or small paper shapes to create paths, starting points, or finishes. Add a die, spinner, or pile of movement cards, and buttons or coins as tokens. Children can play these games in small groups, in pairs, or independently. Shirt box lids work well for games that children share. More than one child can play a small Box Lid Game if each has his or her own lid for die-rolling and token-moving. This more individualized play is well suited to younger children who have not yet mastered the skills of sharing and cooperating.

Children will enjoy taking Box Lid Games home to share with parents. Use the box itself to store the game pieces and replace the lid to keep everything intact. This also is a great way to store Box Lid Games in the classroom. You can also make board games out of manila folders. Use the inside of the folder (when opened flat) as the game board and keep pieces in an envelope or paper pocket attached to the folder with tape or glue.

Apple Picking Box Lid Game

Cover the playing area with green paper. Draw a basket at one end of the box lid and an apple tree at the other. Label each. Cut red circles for a path and glue only the upper edge of the circle onto the lid. Under each circle, draw a tree, an apple, or another piece of fruit. Label each.

Object of the Game: Take your basket to the apple tree. Play the game by rolling a die or spinning a spinner and moving a token up the path. Look under the apple on which the token has landed. If it is a tree, stay there. If it is an apple, move ahead 3 spaces. If it is another fruit, go back 1 space.

Basketball Box Lid Game

Cover the playing area with brown paper. Draw a zigzag path with a rectangular "court" at the top. Divide the path into approximately 1" segments. Make a ball at one end of the court and a net at the other. Label each. Cut twenty-four 2" x 4" cards from white construction paper or index cards. Make an X and print the word FOUL on three cards. Make an athletic shoe and print the word JUMP on three more cards. Write the numerals 1, 2, and 3 on the remaining eighteen cards. Place the card pile in the rectangular "court."

Object of the Game: To "bounce" up the court and "dunk" the ball. Play the game by selecting a card from the pile and moving up the court the number of spaces shown on the card. If a FOUL card (with an X on it) is chosen, go back and start again. If a JUMP card (with an athletic shoe on it) is chosen, "bounce" ahead 3 spaces. Place the cards on the bottom of the pile after taking a turn.

Car Trip Box Lid Game

Cover the playing area with gray paper. Draw a car at one end of the box lid and a house at the other. Label each. Draw a curved path, divided into 1" segments, between the car and the house. Print the words STOP and GO intermittently along the path.

Object of the Game: Drive your car home. Play the game by rolling a die or spinning a spinner and moving along the road. If you land on STOP, go back 1 space. If you land on GO, take another turn.

Rainbow Run Box Lid Game

Cover the playing area with white paper. Holding the box lid horizontal, draw a cloud in the lower left corner and a sun in the lower right corner. Label each. Draw an arching "rainbow" path from the cloud to the sun. Divide the arch into 1" segments. Color the rainbow segments with six different colors (red, orange, yellow, green, blue, purple). Cut twenty-four 2" x 4" cards from white construction paper or index cards. On three cards, draw a raindrop with the word RAIN. On three more cards, draw an umbrella with the word UMBRELLA. Place a color square on the remaining eighteen cards: Three cards will have a red square, three will have an orange square, and so on. Place the card pile under the arch.

Object of the Game: To run from the clouds to the sun without getting wet. Play the game by selecting a card and moving to the corresponding color. If a RAIN card is chosen, go back to the cloud and start over. If an UMBRELLA card is chosen, take another turn. Place cards on the bottom of the pile after taking a turn.

Telephone Talk

A telephone book is an excellent example of print combined with numbers. Most children are familiar with phone books, have one in their home, and have observed adults using them. Given this familiarity, telephone books make useful classroom props for play and adult modeling.

Classroom Telephone Book

Bring in several outdated telephone books or collect a few extras from the local phone company. Find each child's (parents') name and highlight it with a marker or circle it with a red pen. (If there are parents with unlisted numbers, ask those children to look up a relative, a neighbor, or a friend.) Attach (tape) a small tab to the edge of each page containing a pertinent name. Print the first initial of the child's name on the tab. This will help children locate their own name, address, and phone number in a book that might otherwise be overwhelming. To make this print tool even more user-friendly, remove the pages relating to the classroom, the telephone book cover, some of the emergency numbers in the front, and some of the Yellow Pages. Fasten the pages inside the cover, creating a smaller version of a real telephone book.

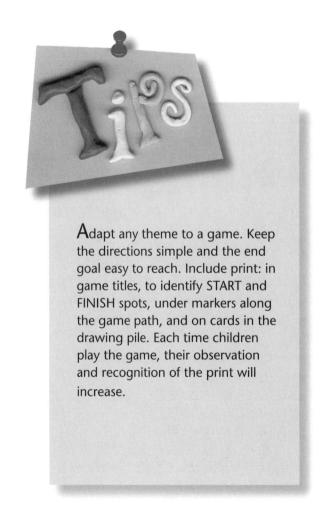

Adapt any theme to a game. Keep the directions simple and the end goal easy to reach. Include print: in game titles, to identify START and FINISH spots, under markers along the game path, and on cards in the drawing pile. Each time children play the game, their observation and recognition of the print will increase.

Add telephones, cell phones, real telephone books with tab-marked pages, and Phone-Friend Books to dramatic play areas. Set up telephone areas with small tables and chairs in classroom corners. Add a telephone phone book inside, and hang phone number signs:

- EMERGENCY: DIAL 911
- OPERATOR: DIAL 0
- Children's names and numbers

Phone-Friend Books

Let children make their own telephone books containing the telephone numbers of friends. Fold five pieces of paper in half to make a ten-page book. Cut construction paper of the same size for a cover. Fasten the book on the left. Children may wish to draw a telephone or pictures of friends on the front cover. Have them write emergency numbers and their own telephone numbers on the first pages and collect their classmates' telephone numbers on the remaining pages. Help children write their own phone numbers as necessary. Friends can fill up the additional pages by writing their own names and telephone numbers. Encourage each child to copy his or her telephone number from the front of his or her own book. Help with numbers if necessary. If possible, have the Yellow Pages from old telephone books available so children can cut ads for places they know (restaurants, stores, service stations, etc.) and glue or tape them in the back pages of their telephone books. For a fun variation, make Phone-Friend Books out of paper cut in the shape of a telephone or cell phone.

Make Cell Phones

Wash and dry the inside of small metal mint tins. Cut four pieces of craft foam to fit the top, bottom, and inside sections of the tin. Glue the craft foam in place. Use a thin-tipped permanent market to write the child's name and "cell phone number" on the craft foam on the front of the tin. On the two pieces of craft foam inside the tin, write the following: In the top section, write 1, 2, 3 on the first row and 4, 5, 6 on the next row. In the bottom section, write 7, 8, 9 on the first row and *, 0, # on the next row. Children can open the tin cell phone, touch the numbers to make a call, and close the tin when finished.

Serve Yourself Snacks

If a snack time is part of the daily routine, set it up to encourage independence as well as awareness and use of print.

Set the snack on a vinyl placement, along with instructions for the children. Instructions should include the name of the snack and the number of items children may take. For younger children, tape a row of paper circles showing how many snacks to take; this lets them match one to one. For example, if children may take five crackers, tape five circles on the mat with the word TAKE. Demonstrate how to use this new "serve-yourself" snack set-up and children will understand the meaning of the paper circles the next time they are used. Make napkins and plates or bowls available. Finger foods work best. Children will enjoy the opportunity to count out their own snack.

Measuring and Comparing

Activities involving measurement and size comparison help make math concepts meaningful and provide opportunities to use print in a purposeful way.

You will need three placements or three separate pieces of paper for this activity. The middle mat holds the object that serves as the standard against which other items will be measured and compared. Tape this object directly to the mat or paper so that it cannot be moved. Write the name of the object directly on the paper or tape a label to the placemat. Place a container of objects to be measured or compared on the middle mat with the standard. On either side of the standard, place a mat with a size word (for example, THINNER/WIDER) written on or taped to it. Children will compare objects in the container to the standard and place them on either side of the two end mats. For example, tape an unsharpened pencil to the middle mat with the word PENCIL. For the two end mats, write LONGER THAN THE PENCIL on one mat and SHORTER THAN THE PENCIL on the other mat. Tape a piece of yarn under the print on each mat as a visual explanation of the size words: one piece of yarn longer than the pencil, one piece of yarn shorter. Fill the container on the middle mat with other lengths of yarn, pencils (sharpened and unsharpened), pieces of rope, plastic snakes, crayons, markers, a craft stick, a tree branch, a comb, and a rules. Children will compare each object in the container with the pencil and decide whether it is longer or shorter than the pencil, placing it on the corresponding mat. Most children will recognize the purpose of this activity and will be able to engage in it independently. Comparison activities can also be introduced during a circle time. Follow the same procedure for comparisons such as:

BIGGER—SMALLER

WIDER—THINNER

HEAVIER—LIGHTER

TALLER—SHORTER

MORE—LESS

Graphing

Graphing offers children experiences with rote counting, one-to-one matching, comparing, and sorting or classifying—all in one activity. It also provides a great way to incorporate print and make connections to literacy. Graphing is best done during a circle time or in a group setting so that all children can have a turn, observe peer interactions with the graph, and take part in teacher-initiated counting and comparing.

Use large chart paper or newsprint for graphs. Print the title of the graph at the top and divide the paper into columns, either vertically or horizontally. For vertical graphs, label each column at the bottom; for horizontal graphs, at the left. The number of columns needed will depend on the topic and purpose of the graph. For example, if children are graphing FAVORITE COLORS, divide the paper into eight sections; for FAVORITE SEASONS, divide the paper into four sections.

Give each child a square of 2" x 2" paper. Children will use the squares to designate their choice by attaching it to the graph in the proper column. Print each child's name on the square or have children write their own names. For a favorite colors graph, for example, children will place their square in the RED column if their favorite color is red; for a favorite seasons graph, children will place it in the SUMMER column if this is their favorite season.

Make sure that all squares placed on the chart are the same size and are next to one another so that the finished graph provides a true representation of the group as a whole. As the group uses the graph, refer to the title and labeled columns frequently.

Display completed graphs at children's eye level. This way they will be able to find their own name or names of friends, practice counting, and draw their own conclusions.

Try these Graph subjects:

♦ Favorites: colors, seasons, dinosaurs, fruits, shapes
♦ Personal Traits: hair color, height, age
♦ Family Information: color of house, number of brothers or sisters, pets
♦ General Topics: weather, animal habits, plant-eating and meat-eating dinosaurs

Make these classroom Graphs:

♦ Plant growth
♦ Number of books read
♦ Bow-tying accomplishments
♦ Science experiments
♦ Do you have gloves or mittens?
♦ How do your shoes fasten?

For younger children, prepare a graph listing the names of all children on the left. Have each child place a symbol next to his or her name representing a particular quantity. Try graphs of these topics relating to the quantity:

♦ People in My Family
♦ How Many Books Did You Read?
♦ How Many Windows Are in Your Bedroom?
♦ Brothers and Sisters
♦ Pets

Children will place one symbol next to their name for each family member, book read, window, brother or sister, and pet.

Room Schedule

Make an hour-by-hour Room Schedule. Include the time, written in number form and shown on a clock, with the activity printed next to it. Next to the activity name, add a symbol: a paintbrush for art, a spoon for lunch, a block for free play, and a ball for outside play. Make schedules in the form of a horizontal time line and hang at children's eye level. To make the schedule more appealing, use a colorful background or a realistic object:

♦ a long snake with the body divided into hourly sections
♦ a train with each car representing a different time of the day
♦ a garden with a row of flowers, one for each hour of the day

Maps, Math, and Literacy

Many children have a fascination with maps. More importantly, children who have little interest in numbers, but who show an avid interest in vehicle or block play, often find maps exciting. Make the most of this situation by integrating maps, which combine numbers with print in a unique way, into the curriculum. As children work with maps, the concepts of space, distance, and time are also enhanced.

Make maps of all kinds available in the Math and Art areas. An atlas is a useful addition to bookshelves or the classroom library. Small maps on travel brochures and pamphlets present many opportunities for children to observe streets, roads, and highways with numbers and names. Local maps will be an important resource, because these contain the names and areas that are most familiar to children. Find local maps at community centers and municipal buildings. Bus schedules and telephone books are also wonderful sources of maps of individual states, counties, and neighborhoods. These maps tend to be simplified and thus are easier for children to understand.

Use maps in a variety of ways in the classroom. Each use should combine numbers and print, focusing on the practice of "reading" a map.

Familiar Maps

Trace maps from telephone books or bus schedules onto plain paper. Include only minimal detail, such as the outline of the area and several streets, roads, and bodies of water. Encourage children to complete the maps as they choose. Offer to add print, such as street and building names, the numbers of friends' or relatives' houses, and other identifying features. Some children will add their own invented writing and numbers. Others will request spellings for print they wish to add. Meet any of these connections to literacy with enthusiasm. Allow children to seek their own comfort level with these emerging skills.

"Where We Live" Classroom Map

Using a large piece of newsprint or craft paper, draw a neighborhood map showing the school and surrounding area. Add a few streets and buildings yourself, but fill in most of the map with children's help. Insert each child's house and any identifying buildings and landmarks along the way. Display the map in the classroom where children can look at it and trace routes from their house to friends' houses and school. This is an excellent way to relate children's names, numbers, and other print to something familiar. Use this type of map when field trips are planned.

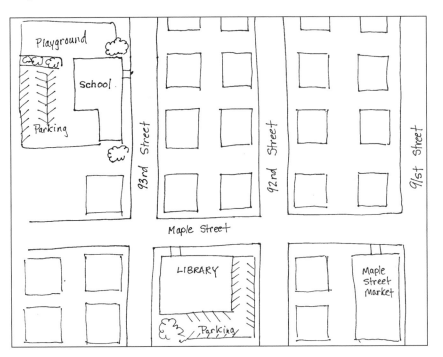

Individual Maps

Encourage individual map-making by responding to stories about trips, traveling, and visitors this way: "How did you get there?" "How far away do your grandparents live?" "What did you see along the way?" Follow up with questions such as: ""Would you like to make a map about it?" or "How would you show that on a map?" Children may request help with spelling or labeling.

Shopping Game

In a world replete with malls and shopping centers, many children have had experience observing adults involved in a variety of literate behaviors while shopping. Re-create this experience in the classroom by using pictures from store circulars and catalogs to create a tabletop mall. Be sure to involve children in the mall's construction; they will have more fun and better understand the activity.

To make the mall, fill large pieces of paper, each of which corresponds to a store, with pictures of items that the "store" sells. Label the paper before using it or invite children to decide what stores will be in their mall: shoe store, toy store, clothing item, pet store, bookstore, furniture store, grocery store. Glue rows of pictures on the paper corresponding to each item. Print the name of the item under each picture. In the corner of the same paper, make a "price list" that names everything in the store and its cost. Each price should be different. If there are twelve items pictured in the "store," there should be twelve prices (perhaps ranging from $1 to $12). When children "buy" something at the store, they need to find the matching item name on the list to know the price of the item. They pay the amount by counting out pretend money and go on to the next store.

Flea Market

Following a procedure similar to that for the pretend shopping mall, set up a classroom Flea Market. Send home a letter telling parents about your plans for a Flea Market and requesting that children bring ten pennies and one or two small items—pencils, stickers, novelty erasers, books, dress-up jewelry, bookmarks, small cars, plastic animals, key rings, and balloons—to school. Stress that items need not be new, just in good condition.

Give each child a small cup or envelope (labeled with the child's name) for their pennies and set the coins aside for "Market Day." Add several small items of your own to those that children have brought. Group similar items in separate containers and make signs with children naming each item. Tent Labels work well. Make a price list naming all the items being sold and the number of pennies needed to buy each of them. Use large paper for this list so it will be easy for children to match items and prices. When children choose an item to buy, they need to find it on the price list and count out the correct number of pennies to buy it.

Tips

Plastic coins, chips, or paper money can be used in shopping games. Add wallets, purses, cash registers, and shopping bags to this activity for more pretend fun. Encourage children to take turns being customers and salespeople.

The amount of time spent organizing and setting up the Flea Market will depend on how involved children get in the project. A List or Time Line (see p. 54) will adapt well to the Flea Market activity. Donate collected pennies to a community project, such as a local library or animal shelter.

Music and Movement

Music plays an important part in any early childhood curriculum. It can start a day, end a day, be the focus of a fun circle time, help children with transitions, suggest a feeling or a mood, add to a celebration, and provide a variety of background sounds. And any medium as versatile as music can certainly accommodate literacy inclusions.

In addition to activities that combine music and print directly, don't miss the opportunity to use a label to identify music you play in the classroom. Create a Stand-up Label (see p. 18) or Tent Label (see p. 21) bearing the name of the song, cassette, record, or compact disc. Once you make these signs, they can be used each time you play that music. Keep signs in a folder in the music area. Include the artist's name, and stand or lay the CD or cassette box next to the sign. Place at children's eye level so they have an opportunity to hold the music container for closer inspection.

Welcome music that children share from home and include this information on a small Tent Label: MUSIC FROM MARY'S HOUSE. Incorporate as much music and as many different types of music as often as possible throughout the day.

Musical Preferences

Provide a "Do You Like This Music?" chart. Title the paper and divide it into two columns. Head one column YES with a happy face and head the second column NO with a frowning face. Fasten the paper to a clipboard. Children can write their names in the appropriate columns or elicit help to write it. Make this a free-choice literacy activity available anytime music is playing. As an added benefit, children come to better understand their own musical preferences and learn to appreciate music other children share.

Make a song-cheering pompon by first cutting sheets of tissue paper into 1" strips. Lay the strips together in a pile and tie a piece of yarn or string around the middle of the pile. Tie the tissue pompon to a rhythm stick or ruler, or knot the ends of the yarn so that children can slip the pompon on their hands and hold it.

Cheering on a Song

Before singing a song, encourage children to join in a Cheer. As a transition between activities, this is a fun way to strengthen group participation, get voices ready to sing, and provide a reference to literacy.

You will need a set of alphabet cards for the activity. The cards should be large enough for children to see during circle or group time. Depending on the word being cheered, you may need duplicate letters.

Choose the principal word in the song and lead children in a letter-by-letter Cheer. Immediately following the Cheer, start the song. As children become familiar with the Cheers, they will begin to remember which song follows.

Before singing "Eensy Weensy Spider," for example, cheer the word *spider*. Hold up or point to each letter as it is cheered.

Your words	Children's response
"Give me an S."	"S"
"Give me a P."	"P"
"Give me an I."	"I"
"Give me a D."	"D"
"Give me a E."	"E"
"Give me an R."	"R"
"What's that word?	"SPIDER."

Once they are familiar with the procedure, invite children to lead the cheers. A tissue paper pompon for the leader of the cheer will add more fun to this activity.

Felt Action Shows

Use a combination of words and pictures to illustrate any favorite classroom chant or song. Counting songs and multi-verse repetitions work particularly well for this print-rich music activity.

A felt board serves as the display area for felt illustrations and print. If a felt board is not part of the classroom, you can make one easily (see instructions below). Use the felt board over and over each time you listen to a new song. The board should be large, colorful, and eye-catching enough for a circle time but also durable and easy for children to use independently. The felt pieces for the board should be easy to store and child-friendly. They must stand up well to much handling and repetitive use.

To illustrate a song or chant with felt, first choose several key characters or objects in the song and cut them out. Make the outline of the shape on the felt; do not be concerned with adding too much detail. Ready-made sets often include many of the needed shapes and objects. If not, children's stencils and cookie cutters make helpful patterns. Then choose two or three repetitive words or numbers to add to the Felt Action Show. Cut out light-colored felt rectangles and print directly on the felt with dimensional fabric paint (a "puffy" paint that is available in an assortment of bright colors) or with a black permanent marker. When preparing numbers, include the numeral and number word on the same felt rectangle. A group of dots corresponding to the number shown next to or under the numeral will be useful to children when using the felt board on their own.

Most of the songs and chants for the Felt Show will require several duplicate shapes and two or three words. As children sing the song or chant, move the felt shapes and words on and off the felt board or point to them at the appropriate time.

After presenting it to the group, be certain to make the Felt Action Show available to children for individual or small-group use. Children will imitate your actions and, in so doing, interact in a pleasurable way with the pictures and print. When two or three children use the Felt Action Show together, they will learn from and teach one another. Encourage such use of the materials, as children will gain valuable print-handling experiences.

Adapt any classroom song or chant to a Felt Action Show. Try these all-time favorites:

♦ "This Old Man"
♦ "Six Little Ducks"
♦ "Five Little Monkeys Jumping on the Bed"
♦ "The Ants Go Marching"

Felt Action Shows work well with other children's songs too:

♦ "B I N G O": Illustrate with a farmer, a dog, and the five letters. Remove one letter at a time as the song is sung.
♦ "Old MacDonald": Illustrate with a farmer, a variety of animals, and print that includes the word FARM, animal names, and E - I - E - I - O.

Although the print is minimal in this musical activity, it is important. As an integral part of the song, children will pay attention to it as it appears along with the pictures. The print takes on even more significance when children interact with felt pieces independently. Perceived as part of the song, children will handle the print and attach meaning to it as it relates to the song and surrounding pictures.

Making a Felt Board

Use a large rectangular carton to make a self-standing Felt Board for a circle or group time, a Story Time, or independent use. Set the carton upright, with the opening at the top. Remove one long side of the carton. Cut the two shorter sides diagonally from the top inside corner to the bottom outside corner. Turn over the box, placing the opening on the table or floor and creating a stand-up tent structure. Cover both long sides with felt. Use one long piece of felt and tuck it under the bottom or attach individual felt squares. Cover each side with a different color of felt, if you choose. Set on a classroom table, children can use both sides of the box; on the floor, two children can use the felt board together, one on each side.

Playing in the Band

Identify each musical instrument in the Music Area with a label attached with tape or clear Contac® paper. When an activity includes musical instruments, make use of the labels in a number of ways:

♦ As you distribute instruments to children, familiarize the group with the name of the instrument and draw attention to the label.

♦ Once children are familiar with the names of instruments, encourage them to choose an instrument by name. Verify their choices by looking at the label.

♦ Sort the names of the musical instruments by grouping together those that begin with the same letter or arranging the instruments alphabetically. Classify instruments during a circle time before or after a music activity.

♦ Use the labels as a means of collecting instruments after playing time. "If you have an instrument that begins with the letter T, please put it away. Yes, the triangle and the tambourine can be put away."

Silent Conductor

Make a second set of musical instrument labels for this activity. Give each child a labeled instrument. You are the conductor, holding up the name of an instrument. The "musicians" play their instrument when they see the name displayed. They continue playing until the name label is no longer displayed. In addition to the label on the musical instrument, try giving children a label naming their instrument to keep in front of them for more immediate matching and playing. This works particularly well with very young children. Have fun by varying the amount of time you display the instrument label—from very quick periods of time to much longer ones. Try displaying the names of two instruments at a time, so that two "musicians" can play together. When children are familiar with the game, invite them to take turns being a Silent Conductor.

Rebus Movement Game

Children love to move. They also have fun pretending. Combine these pleasures with pictures and print to create a music-and-movement experience that everyone will enjoy.

The object of the game is to pretend to be or do what is pictured on a Rebus Movement Game picture card. Make a group of picture cards with the names of the pictured items printed below the pictures. Animal pictures work especially well. Also try pictures of vehicles and people; both require children to be more imaginative in their movements. Pictures of people playing various instruments (or pictures of the instruments themselves) may inspire children to pretend to play imaginary instruments. Sports pictures may find children moving like a tennis player, a swimmer, and ice skater, or a baseball player. Shown occupational pictures, children may imitate a police officer directing traffic, a ballerina dancing, or an astronaut in space. Include print with any picture you show. As children look at the picture, they also see the print.

Play instrumental music in the background for Rebus Movement Games. Be sure to hold the pictures so that all children can see them. Encourage children to move in whatever way they feel suits the picture. Be certain there is enough space to promote freedom of movement.

Create an area for Sound Investigation in a corner of the Music Area. Tie a piece of yarn around a number of objects: metal spoons of all sizes, forks, wooden and metal cooking utensils, tools, chopsticks, and lengths of plastic beads. Place several of each object in separate shoe boxes labeled SPOONS, FORKS, BEADS, TOOLS, and so on. Hang a rope or clothesline corner to corner and provide a basket of clothespins. Children can choose objects to hang on the rope and listen to the different sounds they make together (much like a wind chime). When they are finished, children should replace the objects in the labeled boxes.

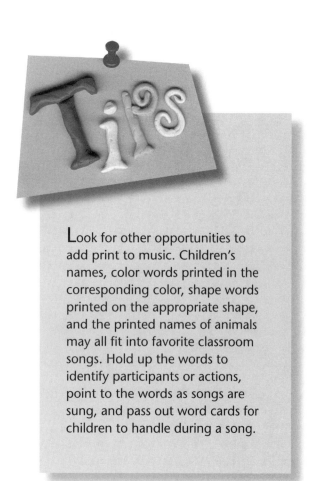

Look for other opportunities to add print to music. Children's names, color words printed in the corresponding color, shape words printed on the appropriate shape, and the printed names of animals may all fit into favorite classroom songs. Hold up the words to identify participants or actions, point to the words as songs are sung, and pass out word cards for children to handle during a song.

Write a New Song

Take a familiar favorite and change some of the key words to create a new version of the song. Use chart paper or easel paper to write children's suggested substitutions. Extend children's thinking by asking open-ended questions. Contribute a new title and some new words to get things started or help clarify ideas. Once the new song is written, sing it through several times, pointing to the new words as the children sing them. Remember, the goal is not to "teach" words; you do not expect children to read the words as you point to them. Rather, the goal is attention to print and children's growing understanding that the print represents the words they are singing.

The class-written "new" songs have many uses, such as:

♦ Save the song and use it again during any gathering or circle time.

♦ Have a sing-along with a selection of old songs and their new versions.

♦ Illustrate the paper containing the new song with magazine pictures and children's drawings. The pictures help children remember the subject of the song and recall the new words.

♦ Punch holes in the top or sides of the paper and put binder rings or yarn through the holes for a "Songs We Wrote" book, to which new songs can be added.

Try the following songs or some of your own classroom favorites. For a list of more songs that are easy to re-create, see Appendix 17.

♦ "B I N G O": Change the title word to any five-letter word and substitute other words as necessary. For example, change the title to "L U N C H" and sing it before lunchtime. "This is the time of the day we all sit down to eat our lunch—L U N C H." Or, "We have a bear we love so much and Teddy is his name—T E D D Y" (an especially fun song to coordinate with the "Traveling Teddy Bear" activity in the Language section (p. 68).

♦ "Old MacDonald Had a Farm": Change "Old MacDonald" to any name and "farm" to any other animal setting, such as "pet store," "zoo," "ocean" or "aquarium," "forest," "rain forest," or "desert." Sing about animals found in each area and supply the appropriate animal noises. For example, "Our friend, Roberta, has a pet store. E-I-E-I-O. And in her store she has a fish...."

♦ "The More We Get Together": Change the word get to any school activity—for example, "The More We Sing Together,"

" ... Draw Together,"

" ... Play Together,"

" ... Read Together."

♦ "Where is Thumbkin?": Change the name "Thumbkin" to the name of any child in the class, encouraging that child to sing back, "Here I Am, Here I Am." Finish the song by alternating group and individual singing. For example, the group sings "How are you today, _____?" and the child sings "Very well, I thank you." All sing, "Run away, run away."

Science

Science in the early childhood classroom should promote open investigation and individual discovery. Providing hands-on experiences at a Science Table or in a Science Center is one of the best ways to make this area of the curriculum a popular one. Make the Science Area more inviting by providing a variety of magnifying glasses, tweezers, tongs, and other science materials. Enhance literacy in this area by labeling utensils and items for investigation; provide clipboards for your use or children's use in recording children's words.

Science Collections

Collecting and categorizing activities are an effective means of bringing science concepts into the curriculum and fostering an awareness of and appreciation for nature in young children. A "Tree Study" is an excellent example of such an activity. Best done in the fall when leaves are plentiful, it also works well in the spring or summer in climates that do not experience fall foliage. Collect leaves, branches, nuts, pieces of bark, or pine cones. Involve children in the collection process, either in the schoolyard or by sharing things collected from home yards. Stress finding or looking for items on the ground, not picking them from the trees. Use box lids (shirt box size) as the categorizing devices. Equip each with a

picture of the tree and the names of various items to be collected, such as LEAF, BARK, BRANCH, NUT, or ACORN. Use the finished collections to identify and learn more about trees. Mix items and sort as often as desired. Include books about trees and leaves with the collection. Make this an ongoing activity, with new items added and categorized daily or weekly.

Use plastic sandwich bags or polystyrene foam food trays to sort leaves to show where they were found. Label bags or trays LEAVES FROM OUR PLAYGROUND, LEAVES FROM KELLY'S YARD, and LEAVES FROM MEI'S YARD. Children will take pride in seeing their name associated with the leaves from their own yard.

Use the collection procedure when putting together collections of a variety of other items. Think of ways to sort and categorize, adding print and labels liberally. Include books that relate to each item in the collection. Collections might include insects, rocks, seashells, seeds, or wildflowers.

Record children's observations about the collections, paying particular attention to their questions. Read these aloud once a week during a circle time, discussing questions and answers as a group. Questions that are left unanswered might become the focus of a Story Time or a demonstration of proper use of a reference book,

or they might result in the inclusion of something in the Science Area that will help children find the answer themselves. Children's observations might take this form:

♦ Daichi wonders, "Does Julie ever get apples on the tree in her yard?"

♦ Cody thinks, "Here are some rocks that look like they might write on the sidewalk."

♦ Maria asks, "What kind of little animal could have lived in this shell?"

♦ Nicole wonders, "Can we keep the wildflowers without putting them in water?"

♦ Raul notices a split in one of the seeds, with a little white thing coming out and thinks, "Is this how it grows?"

All of these questions, observations, and ideas can be discussed, looked up in a book, or "tested" scientifically. This kind of informal exploration and focused follow-up makes science meaningful and enjoyable to children. Because much of the investigation and discovery is independent, print provides a necessary link between the process and the dissemination of information and observations among the group.

Nature Boxes

Many early childhood classrooms provide a Nature Box for the collection of items children gather outdoors or bring in from home. This serves as a useful repository for the many items that find their way into children's pockets while they are outdoors, but it can also provide a variety of materials for scientific investigation. If you make such a box a part of the classroom, decorate it and label it: NATURE BOX.

When the box is fairly full, set up a sorting activity. Divide a large piece of chart paper or newsprint into sections. Label each section with the name of a nature item and glue or tape a representation of the item next to the print. Have children sort through the objects in the Nature Box and place each object in the appropriate section. Replace the objects so that other children can engage in the sorting activity. When most have had a turn, move the objects to the Art Area for use there or store them with other Science materials. The Nature Box is now ready for newfound items.

Science Rebus

Write a short rebus story with a science theme, perhaps about an item in the Science Center. Include as many pictures and repeat as many words as possible. Write about things in which children have shown an interest. Include children in the Science Rebus by encouraging them to finish sentences that you have started.

A Science Rebus about dinosaurs might feature several dinosaurs with relevant facts. Words in parentheses should be rebus pictures:

(Stegosaurus) is a dinosaur.
It is a (plant) eater.
(Stegosaurus) has (4) big (legs).
It has a small (head).
(Stegosaurus) laid (eggs).
(Tyrannosaurus) is a dinosaur.
It is a (meat) eater.
(Tyrannosaurus) has (2) big (legs) and (2) small (legs).
It has a big (head).
(Tyrannosaurus) laid (eggs).

A Science Rebus about plants can include as much information about plants as children can offer:

A (plant) needs (sun).
A (plant) needs (water).
A (plant) is (green).
A (plant) has (leaves).
A (plant) has (roots).

Use the same Yes and No procedure for a variety of other investigations:

- IS IT MAGNETIC? YES or NO? On a large tray, place a magnet and a number of items for children to try with the magnet.

- WILL IT GROW? YES or NO? A large tray will hold a number of seeds and other small items such as beads, nuts, leaves, and stones.

- IS IT HEAVIER? YES or NO? A large tray will contain a number of items to be weighed and a balance. On one side of the balance scale, place an item to serve as a standard against which the others will be compared. Children will compare items to it by placing them, one at a time, on the other side of the scale to determine whether or not they are heavier. Follow the same procedures for an IS IT LIGHTER? YES or NO? investigation.

"What Will Happen" Prediction Charts

Title a chart or piece of paper. "What Will Happen" or "What Happened? and Why?" List children's names down the left side of the chart. Next to the chart, on a separate tray or placement, place an experiment or a "curiosity." Invite children's predictions, analysis of results, or questions. Pique children's curiosity and problem-solving ability using ordinary items or mixtures. Provide an introduction to the activity and/or purpose of the exploration at a circle time or individually, as children investigate the Science Area. Try these and other "curiosities." (For more possibilities, see Appendix 18.)

- Place a damp paper towel in a jar with a lid. (Condensation will form.)
- Place several items such as a key, a coin, a plastic animal, or a thick piece of rope on a piece of dark construction paper directly in the sun.
- Set two flowers on the tray—one in a vase of water, the other in an empty vase.
- Stand a stalk of celery in red colored water.
- Position lima beans in a jar between the inside wall of the jar and a damp paper towel. Water as the beans sprout.

Yes and No Investigations

Label two trays: one with the word YES and one with the word NO. Put these to use in a number of ways in the Science Area. Any activity that offers children an opportunity to explore and experience materials independently is well suited to a Yes or No Investigation. Children can carry out many of these investigations without formal instructions; others may require a presentation or brief explanation at a circle time or when children are in the Science Area.

Sink or Float Investigation

Gather a number of small objects, such as a cork, a penny, soap, a sponge, a metal spoon, a plastic spoon, a feather, a block, a seashell, a piece of paper, a pencil, a crayon, a toothpick, a plastic boat, and a piece of aluminum foil. Display the items on a large tray with a bowl of water. Add a Tent Label that reads DOES IT FLOAT? Let children investigate the items, placing them in the water and then on the appropriate YES or NO tray; YES if it floats, NO if it sinks. Provide paper towels for wiping hands.

Sensory Activities

The sensory activities described here will overlap with many other areas of the curriculum. Children need every opportunity to use, explore, and "wake up" their senses. Use of Tactile Labels is one way to include print in any sensory experience. Also, children are often quite vocal during sensory encounters; be alert to these verbalizations and record them.

Each of the five senses offers a variety of opportunities to include print in everyday sensory experiences. Sensory activities lend themselves especially well to the Yes and No Investigations described in the preceding section. Be sure to check with parents regarding children's food allergies before undertaking tasting activities.

Hearing

Listen and Find

Divide a 6" x 6" piece of cardboard into nine 2" x 2" squares. Glue pictures from old magazines or catalogs into each square (nine pictures in all). Label each picture in bold black print. On a tape cassette, record the names of the objects pictured in random order. Play the tape for children, asking them to listen for each object name and mark it with a token, such as a button or paper circle. If you are facilitating this activity as a large-group game, each child will need his or her own picture boards; if the children are at an interest area, several picture boards will do. Make the listening activity more challenging by supplying clues or a sound instead of naming the picture. Attention to and awareness of print is informal.

Match and Sound

Place a handful of rice in five or six peanut cans, potato chip cans, and/or margarine dishes. Fasten lids securely. Place an assortment of other materials in five or six additional cans. Choose materials that sound distinctly different than rice, such as stones, marbles, coins, a golf ball, bells, and dried beans. Put one type of material in each can. Cover one can of rice with red paper and cover the remaining nine to eleven cans with blue paper. Place the red can on a piece of paper labeled RICE and place a second piece of paper labeled NOT RICE next to it. Place all blue cans in a box lid. Let children shake each can in the box lid and place it on the appropriate paper—RICE or NOT RICE—depending on how it sounds. Rotate the contents of the red can frequently so that children have a chance to match the sound of stones, bells, a golf ball, and so on.

SUPER PRECISION ANTI-RESONANCE CASSETTE MECHANISM

Feeling and Touching

Rough or Smooth?

Gather an assortment of objects that feel rough or smooth. Arrange them on a tray in the middle of a table. Place one piece of paper on either side of the tray. On one piece of paper, write the word ROUGH, and on the other, SMOOTH. Next to each word, attach an item for children to feel, such as a piece of sandpaper and a piece of foil. Have children touch and explore the objects on the tray and sort them according to how they feel, placing the objects on the appropriately labeled paper. Follow the same procedures for HARD and SOFT or WET and DRY.

"What's in the Box?"

Put several objects in a Touch Box (see instructions on p. 107). On a clipboard or a piece of paper next to the Touch Box, record children's responses to the "What's in the Box?" question. Make sure children understand that they are not to remove anything from the box. They simply reach in, touch and feel the objects, and guess what they are. Read children's guesses during a circle time, discuss the answers, and reveal the contents of the Touch Box.

Yes and No Game

Gather two identical sets of objects. Place one set in the Touch Box. Next to the box, place a pile of YES and NO cards, ten of each. To make the cards, print YES on ten red pieces of paper and NO on ten blue pieces of paper. Use the second set of objects to make a checklist for children to follow. Title the list WHAT IS IN THE TOUCH BOX? On the list, include the mate to each object in the box and next to each object, print questions:

♦ Is there cotton? (glue on a piece of cotton)

♦ Is there a car? (tape on a toy car)

♦ Is there a paintbrush?

♦ Is there a stone?

♦ Is there a snake?

Add five to seven more objects that children will not find in the Touch Box. This will enable children to discriminate between the YES and NO cards.

After children have had ample time to investigate the Touch Box, gather for a group time. Read down the list of items. Encourage children to draw on their memories and offer their opinions as to whether the items are or are not in the box. Take everything out of the Touch Box to show what is inside.

Making a Touch Box

Tape both ends of a medium-sized box closed. Cut a circular opening in one end. Remove a sleeve from an adult-size sweatshirt. Cut the sleeve about 4" long, including the cuff. Attach the wide part of the sleeve to the opening in the box with fabric tape. If you wish, stitch around the opening of the sleeve with yarn and a sturdy needle before taping. Although you can use the Touch Box without the sleeve, this addition adds a little more excitement to the activity and ensures less "peeking." Cover the box with plain construction paper. Use a marker or letters stenciled out of sandpaper to label the box TOUCH BOX. Glue several different textures to the sides of the box, such as a piece of cotton, foil, polystyrene foam, sponge, or fur. Show children how to use the box by inserting one hand into the sleeve, through the cuff, and into the box, to feel what is inside.

Squeeze-It Balloons

Take dictation as children delight in some fun-filled balloons. Fill several balloons with a variety of materials: salt, sand, soil, flour, cornstarch, pebbles, dried beans, marbles. Use balloons that are fairly large and sturdy. A funnel or paper cone with the end cut off will help with filling. Fill until the balloon is about the size of a tennis ball. Tie a knot in the balloon, making sure the balloon is firm and that there is little unfilled space. The elasticity of the balloon allows it to stretch and give a little as children manipulate it.

Arrange a time for children to explore the Squeeze-Its. Try handling as an independent activity, with opportunities for children to dictate reactions, comments, and guesses. A circle time is another fun way to present these sensory balloons. Pass the balloons around the circle and record individual comments and guesses as to the contents. Write these on paper in front of the group. If you present balloons during a circle time, prepare three or four balloons of each type so they make their way quickly around the circle, yet children have adequate time to explore them. Color-coding the balloons as to contents (salt in red balloons, flour in green, and so on) helps in keeping track of the actual contents.

Seeing
Color Mixing Paint Bags

Place 8 tablespoons of yellow tempera paint and 3 tablespoons of blue tempera paint in a resealable plastic bag (play with the measurements until achieving a desirable shade). Encourage children to touch, squeeze, and handle the bag. Record comments, predications, and discoveries. Do the same with red and yellow tempera paint and red and blue tempera paint. Try adding white tempera paint to a bag containing any color of paint. When children have finished handling the paint bags, read the comments to the group and discuss the resulting colors. Lay the paint bags on newspaper and cut them open. Allow children to dip brushes into the paint mixtures and use them to make a painting.

Color Match Game

Include print in any Color Match game by adding the printed color word to the game. Children will still play the game in the same way, but will be handling print as they play. A Color Memory Game, a Go Fish card game, or even a color-themed board game such as Candyland can easily accommodate color words added directly to the game cards.

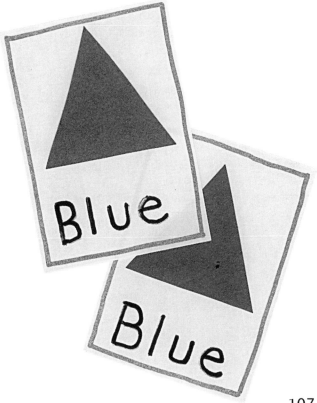

Smelling

Fruity Clay

Handling clays and doughs is a favorite activity of young children. It is one of the best feel-and-touch sensory experiences you can provide. For a clay experience that also excites the sense of smell, make Fruity Clay and combine it with print.

Prepare Fruity Clay according to the following recipe. Make three or four flavors. Roll each flavor into small balls and place the balls on paper plates, one for each flavor. Place each plate on a separate tray. On each try, include a spoon and a label naming the flavor. The fruit drink mix can or package may also be placed on the tray. Use a permanent marker to place a numeral on the spoon, telling children how many balls of clay to take. Provide a bowl, tray, or mat where children can place the clay balls they retrieve. Let children use their sense of smell to decide which Fruity Clay they like best. Their awareness of the labeled flavors on the trays and the different colors of the clay balls help children distinguish between Fruity Clays.

A graph with this activity is another way to introduce print. Title the graph FAVORITE FRUIT CLAYS and print the name of each flavor across the bottom. Divide the graph into three or four columns depending on the number of flavor choices. Also divide the graph horizontally, making individual rectangles in each column. Let children color in the square that corresponds to their favorite flavor. This requires a connection between the print on the tray and on the graph. Review the chart at circle time, counting, comparing and attending to print to see which flavor was the classroom favorite. Label a large container for each flavor and make it available at circle time. Have each child add their clay balls to the larger labeled container.

This is a wonderful exercise in quantitative comparisons and literacy when discussed in conjunction with the chart. Keep the Fruity Clay on hand for other uses. If the flavors are mixed during play, use one container for collection and use the clay in the art center.

Fruity Clay

1-¼ cups flour

½ cup salt

1 teaspoon oil

1 cup boiling water

1 package powdered fruit drink mix

Mix the dry ingredients. Add the oil and water. Knead. Make three or four separate mixtures, using different fruit drink mixes.

Soap Writing

For an new writing experience, provide bars of soap of all different kinds and dark-colored construction paper. Label the soap. Include several samples of your hand traced with soap. Let the fun begin! Some children will draw with the soap; others will follow the samples, tracing around their hands and printing their names. Hang labeled Soap Art in children's bathrooms and near classroom sinks.

Chapter 2: Curriculum

Tasting

Note: Check with parents regarding food allergies before implementing any food activities.

Apple Tasting

Provide three to five varieties of apples. Display the whole apple, along with a label naming the apple variety. In front of each whole apple, place a dish of apple pieces and a list of children's names. Next to each name, write YES or NO. Title the lists of names "Do You Like Granny Smith Apples?" or "Do You Like Golden Delicious Apples?" Include two faces: a happy face over the YES column and a frowning face over the NO column. Have children taste the apple and circle YES or NO. If children are beginning to print letters, they may print YES or NO next to their name instead. Share the results with the classroom. Results might also be graphed, counted, and compared during a circle time.

Other tastes to try include:

♦ several kinds of honey (paper mini muffin cups or thoroughly washed plastic liter soda bottle caps work well for this kind of tasting)

♦ a pickle assortment

♦ a vegetable or fruit assortment

♦ several varieties of berries

What Do You Taste?

Present a food and invite children to describe the taste. Include print by displaying a list of ingredients that may or may not be in the food. Place a picture of the food next to the print. Magazines and grocery store circulars make excellent picture sources. Use 1" x 2" paper to make YES or NO cards, printing YES on red paper and NO on blue paper. Have children taste the new food and go through the list, placing YES next to the ingredient if they taste it and NO if they do not.

Try adding a little something extra, such as shredded coconut to Peanut Butter Balls or honey to Vegetable Dip; try any number of other classroom favorites. Remember to prepare food out of children's sight so the ingredients remain a mystery. This will be a challenging activity for children but a good exercise in thinking about tasting. Awareness of and attention to print occurs naturally, as part of the process.

Other Sensory Activities

Sand and Water Table

Do not overlook this area of the classroom when planning Sensory Activities, because play at the Sand and Water Table draws on so many senses. Print is not usually found here, making print inclusions much more noticeable.

Sand Table

Enhance sensory play while giving function and meaning to print by adding an assortment of signs to the Sand Table. Make road and street signs, traffic signs, and other signs associated with the town or city. Add cars and people to the Sand Table. Signs that relate to construction and digging sites are especially well suited to sand and other digging materials. Add signs naming buildings and animals when you include blocks, plastic animals, or molds at the Sand Table.

Make signs from construction paper or cardboard; print clearly with dark-colored markers. Attach the signs with tape to one end of a craft stick. This way, children can place sticks directly in sand, especially if it is damp.

Label containers, shovels, scoops, sifters, funnels, cups, plastic bottles, sponges, and pitchers used for water, sand, rice, and other materials. Use a permanent marker and write directly on the objects.

If the material(s) in the Sand Table will not support a craft stick sign, mount the stick in a clay (drying dough) base (see recipe at right). Use a clay that hardens and place the craft stick in the ball of clay before it dries. Press the ball of clay against a hard surface to flatten the bottom. Use signs with bases in any Sand Table mixture. Change the print on the paper taped to the stick to relate to any type of play.

For more fun (and print) at the Sand Table, print the names of bakery and restaurant items, foods, and recipe ingredients directly on polystyrene foam food trays, paper plates, and bowls. Add labeled spoons, scoops, hand mixers, and other utensils. Copy short recipes or cut them from magazines. Slip recipes into plastic sandwich bags, or cover on both sides with clear Contac® paper. Children will have fun pretending to mix, cook, and "read" recipes.

Drying Dough (for base)

2 cups flour

1 cup water

craft sticks

Stir flour into water until ingredients are completely combined. Form into bases for signs. Allow to dry four to six hours before inserting craft stick. Dry an additional twelve to eighteen hours or overnight.

Water Table

Include some of the same labeled cooking and mixing utensils as you did for sand table play. Add funnels, cups, pitchers, and plastic bottles with various pour spouts. Use a permanent marker to label these items. Include recipes in plastic bags, as desired.

Cut fish, frog, and turtle shapes from sponges. Print the name of each directly on the sponge shape. Include seashells in the Water Table. Print the name of each on the smooth side of the shell.

Make several trays of ice cubes for Water Table play. Freeze small plastic alphabet letters in the ice cubes. Or, use a permanent marker to write letters and children's names or initials on plastic chips or bread fastener tabs; freeze these in ice cubes for more fun.

Outside Fun

Print and connections to literacy can occur outdoors on a playground in many of the same ways it occurs indoors in the classroom. The observant teacher will notice where children tend to play and how they use outdoor play equipment. He or she will adapt print, labels, and other literacy props to fit into the areas and scenarios of children's outdoor play.

Print for Vehicle Play

Using chalk or any of the outdoor labels discussed in the Labeling Section, construct traffic signs, road signs, signs that read PARKING LOT, and signs for buildings, such as SCHOOL or HOSPITAL.

Make pretend driver's licenses and license plates in the classroom with children. Use them outside with bikes, wagons, and other riding toys. Send drawing paper and notes home to parents asking them to help children make a crayon rubbing of the family car's license plate. Collect license plate rubbings in a classroom book of "Family Car License Plates." Compare letters and numbers on plates and include the collection book with other books taken outdoors. Give children who may not have a family car an opportunity to make a rubbing of the teacher's license plate or old license plates.

Use string to tie print and signs on bike handles and wagons, such as POLICE CAR, AMBULANCE, FIRE TRUCK, TAXI, BUS, DELIVERY TRUCK, CEMENT MIXER, AIRPLANE, HELICOPTER, TRAIN ENGINE, or MAIL TRUCK. Print the signs on construction paper or cardboard, punch two holes in the top of each sign, and add yarn.

Playground Treasure Hunt

Prepare this activity before introducing it to children. On the playground or in the outside play area, hide a bag containing "treasures" for each child (stickers, balloons, bookmarks) or one thing for all to share (a new playground toy, a new book, chalk). Write messages on 4" x 4" (or larger size) paper. Hang on branches, tuck under rocks, and place them anywhere children play. Use six to ten messages, depending on playground size and the age of the children. Write the messages rebus style, guiding the children from one spot to another until they reach the "treasure."

sand box

Excavation Sites

Turn sandboxes and digging areas into excavation or construction sites. Make small signs attached to craft sticks and larger signs attached to rulers, dowel rods, or branches.

Use construction site signs with large or small vehicle play, shoves, buckets, stones, and pebbles. For excavation sites, include signs that read DIGGING SITE and CAMP. Add collection containers and different kinds of digging implements, such as scoops, spoons, spades, and forks. Label containers and implements so as to relate to the scenario. Add more fun and purpose to the play by mixing "finds" into the sand or soil area before bringing children out to play, such as:

♦ Paint small stones with gold and other metallic colors or dab them with glue and sprinkle on glitter. Label collection devices GOLD and STONES to encourage visual discrimination.

♦ Mix metal objects into sand and include magnets with the tool assortment.

♦ Add rubber or plastic insects or small dinosaurs to the digging area.

Garden with Children

A garden, no matter what the size, presents a natural setting for purposeful print. Fence off a small area and plant seeds, or move plants started indoors to the garden.

Children can help make a sign identifying their garden. Stencil a few words, such as OUR GARDEN, on a smoothly cut and sanded square of wood. Let children paint the stenciled letters with acrylic paint and help nail the sign to a 12" plank that will anchor the sign in the ground. Use a picket fence to border the garden and let each child write his or her name on one picket with a permanent marker. Or, enclose the garden with a row of flat stones or bricks. Paint the top surface of each stone with white acrylic paint. Let each child use a darker color of acrylic paint to print his or her name or first initial on a stone. If the garden is large enough, lay the stones or bricks in a steppingstone path through the plants or flowers.

Whether the garden consists of flowers or vegetables, label it. Labels help distinguish plants, especially when they are just beginning to grow. More importantly, garden labels offer one more opportunity for children to see meaningful print in the outside world. This print serves a purpose and meets a need. ("How can we tell these little green plants apart?") A florist or garden shop may give you garden sticks that children can help label. Pickets from a fence also work well. If you grow plants from seed, use the seed packets as garden markers. Glue a plain piece of paper to the back of the seed packet and write the name of the plant on the paper. Enclose the packet in a plastic sandwich bag and tape closed, or cover with clear Contac® paper, for protection outdoors.

Record children's observations about the garden. Use graphs to chart plant growth. Add relevant classroom books (protected with plastic) to the garden.

Sandbox Kitchen

Occasionally, move props from the dramatic play centers to the sandbox. Labeled dishes, kitchen containers, and cookware can turn ordinary sand play into a new adventure. Relate craft-stick signs to kitchen, restaurant, or bakery play. Add plastic-bag-protected recipes and cookbooks. Play scribe and write children's "sand recipes" on the spot, if possible.

Consider what items might extend the play, and provide them. Not only will the play become more realistic and purposeful, but there will be new opportunities for literacy connections. Adding a table and chairs next to the sandbox might encourage children to engage in restaurant play. As children define their roles, include additional print props, such as a menu or a pad and pencil for taking orders.

Try other scenarios for a sandbox setting and offer opportunities for print inclusion: grocery store, pizza shop, or camping site.

Outdoor Role Play

Consider any activity that normally occurs outdoors and re-create it on the playground. Add appropriate props, print, and literacy connections.

A Camping Site might include props from the dramatic play area, such as backpacks, cameras, binoculars, flashlights, and fishing rods (made with branches and string). Print opportunities include maps, written directions, instructions for cameras or tents, signs (CAMP SITE, NO FISHING, PARK HERE), nature guides, bird and fish identification books, and blank books for "Nature Journals."

An Outdoor Barbecue requires only some basic picnic supplies: aprons, plastic food, cooking utensils, picnic basket, blanket, dishes. Use a box or a similar structure for a pretend grill. Or, look for an old tabletop charcoal grill that can be cleaned up. Gather stones and place them in a bag labeled CHARCOAL. The literacy opportunities here include recipe books, labeled props, food packages (such as plastic barbecue sauce bottles), and magazines.

A Sporting Event, such as a softball game or game of golf, is easy to re-create. Take any equipment normally used on the playground and adapt it to the game. Child-sized equipment is available at most discount stores. Although this equipment is plastic and not durable for everyday play, it is well suited to limited specialized play. Set up team and spectator areas and label all equipment. Provide other connections to literacy by including tickets (and a ticket booth), scorecards, sports magazines, rule books, banners, pennants, and labeled storage containers for equipment. Scenarios such as these help you foster children's awareness of the need for print even in the games people play. Children who are not particularly aware of print in other areas often find this functional use of print very interesting and appealing.

NO FISHING

Chalk Print

A piece of chalk and a length of concrete offer endless possibilities for incorporating print outdoors. Although temporary, chalk print is easy to reproduce; it also lets you (or children) add print to an area almost immediately. Set up chalk print areas before children go outdoors or ask their participation.

Chalk and Riding Toys

If children play with bikes, wagons, and other riding toys on the playground, use chalk to identify roads, traffic signs and directions, parking areas, and community buildings. Mark BIKE LANES and NO BIKES when riding toys are used in conjunction with other outdoor activities. Identify all areas and "roads" with chalk lines and print, such as ONE WAY, PARKING, and STOP.

Chalk and Balls

Identify ball-playing areas in much the same way. Use chalk print to identify each area's use:

♦ A large chalk square labeled BOUNCE BALLS.

♦ A chalk lane with a bin or box at the end labeled ROLL BALLS.

♦ A chalk line several feet from a wall directing children to THROW BALLS. Children can stand behind the line, throwing balls against a wall and catching them.

Try some of the same ideas with beanbags. Children may need a general "walk around" introduction to chalk print activities. They may also be left to discover chalk print activities on their own, interpreting the print themselves or seeking a response to "What does this say?"

Chalk Games

Incorporate print in many traditional chalk games. For example, turn Hopscotch into Thought Scotch. Prepare any Hopscotch pattern. Choose a theme for the game and, instead of a number in each square, print a word relating to the theme. If "favorites" is the Thought Scotch theme, print ten words (one per square) that relate to personal favorites: COLOR, ANIMAL, HOLIDAY SEASON, CEREAL, FRUIT, VEGETABLE, ICE CREAM, BOOK, and SONG. Children play Thought Scotch the same way they do the traditional game, but when landing on a (category) square—such as COLOR, they tell their favorite color. Rather than a win-or-lose game, this is a game of movement, turn-taking, language, idea sharing, and attention to print. Try any theme with Thought Scotch and encourage children to offer suggestions.

♦ **Name Game Theme**—Print an animal category in each square, such as BIRD, FARM ANIMAL, INSECT, and so on, and name something in each category.

♦ **Color Theme**—Print a color in each square and name something for each color.

♦ **Dinosaur Theme**—Print a dinosaur name in each square and tell something about each dinosaur.

Chalk Body Tracings

Use chalk to trace the outline of a child as he or she lies on the playground. Label body tracings with print: the child's name, the parts of the body (arm, let, etc.), and a balloon caption that records what the child wants to say.

Chalk Obstacle Course

Playground equipment or outdoor toys can be arranged into an Obstacle Course that children will enjoy. Add print at each obstacle point or "station," giving children an encounter with literacy each time they go through the course.

Use as much space as the outdoor area will allow, spacing obstacles at least six feet apart to allow movement in between. Set up a balance beam, a tube tunnel, steppingstones or blocks, a tire walk, and a tumbling mat. Add ball-rolls and beanbag-tosses; incorporate climbers and slides. Even bikes and wagons can be part of the course: Have children ride the bike or pull the wagon from one point to another, or in and out of barriers. At each point, use chalk to label the course with directional words: START, CLIMB, UP AND DOWN, WALK ACROSS, CRAWL THROUGH, IN AND OUT, ROLL THE BALL, TOSS THE BAG, and FINISH. Add numbers to help children follow the course in a sequential order. The goal here should not be a race or a rush to the first or best, but an enjoyable exercise that inspires an awareness of print.

Grass Print

Even playgrounds with more grass and soil then concrete offer numerous opportunities to incorporate print. Adapt many of the same ideas suggested under Chalk Print to grass play.

Create cardboard signs for riding toys, balls, and obstacle courses. Attach the cardboard to dowel rods, rulers, or sturdy branches and secure in the ground. It's easy to remove the signs at the end of the day or at the start of an unexpected shower, and replace them the next day, or change them to reflect a new type of play or new toys available.

Even games such as Thought Scotch can be adapted to grass. Use rope or clothesline to lay out the game squares. Make squares slightly larger than usual so children have enough space to jump into and out of them without moving the ropes. Print the categories on cardboard and lay them in each square. With these minor adaptations, children can play the game as they would on concrete.

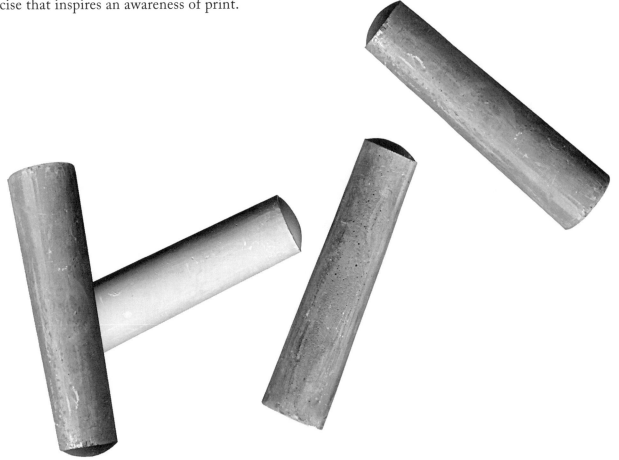

Dramatic Play

Themes and Props to Actively Practice Literacy in a Play Setting

Dramatic play is an integral part of the early childhood curriculum. A separate section devoted solely to this area of the curriculum reflects the important correlation between this form of pretend play and the emerging literacy of the young child. The Dramatic Play Center is one of the most effective integrated learning areas of the classroom, and the props included here reflect all areas of the curriculum from manipulatives and numbers to art and music. With a natural instinct for pretend play, an innate desire to control the environment, and a need to act out familiar roles, children are drawn to Dramatic Play Centers. So attractive is this area to children that it is essential that educators use it as a means for exposure to the tools and uses of literacy.

Selecting, Using, and Changing Centers

Dramatic play affords children an opportunity to practice a variety of social skills and exercise imagination and creativity. Here they learn to get along, share, bargain, compromise, and make decisions. Provide children with a few housekeeping props and expect to observe any or all of these behaviors. Literacy skills such as verbal and written communications are enriched in the process. Props themselves contribute to early literacy as children transfer meaning to objects and use objects to symbolize play. Add more props and include literacy materials, and you increase the likelihood that children's play will promote literate behaviors.

Dramatic, or Symbolic, Play is one of the easiest and most effective ways to incorporate positive experiences with literacy into the classroom. Dramatic Play settings provide children with countless opportunities to explore the functions and uses of print. Here, children can engage in reading and writing experiences that are relevant to the play scenario. In the early childhood classroom, Dramatic Play and related literature behaviors involve a high degree of self-initiation and self-direction. Children recognize the need to perform literate behaviors on their own. They engage in them for no other reason than to extend or enhance play. This is the natural acquisition of literacy skills, not taught or imposed, but self-selected and necessary to play. Literacy behaviors in this setting have meaning because they are chosen and perceived as necessary by the child, not the adult. In contrast to adult-directed exercises, there is no right or wrong here and no possibility for failure.

Add literacy props such as pictures of restaurant workers and customers, menus, small pads of paper for taking orders, pencils and pens, cash register, money, and signs (OPEN, CLOSED, TODAY'S SPECIAL, PLEASE WAIT TO BE SEATED, etc.), and the restaurant becomes authentic. Hence, the play becomes more real and the use of literacy becomes more natural. Literacy will be necessary in the course of play. The setting will seem more familiar to children's own experiences with restaurants. Children will make use of these literacy props just as they use the play food and dishes. They perform more literate behaviors: "reading" menus and signs, "writing" orders and bills, "counting" money, and communicating with more literate actions.

Selecting a Theme

Dramatic Play settings can be independent of classroom curriculum or reflective of it, such as a restaurant, police station, or bank setting for a Community Helpers or Occupations theme and a pet shop or veterinarian office during an Animals unit. The Dramatic Play themes included in this section and the suggested props are intended to be a guide only. Do not feel that all centers must be tried or all props must be included in order to present an effective play situation. Be alert to other meaningful centers and other items available through community or parent sources. In selecting props to enhance the theme, try to achieve a balance of literacy props, such as pencils, paper, cookbooks, or typewriters, and props related solely to the theme, such as photographs, dishes, stuffed animals, or jewelry.

Materials for Dramatic Play

These are as varied as the themes of the play areas themselves. Many props are available within the classroom or easily made. You can gather others, especially literacy-related props, in a number of ways. School staff and parents can contribute much to the prop collection. Thrift shops and yard sales offer a fine assortment from which to choose. Perhaps some of the best sources of literacy props are the community businesses in the area. Here parents will again be a valuable source. Each parent's workplace and those of other family members are possible contributors to the classroom prop supplies. Before the collection of props begins, a survey of parents' occupations and workplaces will be a time saver (see the letter samples in Appendices 19 and 20). This will help in choosing interest areas to start with and guide the collection of props.

Involving Children

Once the theme has been determined, brainstorm and list appropriate props. Involve the children in the preparation of the Dramatic Play Area. Discuss the area to be set up, encouraging children to share their experiences that relate to the Dramatic Play Theme. With children's help, make a list of props that are needed in the Dramatic Play Area.

Use large paper and markers to write ideas as children dictate them. Decide how the furniture is to be arranged and what clothing will be used. Use the list as a guide for collecting. Put the list to use again when the area is set up for play. When you introduce new materials, display the list and check off or circle the props that have been collected for the area. This is a cooperative activity that demonstrates to children how printed words can be used to represent objects. It also provides a functional or purposeful use for print.

Props

Using the Center

In engaging in literate behaviors, children begin to understand how the printed word can be useful and meaningful. They use the materials, "reading" and "writing" for real-life purposes. Note that the terms *reading* and *writing* as they relate to preschoolers refer to a child's play "reading" and "writing." Children may read and write a few recognizable words or the reading and writing may be completely invented, symbolic, or even scribbled. The value here is in the doing. The act of engaging in literate activities, not the conventional reading and writing of words, is the desirable outcome.

When children have the opportunity to explore and interact with authentic materials, they easily lose themselves in their roles and experience complete enjoyment in their play. This pleasure contributes to the development of positive attitudes toward the functions and materials of literacy. Because this type of pretend play has no risk of failure, all children can feel successful engaging in literacy behaviors. The sense of accomplishment and competence they feel will extend to other classroom experiences as they become comfortable with the materials and routines of literacy.

Changing the Theme

To maintain interest in Dramatic Play Areas and to multiply the different types of experiences children will have with literacy props, change the theme periodically. As the themes change, so will the play materials and literacy props. Many of the literacy materials will be the same even though the theme of the area changes. However, the materials may be used in different ways, for different purposes, and to meet different needs. For example, the small pads of paper children used to take orders in restaurant play may be used to make lists in grocery store play or write out prescriptions in doctor play. Repeated uses with the many tools of literacy give children the opportunity to see new possibilities for materials and sharpen their skills with each use. Therefore, though changing Dramatic Play Areas periodically is important, take care to keep the area in the room long enough to permit repeated uses of the materials by all children. Take cues from the children themselves and, when it seems that they have used the materials enough or taken the play scenario to its limit, it may be time for a change. Often children will change the direction of an area on their own. The restaurant theme is forgotten and housekeeping play is initiated or "robbers" invade the restaurant space. This is an indication that the play theme may be ready for a change. Some children may object to the absence of certain props. Most children will be satisfied by your assurance that the props will be used again, the presence of new theme settings, and the reintroduction of the popular props later. Allowing props in Dramatic Play Areas for long periods of time, even very popular items, may cause the area to become stale, the props to be misused, or the attraction of the prop to detract from the intended scenario.

Setting Up Centers

Try to maximize classroom space to permit the inclusion of more than one Dramatic Play Center at a time. Ideally, you will be able to set up new Dramatic Play Centers in other areas of the classroom, thereby enabling the Home and Family Center to remain intact. Much interaction occurs between Dramatic Play Centers. A Grocery Store Center, an Office Center, and a Home and Family Area set up in the same classroom at the same time present the potential for print-rich and pleasurable interactions among many children.

Getting Started

In setting up the centers, you'll find a variety of suggestions for creating boundaries. (Refer to Chapter 1, "Defining Space" on p. 23, for a more thorough discussion.) Remember, when counters are suggested, this may be the tops of classroom furniture or it may mean the tops of boxes stacked two high. Similarly, shelving may be classroom bookshelves and toy shelves or a grouping of open shelves. A Natural Boundary may be classroom plants or it may be a row of constructed paper trees. Use what is available first, and make additional materials to complete each setting.

Each different Dramatic Play Center should have an Interest Center Label hanging or placed on the floor. Try cutting Interest Center Labels into a shape relating to the area. Labels that stand on the floor may be Free-standing Labels, Paper Bag Labels, or cardboard Tent Labels. (Check Chapter 1 for labeling ideas for each center and complete instructions for making a variety of labels.)

Equip the Home and Family Center with the furnishings, dress-up props, scenario props, and literacy props found in any home. Make this center a permanent part of the classroom and available for imaginary play throughout the day. The prop list in the "Home and Family Center" section will suggest inclusions for this area.

Types of Props

Center Props

Photographs and pictures enhance the appearance of the center. Separate photograph and picture files will help you locate photos and pictures for each center quickly. Photos and pictures should relate directly to the setting and include a label.

Photographs

Ideally, photographs will portray parents at work and children with their families engaged in activities that relate to the center. These are not difficult to obtain. Request family photos each time you introduce a center. Supply a camera (disposables work well) with a note asking parents to take the camera to work with them and have a colleague take a quick photo. Give each family a turn to use the camera for a few days or a weekend. Have the film developed and add the photographs to a photograph file. Consider asking community members if they will supply a photograph of themselves at work:

♦ a pediatrician
♦ a local dentist
♦ a police officer
♦ a veterinarian
♦ a school secretary
♦ a librarian
♦ a teacher (don't forget yourself!)

Display photos on a display board or on walls and furnishings throughout the center.

♦ Small Lucite photo frames are inexpensive and available. They make a fun and easy way to share photos of children and their parents throughout the classroom.

♦ Follow the instructions for making Stand-up Labels with easel backs to make self-standing frames for family photos.

♦ Create a large photo cube using a large cardboard box or carton (2' x 2' or larger). Cover the entire box with brightly colored paper or gift wrap. Attach photos on all four sides of the box. First place strips of clear tape on the box; then attach photos to the tape strip using rolled-up pieces of tape or double-sided tape. Then the paper on the box won't tear when photos are changed. Add small labels to title each photo. Place a label on the top of the photo cube reading "Our Families."

Pictures

Use pictures throughout every Dramatic Play Center. In addition to being a quick and easy way to change the environment, pictures are visually stimulating and add to the realism of the setting. Animal pictures hanging in the Pet Shop or Veterinarian Office, pictures of police officers and vehicles in the Police Station, or pictures of desserts and breads in the Bakery set the mood for play and give children a visual reference for roles they play and actions they perform. Pictures also display print, because each picture should be labeled. Sources include:

♦ magazines
♦ catalogs
♦ calendars
♦ newspapers
♦ store circulars
♦ postcards
♦ travel brochures

Dress-up Props

Clothing is included on some prop lists, but not all. Use your discretion as to when to include dress-up clothes and accessories in a Dramatic Play Center. Often, a modest selection of clothing props is sufficient to add realism to the play: hats, aprons, vests, badges, and other items that suggest an occupation or theme. When too many dress-up items and accessories (such as jewelry, wallets, purses, and shoes) are available all of the time for every setting, the dress-up props often become the focus of the play and the real purpose of the center is lost. Indeed, Dress-up Props have more appeal and serve a better purpose if they are brought into some Dramatic Play settings, but not all.

Literacy Props

Literacy Props consist of all the tools, materials, and print that an adult might be expected to use in a similar setting. Community resources and parent donations will be important sources of these materials. Many can also be made and adapted from one center to another and have uses in more than one area. For example, small note pads or clipboards may be used in Restaurant Play, Hospital or Doctor's Office Play, and Office Play.

Scenario Props

Scenario Props are all of the other materials, furnishings, and toys that are usually present in most Dramatic Play settings. Though these are, for the most part, non-literacy related, they greatly enhance the realism of the play. Examples of scenario props include dolls, stuffed animals, dishes, cookware, clothing and accessories, cash registers, tool kits, telephones, and tables and chairs. Because the authenticity of materials can greatly enhance the realism of the play, supplement "toy props" with real ones as much as possible. A toy typewriter is an asset to any Office setting; one made from a box lid will certainly meet the needs of children's play if a toy typewriter is not available. But a real typewriter, even one that does not work, makes the actions performed in the Office and the role playing in the Office that much more real.

Mount pictures on colorful construction paper or posterboard to make them sturdy and more noticeable.

Though large pictures are preferable, smaller pictures grouped together on 9" x 12" (or larger) construction paper and individually labeled work equally well.

Hang most pictures at children's eye level, though hanging some higher make them more visible throughout the classroom and add to the center's appeal.

If bulletin boards or wall space is scarce, use any flat surface in the center, such as the sides and backs of furniture, shelves, or boxes.

Don't forget children's artwork and easel paintings as a source for pictures. Mount, label, and hang them with other pictures.

Linking Props

Scenario Props and Literacy Props should be strongly linked in Dramatic Play settings. One provides the authentic connection to the real world, while the other confers meaning on the play. When added, Dress-up Props further enhance authenticity and can even provide literacy connections if name tags, emblems, or badges are included. Take a Pizza Shop, for example. Children have the kitchen props they use for House Play and the cues and suggestions you provide. Play is enjoyable here, with everyone "making" and "eating" pizza. The addition of Scenario Props changes the play significantly. Add a few empty pizza boxes, pizza cutters, a cheese grater, a telephone, and a cash register, and the "shop" becomes more realistic. Aprons, hats, purses, and wallets further enhance the play. Language and social interactions are enhanced as children assume roles and recreate past experiences in this or a related setting.

Now, consider Literacy Props. Interestingly, some children seem to recognize the need for print in Dramatic Play settings. Once Scenario Props are part of the play, children may be observed pretending to write on their hand with a finger or looking at the wall as if reading a menu. Add Literacy Props, and roles become more realistic and communications more clear. Telephone books, memo pads and writing utensils for orders, menus from actual pizza shops, signs showing prices and toppings, name tags, and paper money add meaning to the play. As children engage in literate behaviors with these props, they gain an awareness of print and an understanding of its many functions.

Dramatic Play Prop Storage

Each different Dramatic Play Center should have a storage box, or Prop Boxes containing the Scenario, Dress-up, and Literacy props that relate directly to the area. Label each box and add the contents to the play area only when appropriate. Store Literacy Props that will be used in more than one area separately, in one or two boxes. This leaves more space in the Prop Boxes for the collection to grow. It also makes it easier to add a variety of literacy tools and props to each play setting and to replenish paper, forms, and writing utensils as necessary.

Center Activity and Tips

Each Dramatic Play Center description includes a Center Activity and Tips. The Center Activity will be one in which children can engage while playing and pretending in the setting. Depending on the theme of the center, the activity will combine print with art, music, math, language, science, or sensory projects. The activities are designed for independent use, with the dual purpose of involving children more directly in the theme of the center and providing additional experiences with print. The Tips provide suggestions for locating and making props for the center.

Guidelines for Making Props

Many props will fit a number of Dramatic Play Center themes and can be used in a variety of contexts. Some may already be available in the classroom; others can probably be borrowed. Children will use authentic props in more realistic and, therefore, more meaningful ways, so they are always preferable. But if real props are not available, you can augment play centers with a number of handmade props. Tickets, checkbooks, menus, and a variety of print props are easily made if real props (expired driver's licenses, old credit cards and checks, outdated user's manuals) are not available.

Hats

Hats of all kinds play an important role in any Dramatic Play Center. A hat can help children "get into" a character, role, or play scenario. Hats also enhance interactions between players, helping children respond to one another according to the type of hat being worn. Supplement authentic hats, always the first choice, with hats you create for nearly any play center in the classroom.

One simple and effective way to create hats is to take plain baseball caps and add felt emblems to suggest the play center theme. Use rolled-up tape to attach emblems, so the same hats can be used again with a different emblem.

Another, more personal hat that you can create with children is a Band Hat. The base for this type of hat is a 1½" strip of heavy paper or craft foam that wraps around the child's forehead. The front of the Band Hat can display an emblem, a symbol, or a visor. Try adding two to four additional strips to the Band Hat to fit the crown, or top, of the child's head. Attach larger strips of construction paper or tissue paper to the band to make a larger hat. Make Band Hats with colors related to play center occupations and scenarios.

Carton Cars

Remove the top and bottom of a cardboard carton. Choose a carton large enough to fit over a child's body. Cut two slot "handles" in the top of each side of the carton. Paint the outside of the carton or cover it with paper. Use black paint, a thick black marker, or colored construction paper to "detail" the car, adding headlights, taillights, doors, door handles and other trims. Glue on cardboard wheels that have been painted black or covered with black construction paper. Add different paper/cardboard details to turn Carton Cars into other vehicles: a ladder and bell for a fire truck, a siren and number for a police car, a red cross for an ambulance, and a U.S. mail sign for a mail truck. To "drive" the Carton Car, children hold the side "handles," keeping the car about waist high, and walk slowly or quickly, depending on the scenario.

Checkbooks

Make photocopies of a blank check or a sample check. Cut and gather into small booklets attached at the top with staples. Put into an old checkbook cover or make a paper checkbook cover.

Clipboards

Fasten a binder clip to the top middle of a heavy piece of corrugated cardboard. Small plastic cutting boards also work well. Attach paper under the clip and use pencils or pens for writing.

Computer

Draw a Computer Keyboard on a piece of paper cut to fit inside a shoe box lid. Glue the Keyboard inside the lid. A more tactile and dimensional keyboard can be made by printing letters on small squares of polystyrene foam or craft foam. Glue squares on paper attached to the shoe box lid. Place a second shoe box lid perpendicular to the bottom lid as a "screen" and "cover" for the laptop computer. Add a paper "mouse" and a polystyrene foam food tray or a square of craft foam as a "mouse pad."

Control Panel

Use a large carton to make a Control Panel. A box about 1' high and 2' wide works well. Set the carton upright with the opening at the top (no lid or box flaps). Remove one long side of the carton. Cut the two shorter sides diagonally from the top back corner to the bottom front corner. Turn over the box, with the opening facing the table, leaving a stand-up triangular structure. Cut several ovals, circles, and rectangles from either slanted side of the box. Cover holes with colored plastic or cellophane by taping it under the opening. Make cardboard knobs and attach with brass fasteners or use large beads for knobs. Make two holes where the bead will be placed. Thread a piece of cord or yarn up through one hole, attach the bead, and run the cord down through the second hole. Tie it under the box. Attach pointers and arrows in the same way. Write compass directions around one of the pointers. Write the numbers of a clock around the other. Make a small rectangular "radio" or "telephone" with a piece of polystyrene foam, craft foam, or section of a paper towel tube. Attach it with a long piece of yarn so children can remove it for use. Make a slit where the radio can be placed or cut a hole for the telephone. Lay a small flashlight under the box to "light up" the Control Panel. Cut and assemble shoe boxes the same way, to make smaller, individual Control Panels. Add as much print as possible to the Control Panels: ON, OFF, RIGHT, LEFT, UP, DOWN, IN, OUT.

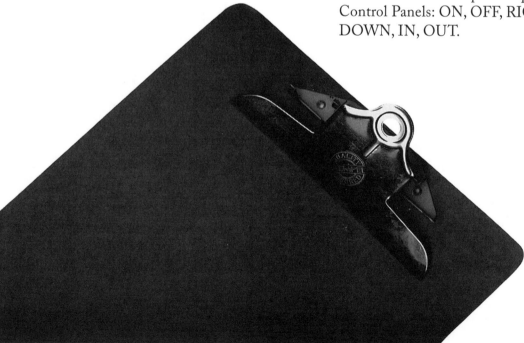

Credit Cards

Cut craft foam into credit-card-sized pieces. Use an ink pen to lightly write the credit card name and expiration date and to draw a logo. A permanent marker also works well.

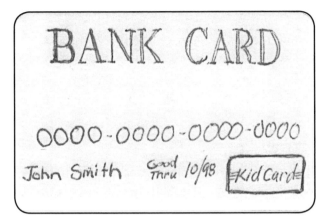

File Cabinet

Use two computer-paper boxes or similar-sized boxes as the frame for a File Cabinet. Arrange the boxes vertically, one on top of the other, with the openings facing front. Attach heavy corrugated cardboard horizontally on the inside of the box to serve as shelves where the shoe box "drawers" will be placed. Cut the shelves as deep as the computer-paper boxes and 4" wider. Make 2" bends on each side of the shelves and use masking tape to secure the shelves in the box. Place three or four shelves in each box, depending on the size of the shoe box drawers. Place shoe boxes (without lids) on shelves horizontally. Children move the boxes onto and off of the shelves to use the File Cabinet. Set two File Cabinets side by side, creating six to eight drawers. Cover the File Cabinets with paper or paint. Label each "drawer" and put cards and folders inside the drawers.

Grocery Bag File Folders

One brown grocery bag will make two file folders. Spread out the sides to flatten the bag and make it wider. Use two file folders as stencils. Lay one folder against each folded edge of the bag. Stagger the folders so that one is against the top of the bag and one is against the bottom. This will also give you space for the top tabs of the folders. Trace around each and cut out. Use the bag scraps to make memo pads or "index cards" by tracing around large or small cards.

Hoses

Cut an old garden hose into a number of 2' and 3' pieces. Wrap silver or gray cloth tape around one end as a nozzle.

Mailboxes

Clean and scrub fifteen half-gallon milk cartons. Remove the pour-spout top so that the top is square and open. Stack the milk cartons on their sides with the openings facing front. Attach them with brass fasteners or double-stick tape. The final divided structure will measure five milk cartons long and three milk cartons high (fifteen individual compartments in all). Cover the outside with paper or invite children to decorate the Mailboxes.

Memo Pads

Staple fifteen to twenty small pieces of paper (about 3" x 5" size) at the top. Attach a heavy piece of cardboard on the back with glue. Make assorted pages, both lined and unlined.

Name Tags/Badges

Adhesive labels serve as useful Name Tags and are fine for occasional use. For many situations, however, you will want to prepare permanent Name Tags. Pins are not safe choices for play centers, so fasten tags in other ways. Make craft foam or construction paper Name Tags that fasten on collars and shirt fronts with a paper clip. Change these for every play situation and for every child who chooses to wear one. Wallet-sized plastic photo holders make fine reusable Name Tags; change them by simply slipping a new piece of paper into the plastic enclosure. Fasten on children with a paper clip. Felt Name Tags also work well. Tape a paper name label onto a felt background or write directly on the felt. Hang the tag around the child's neck with yarn or cut a slit in the top of the felt and attach the tag to a button on the child's clothing. Remember to ask children what name to print. Many children like to have a different name for pretend play. Some children may also want to write their own name.

Make badges, using the same basic techniques. Add stick-on stars, border the Badge with foil, or cut the Badge in the shape of a star or shield. Add numbers as well as names.

Money Props

Make coins by covering buttons, chips, or craft foam circles with aluminum foil and other shiny papers.

Ticket Window, Cashier's Window, Serving Window

Use this prop in many play centers, including the Bank, Pizza Shop, and Fast-Food Restaurant Centers. Start with a large appliance box. Cut the box to a 3' x 3' size. Next, cut the structure in half, leaving one full side and two partial sides on each piece. This makes two "windows." Use them both in one center or decorate them for separate scenarios. Remove a 2' square "window" from the full side, leaving a 6" frame around the opening. Decorate the frame with paint, markers, or paper. To use, tape the "window" bottom to a counter, table, or shelf. Children stand behind the window and use the table for the cash register, telephone, and other supplies. Add print to the front of the structure (above the opening) that relates to the play setting: TICKETS, ORDER HERE, BANK TELLER, DRIVE-THROUGH.

Walkie-Talkies

Connect two paper cups with yarn. Add round stickers or brass fasteners for "buttons."

Tool or Gadget Board

Cut a heavy rectangular box following the directions for the Control Panel. Attach various sizes of screw and bolts to the slated front of the box. Fasten cardboard knobs and arrows. A piece of smooth, well-sanded wood, if available, make an even better Tool Board. On wood, attach wires and door latches as well. Children will enjoy using these realistic items as well as strengthen manual dexterity and fine-motor control in the process.

Typewriter

Use a square box and cut it according to Control Panel directions. On the slanted top, draw square shapes for the keys and print a letter on each key. Follow an actual typewriter layout or arrange letters alphabetically. Cut a narrow slit in the top and tape a piece of paper in the slit.

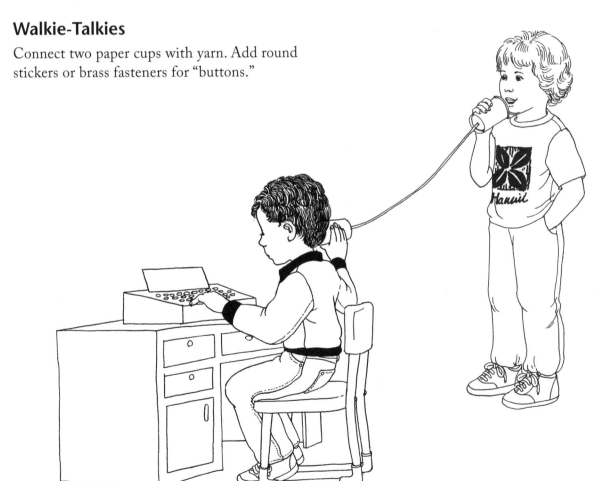

Specific Ideas for Setting Up Centers

This section provides detailed suggestions for setting up and labeling twenty-eight Dramatic Play Centers. Each includes instructions for setting up the center, labeling the center, and making related signs. Props for each center are divided into four categories: Center Props, Scenario Props, Dress-up Props, and Literacy Props. An activity is included for every themed setting, as are Tips providing additional ideas for locating and making props. Use this section as a guide, adding or substituting props and materials as needed, and making the most effective use of classroom space and materials.

Airport Center

Setting Up the Center

Divide the area into two sections. Use chairs and tables, shelves, and rugs to set boundaries.

In one section, place several rows of chairs or lay out mats or rugs for use as seats. This is the Airplane. Set two chairs at a table or counter for the pilot and co-pilot. Assemble the control panel, compass, maps, a microphone, and walkie-talkies on the table. Make pillows, trays, food, and magazines available for the passengers in the airplane. The other section is the Airport Waiting Area. Place the ticket window, a wagon for luggage, and chairs for waiting there. A Snack Bar and Newsstand can also be set up.

Labeling the Center

Use Identification Labels to label items in the center and large Free-standing Labels to identify the Airplane and Airport Waiting Area.

Signs in the Center

- ARRIVALS
- DEPARTURES
- NEWSSTAND
- SNACK BAR
- TICKETS
- WAITING AREA

Airport Center Props

- photographs of families traveling and on vacation
- pictures of airplanes, airports, and people traveling

Scenario Props

- cash register
- clock
- computer
- control panel
- dishes
- headsets
- hole punch (to "punch" tickets for passengers)
- loudspeaker or microphone
- luggage cart (wagon)
- pillows and blankets
- play food
- small rugs or mats
- telephone
- trays
- walkies-talkies

Dress-up Props

- flight attendant name tags
- hats
- luggage and overnight cases
- pilot badges
- wallets and purses

Literacy Props

- books about airplanes, airports, travel, clouds, the sky
- compass
- forms (credit card, reservation, vacation package)
- magazines
- maps
- money, checks, credit cards
- newspapers
- telephone book
- tickets
- travel brochures

Center Activity: Paper Airplanes

Supply paper and completed paper airplanes (as models) for paper airplane folding. Include markers at the table so children can print letters and numbers on their Airplanes. Pictures of airplanes can serve as examples of letters and numbers. Children may want to print their own initials and age on the planes, or the letters USA.

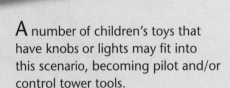

Tips

A number of children's toys that have knobs or lights may fit into this scenario, becoming pilot and/or control tower tools.

Hang blue-and-white cloud shapes on the walls surrounding the Airplane area to add to the feeling of "flying."

A local travel agency may be able to contribute brochures, sample flight plans, forms of any kind, and maps to this setting.

Archaeology Site Center

Setting Up the Center

Set up outdoors, this center can incorporate a sandbox or digging area. Set up inside, it can include a sand table for the digging site. A hard floor without a rug is best for easy sweep-ups. Arrange classroom floor plants in a row and small plants on shelves as a Natural Boundary, or create a paper Tree Divider if real floor plants are not available.

Provide counters, tables, and a sand table. If a sand table is not available, use several large plastic tubs or line cardboard boxes with a plastic trash bag. Fill tubs or boxes with sand, soil, gravel, rice, and other digging materials. Add wagons, dump trucks, and buckets of tools.

Labeling the Center

Use Tent Labels to designate areas on the counters and tables where various jobs will be done. Label tools and containers with Identification Labels. Use Identification Labels attached to craft sticks for soil and sand areas, and attached to sticks anchored in clay bases for gravel and other materials. Print DIGGING SITE, ARCHAEOLOGY SITE, EXCAVATION SITE, and names (SAND, ROCK, GRAVEL) on the labels.

Signs in the Center

- ♦ BE CAREFUL
- ♦ CAMP SITE
- ♦ CAUTION
- ♦ DIGGING SITE
- ♦ DUMPING AREA

Archaeology Site Center Props

- ♦ photographs of actual excavation sites and archaeologists
- ♦ pictures of mountains, deserts, forests, dinosaurs, dinosaur bones, rocks, minerals

Scenario Props

- ♦ clipboards
- ♦ collection bags
- ♦ containers of all kinds
- ♦ dump trucks and other related vehicles
- ♦ pails
- ♦ sand table containing a sand and gravel mixture, containers of digging mixtures
- ♦ shovels, scoops, spades, spoons
- ♦ stones, rocks, pebbles
- ♦ wagon

Dress-up Props

- ♦ boots
- ♦ hats
- ♦ name tags or badges
- ♦ sunglasses

Literacy Props

◆ adhesive labels for collection bags

◆ books about digging, museums, dinosaurs, rocks

◆ labeled muffin tins, egg cartons, ice cube trays for collecting and sorting (label: rocks, minerals, stones, gems, dinosaur names, or any items made available for collection)

◆ maps

◆ nature guides

◆ note pads

◆ writing utensils

Center Activity: Fossil Making

Set up a Fossil Making Area in the Archaeology Site Center. Provide clay (see recipe below), previously mixed and separated into 2" balls. Place one ball in each section of an egg carton and cover the carton with plastic wrap. In another egg carton, place twelve objects that can be used to make an imprint in the clay. Label each object with a small tag taped onto the egg cup. Add crayons and a number of 4" squares of cardboard. Have children write their names on pieces of cardboard and choose a ball of clay and one object. Let children work the clay with their hands, flatten it slightly on the cardboard and make an imprint in the clay with the object they have chosen. Allow the "fossils" to dry. Paint them with a mixture of white glue and water (1 part glue to 3 parts water) for a glossy shine. Children can take the fossils home or add them to a "Fossil Museum."

Fossil Clay

2 cups cornstarch
4 cups baking soda
2-½ cups water

Combine ingredients in a pan and cook over medium heat. Stir until mixture thickens. Cool and knead. Make 2" balls, storing in an airtight container until used.

Mix special "finds" in with the sand, soil, or pebbles in the digging site. Prepare and incorporate one group of items at a time; supply labeled collection devices for "discoveries." Any of the following "finds" help to lend authenticity to an Archaeology Site: stones painted in bright colors, gold- and silver-painted stones, stones with dots of glitter, small plastic dinosaurs, seashells, and fossil rocks. Include metal "finds," providing magnets to use along with shovels and scoops.

Bakery Center

Setting Up the Center

Use furniture props from the kitchen in the Home and Family Center to separate the Bakery from the rest of the classroom. Use shelves for added boundaries. Divide the area into two sections.

One section will be the Bakery Kitchen. Locate the stove, refrigerator, and other appliances here. Stock the kitchen with cookware, cooking utensils, and empty packages of food generally used in desserts and bread making, such as cake mixes, flour, sugar, vanilla, and spices. The other section will be the Bakery itself. Shelves, a table and chairs, and a counter will furnish this area. Add a cash register, a telephone, paper bags, pictures of desserts, and pretend cakes, cookies, and breads.

Labeling the Center

Use Identification and Tent Labels to label furnishings and supplies. Stand-up Labels with easel backs can display pictures and identify Bakery desserts. Tactile Labels are useful in the Kitchen area.

Signs in the Center

♦ Bakery Items: PIES, CAKES, COOKIES, TARTS, BREADS
♦ Kitchen: KEEP OUT
♦ OPEN; CLOSED
♦ PAY HERE
♦ PRICE LIST
♦ TODAY'S SPECIAL

Bakery Center Props

♦ photographs of parents and children cooking; relatives and friends who work in a bakery; and, if the school has a kitchen, school personnel baking in the kitchen
♦ pictures of desserts, breads, bakeries, cooks, chefs

Scenario Props

♦ baking pans of all kinds
♦ bowls
♦ cash register
♦ cookie sheets
♦ cooking utensils
♦ dishtowels
♦ empty packaging from dessert and bread ingredients: bags of flour or sugar; egg cartons; milk cartons; baking soda cans; cake, cookie, and brownie mix boxes; vanilla bottles; spice cans
♦ paper bags and bakery boxes
♦ potholders
♦ rolling pins
♦ scale
♦ sponges
♦ telephone

Chapter 3: Dramatic Play

Dress-up Props

♦ aprons
♦ chef's hat
♦ name tags
♦ wallets and purses

Literacy Props

♦ books about bakeries, cooks, chefs, food, breads, desserts
♦ calendar
♦ cookbooks
♦ recipe cards
♦ pads of paper
♦ receipts
♦ telephone book
♦ writing utensils

Center Activity: Baking Cookies

Make three to five pretend cookie sheets by covering box lids, polystyrene foam food trays, or plastic trays with aluminum foil. Gather three to five or six to ten cookie cutters. Trace cookie cutters onto paper and glue one or two paper cookie shapes on each tray. Add a label naming the shape. If placing two shapes on each tray, divide the tray in half with a piece of colored tape. Make play cookie "batter" out of dough (see recipe below). Add rolling pins and spatulas. Children can roll out the dough, cut the cookie cutters, and move them to the appropriately labeled cookie sheet using the spatula. In addition to a print awareness activity, this is an exercise in dexterity and fine-motor control.

Cookie Dough

2 cups flour
1 cup salt
2 tablespoons oil
9 tablespoons of water

Combine flour, salt and oil. Add water, one tablespoon at a time, until mixture is smooth (up to 9 tablespoons). Mix with a spoon until fairly blended. Knead.

Make "cookies" by cutting 2" and 3" cardboard circles. "Ice" with a Soap Clay mixture (see recipe below). Sprinkle with glitter or confetti. Allow to harden.

Make cakes using two polystyrene foam (1" to 2" thick) circles, 4" and 6" in diameter. Glue the smaller circle on top of the larger one. Cover with soap clay icing and sprinkle with glitter or confetti. To make a birthday cake, add candles before icing hardens.

When visiting a local bakery or grocery store bakery, save bakery boxes and bags and reuse them in the Bakery Center.

Soap Clay

3 cups laundry detergent flakes
2–3 tablespoons water

Pour laundry detergent flakes in a bowl. Add 2 to 3 tablespoons of water. Mix until uniformly moist and mixture can be shaped into a ball. Add more water if necessary to achieve this consistency. Place on cardboard or polystyrene foam "desserts" by the spoonful and spread with a knife just like real frosting.

Bank Center

Setting Up the Center

Use counters, shelves, and tables as boundaries for the Bank Center. Place one or more teller windows in the area and several desks or tables and chairs.

Stocks shelves with paper, notebooks, envelopes, writing utensils, and forms and applications of all kinds. Make calendars, telephones, and cash drawers available. Equip tables with pens, note pads, index cards, check forms. Number cards and an abacus also work well in the Bank Center.

Labeling the Center

Use Tent Labels and Stand-up Labels to identify items on shelves. Use Identification Labels on large items and Cube Labels at "teller windows."

Signs in the Center

- CHECK CASHING
- DO NOT ENTER
- NEXT WINDOW
- OPEN; CLOSED
- THANK YOU
- TODAY IS _____

Bank Center Props

- photographs of relatives and friends who may work at a bank
- pictures of banks, people buying things, coins and money

Scenario Props

- cash drawer
- clipboards
- computer keyboard
- desk sets
- paper clips
- real pennies
- telephone

Dress-up Props

- bank teller name tags
- wallets and purses

Literacy Props

- abacus
- adding machine
- calculator
- calendar
- check forms
- coins
- coin wrappers
- envelopes
- forms and applications
- index cards
- money, checks, credit cards
- number cards
- paper and notebooks
- rubber stamps and ink pads
- typewriter
- writing utensils

Center Activity: Penny Shining

On a table in the Bank Center, place a jar containing 1½ cups vinegar and ¼ cup salt. Label the jar VINEGAR AND SALT. Set the (tightly closed) bottle of vinegar and the box of salt on the table also. Provide a dish of pennies, an empty dish, a spoon, and several paper towels. Label the dish PENNIES. Children drop the pennies in the vinegar/salt mixture and watch as the tarnished pennies begin to shine. After removing the pennies with the spoon and drying them off, they place the pennies in the other dish, labeled SHINY PENNIES.

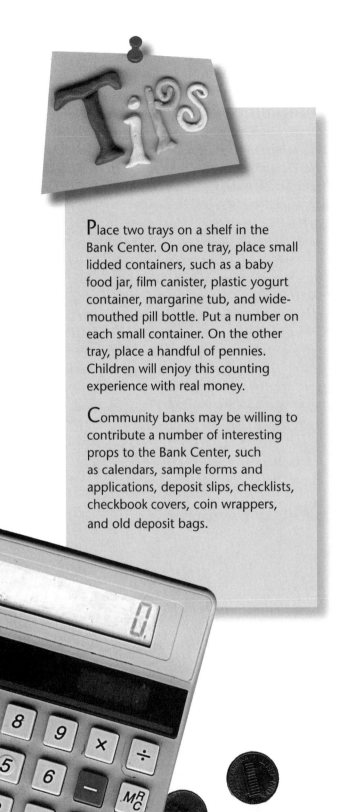

Place two trays on a shelf in the Bank Center. On one tray, place small lidded containers, such as a baby food jar, film canister, plastic yogurt container, margarine tub, and wide-mouthed pill bottle. Put a number on each small container. On the other tray, place a handful of pennies. Children will enjoy this counting experience with real money.

Community banks may be willing to contribute a number of interesting props to the Bank Center, such as calendars, sample forms and applications, deposit slips, checklists, checkbook covers, coin wrappers, and old deposit bags.

Beach Center

Setting Up the Center

Use white clothesline to make boundaries for the Beach Center. Tie the rope between two hooks, two pieces of furniture, or two table legs. Hang beach towels bearing signs naming the area on the rope boundary. Arrange classroom floor plants in a row for a Natural Boundary; make a "Tree Divider" if large plants are scarce. Include a sand/water able as a boundary. Fill the table with sand and add seashells, pails, and shovels for sand play.

Cover one section of the Beach Center with beach towels. Create a Life Guard Station with a chair, life preserver, and first-aid kit. Add an Umbrella Rental Station using a supply of rain umbrellas. Set up a Snack Bar using a serving window and kitchen props. Cover the other section with blue paper or fabric to suggest water. Place boxes on the "water" to use as sailboats. A paper sail attached to a yardstick and taped to the side of a box adds to the realism. Place paper fish and real seashells on the blue paper for fishing and scuba diving.

Labeling the Center

Label the Snack Bar and beach items with Identification Labels. Designate the sand and ocean areas with Free-standing Labels. Hang signs on the boats, Life Guard Station, and Umbrella Rental Station.

Signs in the Center

- ◆ BOAT RENTAL
- ◆ COLD DRINKS
- ◆ FIRST AID
- ◆ LIFE GUARD
- ◆ NO FISHING
- ◆ NO SWIMMING
- ◆ SNACK BAR
- ◆ UMBRELLAS FOR RENT

Beach Center Props

- ◆ photographs of children and their families at the beach or at swimming pools, and enjoying other summer fun
- ◆ pictures of oceans, underwater life, beaches, seashells, sunrises and sunsets, palm trees, sand castles

Scenario Props

- ◆ beach bags
- ◆ beach balls, beach toys
- ◆ beach towels
- ◆ cameras
- ◆ empty bottles of sunscreen
- ◆ first-aid kit
- ◆ food-serving window
- ◆ lifeguard chair
- ◆ life preservers
- ◆ sand table
- ◆ seashells
- ◆ shovels and pails
- ◆ umbrellas

Chapter 3: Dramatic Play

Dress-up Props

♦ beach hats	♦ lifeguard shirt
♦ diving masks	♦ sandals
♦ fins	♦ sunglasses
♦ goggles	♦ whistle

Literacy Props

♦ books about the beach, summer, underwater life
♦ first-aid manual
♦ magazines
♦ maps
♦ nature guides: fish, birds, seashells
♦ Snack Bar menu
♦ sticks for writing in the sand

Center Activity: Seashell Sorting

You will need an assortment of seashells for this activity: at least three distinct kinds, ten to twelve of each. Make a sign showing an example of each kind of shell (either a picture or a real shell attached). Print the name of each. Provide three trays, each labeled with the name of a shell (no pictures) and a box of assorted seashells. Have children sort the shells by matching the shell to the chart and finding the corresponding labeled tray where they can place the shell. Add thin paper and crayons for shell rubbings. Include a tray of soft clay for making shell impressions.

Fill two plastic tubs with water and two with wet sand. In one water tub, place plastic fish, frogs, turtles, and other water creatures. In the other water tub, place sponges cut into beach shapes: fish, turtles, seashells, boats, suns, anchors, life preservers. Print the name of each shape on the sponge with a permanent marker. In one wet sand tub, add sand molds and digging tools; in the second, include a shovel and a variety of seashells. Children can press seashells into the sand and dig them up. Place these tubs on the floor in between beach towels, to add to the beach theme.

Set up a postcard-making area that includes blank index cards and as assortment of pictures of beach scenes. Travel brochures provide an excellent picture source. After tracing the index card directly onto the picture, children cut out the picture and glue it on the index card. Children can write on the blank side of the card. Stamps, stickers, and rubber stamps can be included. Place a box of real postcards (preferably with writing and canceled stamps) with this activity for children to investigate.

Make balls for indoor games:

• Stuff socks with newspaper, dried beans, rice, or cotton. Tie off with yarn or a rubber band. Fold the rest of the sock over the toe (and back again if necessary). Squeeze and form the stuffed sock into a ball shape.

Camping Center

Setting Up the Center

Use a Natural Boundary of floor plants and smaller plants set out on counters and tables. If large plants are not available, use smaller plants and construct a row of paper trees. Use a rope tied between two points in conjunction with plants to help separate the area.

The Camping Center should look rather sparse. Set up one or two tents by draping blankets over a rope anchored firmly between two points or by placing blankets over tables. Assemble branches in piles for "campfires" and designate areas of the Camping Center as fishing, hiking, and cooking areas. Stock each area with related props.

Labeling the Center

Label most items with Identification Labels. Use Free-standing Labels to identify the fishing, hiking, and cooking areas.

Signs in the Center

- ◆ CAMPING SITE
- ◆ DO NOT FEED THE BEARS
- ◆ FIRST AID
- ◆ LOOKOUT POINT
- ◆ NO SWIMMING
- ◆ PACK IT IN; PACK IT OUT
- ◆ PARK RANGER STATION
- ◆ PICNIC AREA
- ◆ PLEASE PUT OUT CAMPFIRES
- ◆ WATER

Camping Center Props

- ◆ photographs of children on camping trips with their families
- ◆ pictures of the following: people camping, hiking, fishing; tents; campers (car dealerships are good sources); forest, mountains, fish

Scenario Props

♦ backpacks
♦ binoculars
♦ branches and leaves from outdoors
♦ cameras
♦ canteens
♦ compass
♦ cookware
♦ first-aid kit
♦ fishing nets
♦ fishing poles made with branches and string
♦ flashlights
♦ food packages
♦ plastic food
♦ sleeping bags
♦ tents or blankets
♦ thermos

Dress-up Props

♦ hats
♦ hiking boots
♦ vests

Literacy Props

♦ blank books for Nature Logs
♦ books about camping, fishing, boating, hiking
♦ camera instructions
♦ driver's license
♦ first-aid manual
♦ fishing license
♦ maps
♦ nature guides: fish and birds
♦ outdoor camping magazines

Center Activity: Branch Weaving

Gather an assortment of V-shaped branches. Place the branches in a large container with a variety of yarn and string. "Campers" can make a branch weaving by working the yarns over and under the V-pattern of the branch. Provide an instruction chart showing children how to weave the branches with the yarn. The chart should consist of rebus-style instructions (a combination of pictures and words). Hang up branch weavings to decorate the Camping Center.

Prepare Trail Mix (see recipe below). Fill individual plastic bags with several spoonfuls of mix for Campers and Hikers to munch. Note: Check with parents first about children's food allergies before preparing or serving Trail Mix.

Turn a large appliance box into a van or camper. Arrange a table, chairs, and other small furniture pieces inside.

Visit or call a local travel agency to gather brochures and maps showing pictures of camping sites and hiking trails.

Trail Mix

1 cup peanuts
1 cup sunflower seeds
1 cup raisins
1 cup dry cereal
1 cup crisp Chinese noodles

optional:

½ cup chocolate chips
½ cup peanut butter or butterscotch chips

Children can help prepare and bag Trail Mix following a rebus-style recipe.

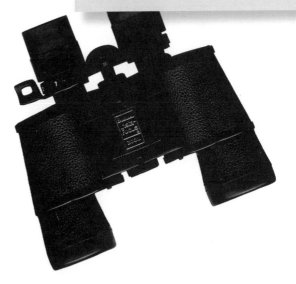

Car Repair Center

Setting Up the Center

Use shelves and counters as center boundaries. If old automobile tires are available, bring three into the classroom and stack them for an additional boundary.

Situate riding toys from the playground, such as bikes, wagons, and large trucks, throughout the area. Stock the shelves and bins on the floor with tools. Stack cans and plastic bottles on shelves. Add other vehicles, small and large, to the Center.

Labeling the Center

Use Identification Labels and Tent Labels to identify furnishings and items in the center.

Signs in the Center

- ◆ DO NOT ENTER
- ◆ GAS
- ◆ KEYS
- ◆ OPEN; CLOSED
- ◆ PARKING
- ◆ PAY HERE
- ◆ TIRE SALE
- ◆ WAITING AREA

Car Repair Center

- ◆ photographs of children and parents in family cars, and parents repairing and washing cars
- ◆ pictures of the following: families in cars; roads; cars, trucks, vans (car dealerships are a good source)

Scenario Props

- ◆ bikes and wagons
- ◆ buckets and tubs
- ◆ cash register
- ◆ cleaning cloths
- ◆ flashlights
- ◆ large trucks and cars
- ◆ coffee can covered with paper and labeled OIL
- ◆ plastic water jugs labeled ANTIFREEZE, WINDOW WASHING FLUID, WATER
- ◆ telephone
- ◆ tires
- ◆ tools
- ◆ watering hose

Dress-up Props

- ◆ baseball hats
- ◆ name tags
- ◆ work gloves

Literacy Props

- books about cars, trucks, and other vehicles
- car manuals
- memo pads
- money
- newspaper car ads
- pencils
- repair guides
- telephone book

Center Activity: Car Collages

On large mural-sized paper, draw the outline of a car. Label the various parts surrounding the outline. Supply magazines and car dealership brochures, scissors, and glue. Let children cut out vehicle pictures and glue them inside the outline, creating a group car collage. Save the finished collage to add to the Car Repair Center next time you set it up.

Include a variety of blocks and boxes so children can construct ramps and inclines.

A Service Station or an Auto Salvage Center will often donate old or broken car parts, such as a steering wheel, an exhaust pipe, wiper blades, a seat belt, or car mirrors for use in the Car Repair Center. Clean these items thoroughly and check for sharp edges. Label them before adding to the center. Children will enjoy the realism these items provide.

If the center will include old automobile tires, check thoroughly for hidden "creatures" before using indoors. Put them to use on the playground once you have disassembled the center. Use them as part of an Obstacle Course, as areas for plants or vegetables, or as part of an outdoor Gas Station Center.

Construction and Building Center

Setting Up the Center

Use large blocks, shelves, and floor signs to divide this area from the classroom. One or two wooden horses and a workbench make fun boundaries too.

Arrange this center as a random selection of activities that suggest building and constructing. Sets of wooden blocks, construction vehicles, a toolbox containing tools of all kinds, sandpaper, wood scraps, and craft sticks are some of the items you might make available to children. Define work areas within the center by laying out several pieces of newspaper in three or four areas. Place a set of blocks on one; wood scraps, sandpaper, and white glue on another; and construction vehicles and craft sticks or wood chips on another. On shelves throughout the center, place supplies such as goggles, work gloves, blueprints, tools, and paintbrushes. Include old paint cans and containers labeled CEMENT and PLASTER. Place small items, such as nuts, bolts, and screws, in egg cartons and muffin tins for easy storage and fun sorting experiences. Provide a bench or table and chairs where "construction workers" can take their lunch boxes and eat.

Labeling the Center

Place Stand-up Labels at each newspaper-defined building station. Use Identification Labels on containers of blocks and tools. Place Bag Labels on shelves containing supplies. Incorporate Tactile Labels made with sandpaper and small nuts and bolts.

Signs in the Center

+ BUILDING AREA
+ CAUTION
+ CONSTRUCTION AREA
+ LUNCH AREA
+ WET CEMENT
+ WET PAINT
+ WORK AREA
+ WORK SAFELY

Construction and Building Center Props

+ photographs of relatives and friends who may work in construction, building, carpentry, or architectural occupations
+ pictures of construction sites, construction vehicles, buildings, woodworking, house repairs

Scenario Props

+ blueprints and floor plans to hang on walls
+ building toys, such as blocks, Tinker Toys, Lincoln Logs
+ busy board with nuts, bolts, and other materials attached
+ construction vehicles
+ cork board
+ craft sticks
+ empty paint cans with lids secured
+ first-aid kit
+ locks and latches
+ lunch boxes and Thermos
+ nuts, screws, bolts
+ paintbrushes
+ sand, gravel, pebbles
+ sandpaper
+ tools of all kinds
+ white glue
+ wooden blocks
+ wood scraps
+ workbenches

Dress-up Props

+ bandannas
+ hard hats
+ overalls
+ safety glasses
+ tool belts
+ work aprons
+ work gloves

Literacy Props

+ blueprints
+ books about construction, building, workers, tools, construction vehicles, architecture, repairs
+ construction, lumber, and carpentry ads
+ first-aid manual
+ floor plans
+ graph paper
+ memo pads
+ newspaper
+ repair manuals
+ tape measures and rulers
+ writing utensils

Center Activity: Build a Town

Wash and dry a number of milk cartons of all sizes: half pints, pints, quarts, half gallons. When cleaning cartons, do not open the spout any wider than usual; the triangular top of the cartons will be an important feature of the finished project. When the cartons are dry, tape the spout closed. Provide three boxes of precut 1" and 2" construction paper squares in nine colors. Label one box HOUSES and one box ROOFS and include red, green, blue, purple, gray, and brown paper squares in both boxes. Label a third box WINDOWS AND DOORS and include white, yellow, and black paper squares. Provide sandpaper and white glue. Place all supplies on a newspaper area on the floor. Children will choose one or two milk cartons and lightly sand, roughing up the waxy coating on the carton in preparation for gluing. Next, they will glue squares from the houses box all over the carton and squares from the roofs box on the triangular top of the carton (which becomes the roof). Finally, children will glue on windows and doors. After children have constructed their building, they can place it on a table, counter, or floor area of the classroom covered with a large piece of craft paper or newsprint. On this large paper, draw roads (colored black) and grass areas (colored green) for the houses and buildings. Make trees with paper towel tubes painted brown; cut green leaf shapes and tape them in one end of the tube; cut four slits in the other end and bend slits out to make the trees stand. Add print to the town, naming streets, roads, and buildings (school, post office, police station).

Include several plastic tubs with a different material in each: gravel, soil, sawdust, small wood chips. Add scoops, shovels, small construction vehicles, and craft stick signs to the tubs. Place these containers on one of the newspaper areas in the center.

Place pieces of polystyrene foam, polystyrene foam peanuts, and toothpicks in a box for structure building. Children can hold polystyrene foam pieces together with toothpicks.

Note: Polystyrene foam peanuts should not be used with very young children.

Include a wagon in the Construction and Building Center. Use it to store wooden blocks in the area; let "builders" use it to haul tools, paint, and other equipment; or fill it with everything needed to work at one of the newspaper areas.

Visit a construction site, a building supply company, a carpenter, or an architect. Request blueprints, charts, paint color samples, wood chips and scraps, sawdust, cans, and packaging.

Dentist's Office Center

Setting Up the Center

Use tables, shelves, and counters to create boundaries for the Dentist's Office. Include a cupboard and sink from the Home and Family Center.

Divide the space into two areas: a Waiting Room and an Examining Room. Use one or two rugs to define the areas and/or place a counter or row of chairs between areas. In the Waiting Room provide chairs, magazines, a few puzzles, a desk or small table for the receptionist, and a variety of office supplies, such as an appointment book, a calendar, a telephone, and a telephone book. A shoe box filing cabinet can also be added. In the Examining Room, provide one chair, a mirror, cotton balls, and dental floss. Hang charts or posters showing teeth, smiles, and toothbrushes.

Labeling the Center

Use Identification Labels and Stand-up Labels to identify items in the Dentist Office. Use Free-standing Labels to identify the Waiting Room and Examining Room.

Signs in the Center

- ◆ BRUSH YOUR TEETH
- ◆ PLEASE BE SEATED
- ◆ SMILE
- ◆ THANK YOU
- ◆ THE DENTIST IS IN/OUT

Dentist's Office Center Props

- ◆ photographs of the following: relatives and friends who may be dentists; children smiling; children brushing their teeth
- ◆ pictures of dentists, toothbrushes, fruits and vegetables, people smiling

Scenario Props

- ◆ cotton balls
- ◆ dental floss containers
- ◆ empty toothpaste boxes, plastic mouthwash bottles
- ◆ paper or plastic cups
- ◆ plastic gloves
- ◆ telephone
- ◆ tissues
- ◆ toothbrushes

Dress-up Props

♦ name tags
♦ wallets and purses
♦ white shirt with buttons or white T-shirt, for dentist and office help

Literacy Props

♦ appointment book and appointment cards
♦ books about dentists, teeth, tooth fairies, fruits and vegetables
♦ calendar
♦ file folders
♦ magazines
♦ memo pads
♦ money, checks, credit cards
♦ newspapers
♦ paper
♦ telephone book
♦ writing utensils

Center Activity: Mix Toothpaste

On a tray in the Dentist Office, place three bowls: one each of baking soda, salt, and water. Label each bowl. Place paper cups, pencils, measuring spoons, eyedroppers, and a choice of several flavorings—extracts such as cherry, orange, and mint—on the tray. Have children follow the toothpaste "recipe" posted on the tray to mix their own toothpaste. They should write their name on a paper cup and use it as a container for mixing. Children can then brush their teeth with the toothpaste they made. Have them bring new toothbrushes from home or let them use a clean index finger to brush.

Toothpaste

1 teaspoon baking soda
¼ teaspoon salt
¼ teaspoon water
1 drop of flavoring

Mix plaster of Paris and pour it into a polystyrene foam egg carton. Fill it to the top so that all twelve egg cups are joined. When dry, peel off the carton and use the plaster of Paris unit as a dentist's plaster cast of teeth. Practice correct brushing and use as a dentist's teaching tool.

Make paper bibs for "patients." Use a paper punch to put a hole in two corners of a paper towel. Tie a piece of yarn through each hole, and tie the bib behind the neck.

A family or community dentist may be a source of posters, pictures, pamphlets, perhaps a few paper bibs, or an X ray of a tooth. Ask for a sample appointment card or page from an appointment book to copy.

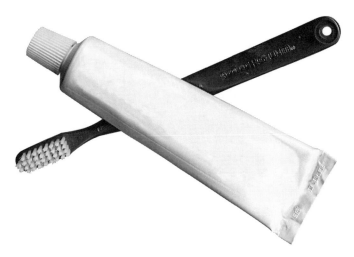

Doctor's Office Center

Setting Up the Center

Define the space for the Doctor's Office Center with counters and shelves. Include a sink and cupboard from the Home and Family Center. Divide the space into two sections using rugs or a row of chairs.

In the Waiting Room, provide chairs, magazines, a few puzzles, a desk or small table for the receptionist, and a variety of office supplies, such as an appointment book, a calendar, a telephone, and a telephone book. You can also add a shoe box filing cabinet. Pictures in the Waiting Room should relate to health and body. In the Examining Room, assemble several types of bandages; empty aspirin, vitamin, and other pill bottles; empty packaging from first-aid products; a first-aid kit; a stethoscope; an eye chart; a scale; and a measuring chart for the wall. A play doctor's kit fits in well. Also include a cot, mat, or sleeping bag, and blankets and pillows.

Labeling the Center

Use a variety of labeling types and forms, such as Identification, Location, and Stand-up Labels to name the objects in the Doctor's Office Center. Try several Tactile Labels made with cotton, adhesive bandages, and round paper "pills."

Signs in the Center

♦ EXAMINING ROOM
♦ FIRST AID
♦ PLEASE BE SEATED
♦ THANK YOU
♦ THE DOCTOR IS IN/OUT
♦ WAITING ROOM

Doctor's Office Center Props

♦ photographs of relatives and friends who are doctors or who work in a doctor's office and community doctors
♦ pictures of doctors, hospitals, children being measured or taking medicine

Scenario Props

♦ bandages, several types
♦ cot or mat, blankets and pillows
♦ cotton balls
♦ dolls
♦ empty aspirin, vitamin, and other pill bottles
♦ empty packaging from first-aid products
♦ eyedropper
♦ eyeglasses frames
♦ first-aid kit
♦ plastic containers and jars
♦ plastic gloves
♦ pretend doctor's kit
♦ stethoscope
♦ telephone
♦ tissues
♦ tongue depressors
♦ tweezers

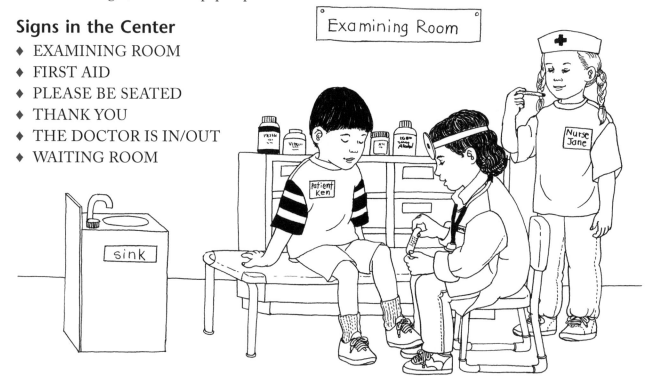

Dress-up Props

♦ name tags
♦ wallets and purses
♦ white shirt with buttons or white T-shirt, for the doctors and nurses

Literacy Props

♦ appointment book and appointment cards
♦ books about health, doctors, hospitals, first aid
♦ calendar
♦ clipboards
♦ eye chart
♦ file folders
♦ first-aid manuals
♦ magazines
♦ memo pads
♦ money, checks, credit cards
♦ newspapers
♦ paper
♦ telephone book
♦ writing utensils

Center Activity: Tongue Depressor Puzzles

Line up eight jumbo craft sticks or tongue depressors side by side. Place a strip of masking tape across both ends of the stick grouping to hold it together. Turn the stick grouping over as one piece. Hold the unit so that the sticks are vertical. Use one color of marker to draw a picture (outline) of a part of the body on the surface of the sticks. Make the lines heavy and draw the picture large enough to fill the whole area. Print the name of the body part, placing one letter on a stick. Draw and color a hand, a foot, eyes, a head, and a body. Pictures of doctor's equipment—a red cross, a bottle of vitamins, or an adhesive bandage—also work well. Place one large round dot in the upper left corner of the first stick. Remove the tape from the back of the sticks and place the individual sticks in a paper cup or a plastic bag. Place the stick puzzles on a table in the Waiting Room for "patients" to put together. Children will arrange the sticks in the correct order to complete the picture. As they line up the sticks, children will also be arranging the letters (one on each stick) to spell the word.

Tips

Make a literacy-rich, child-friendly examination chart on 9" x 12" paper. Draw the outline of a child with a line for the patient's name. Label a variety of body parts. Print the names of the body parts next to each. Make copies of the drawing and attach several to a clipboard. The "doctor" or "nurse" uses the chart when examining dolls or real "patients." The doctor places an X on the body part that is hurting or bothering the patient.

A community doctor or the Red Cross are both excellent sources of posters, pamphlets, first-aid samples, tongue depressors, empty medicine bottles, casts that have been removed, or even an example of an X ray. Ask for a sample appointment card or page from an appointment book to copy.

Fast-Food Restaurant Center

Setting Up the Center

Use kitchen furniture, tables, and counters as center boundaries.

Create two distinct areas, a kitchen and an eating area. Between the two, put a serving window at a counter or table for ordering. Fill the kitchen area with appliances and cooking props. Place a table and chairs, napkins, trays, and trash cans in the eating area.

Labeling the Center

Identification Labels work best in this center. Use them to identify furniture and objects.

Signs in the Center

- ♦ COLD DRINKS
- ♦ DO NOT ENTER
- ♦ DRIVE THROUGH
- ♦ OPEN; CLOSED
- ♦ ORDER HERE
- ♦ PAY HERE
- ♦ PICK UP HERE
- ♦ THANK YOU
- ♦ TRASH

Fast-Food Restaurant Props

- ♦ photographs of relatives and friends who may work at a fast-food restaurant and families eating together
- ♦ pictures of food, food workers, cooks

Scenario Props

- bags
- cash register
- cookware and cooking utensils
- dishtowels
- napkins
- paper plates, bowls, cups
- paper towels
- sponges
- squeeze bottles: catsup and mustard
- trays

Dress-up Props

- hats
- large shirt "uniforms"
- name tags
- wallets and purses

Literacy Props

- books about food, cooks, eating out
- coupons from local fast-food restaurants
- memo pads
- money
- newspaper ads
- receipts
- writing utensils

Center Activity: Burger Building

Use an assortment of paper and cardboard shapes to make a "burger building" area in the kitchen. Cut and label each of the following, keeping them in separate containers: brown cardboard circles for buns, dark brown construction paper circles for burgers, green triangles for lettuce, small red circles for tomatoes, yellow squares for cheese. Add a "Burger Building Chart" for "fast-food workers" to follow. This chart should combine print, numbers, and glued-on shapes. Cut yellow and brown construction paper into strips and serve these "French fries" in a paper cup or French fry container. Children will enjoy this "burger building" activity and engage in a new print experience at the same time.

Create a Salad Bar between the eating area and the kitchen. Line up plastic containers from grocery store salad bars and fill them with plastic fruits and vegetables. Try filling the containers with various colors of tissue paper too: torn green pieces for lettuce; orange strips for shredded carrots, crumpled balls of red, brown, green, and white for tomatoes, mushrooms, broccoli, and cauliflower. Label each container. Provide a stack of bowls and spoons or tongs for "Serve Yourself" salads.

Add "carton cars" or bikes and wagons for use at a "Drive-Through Window."

When visiting local fast-food restaurants, save paperware, bags, and napkins. Request samples of paperware, French fry and sandwich containers, and cups. Some fast-food restaurants use paper hats and aprons; they may donate several of these for the center.

Fire Station Center

Setting Up the Center

Use ropes attached between two points, shelves, and counters as the center boundaries.

Separate the center into two areas: a living space for firefighters and a garage, or firefighting area. Set up the living space using many of the Home and Family Center props. Include cots or sleeping bags. Equip the garage area with shovels, pails, hoses, a first-aid kit, flashlights, and walkie-talkies.

Labeling the Center

Label the living area with Identification and Tent Labels. Use Arrow Labels and Free-standing Labels in the garage area.

Signs in the Center

♦ ALARM
♦ CALL 911
♦ NO SMOKING

Fire Station Center Props

♦ photographs of relatives and friends who may be firefighters
♦ pictures of fire trucks, firefighters, firefighting equipment (avoid pictures of blazing house fires)

Scenario Props

♦ bells
♦ cots and sleeping bags
♦ flashlights
♦ hoses (cut to short lengths)
♦ kitchen props
♦ pails
♦ shovels
♦ stuffed dog "mascot"
♦ telephones
♦ tools
♦ walkie-talkies

Dress-up Props

- badges
- boots
- fire hats
- vests

Literacy Props

- books about fire safety, firefighting, fire trucks
- city maps
- clock
- emergency numbers
- first-aid manual
- fire safety tips
- telephone book

Center Activity: Fire Station Mascot

On large newsprint, make the outline of a dog. Add facial features and a collar. Hang the dog in the Fire Station. On a table or floor space next to the dog, provide sheets of white paper with circles drawn on them. These will be "spots" for a Dalmatian dog and should be about 3" in diameter. Print each child's name or initials on one spot. Include black crayons, scissors, and glue. Children will find the spot with their name, color it black, cut it out, and glue it somewhere on the Dalmatian. Record children's choices for a name for the dog; vote on choices at a group time. Keep this "mascot" with other Fire Station Center props.

A ladder makes an excellent boundary for this center. Set the ladder on its side, leaning the ends against shelves and a wall.

Turn a large appliance box into a fire truck. Remove the ends and most of the top. Let children paint the box red, if you wish. On each side, cut a door to open and close. Inside, set up several chairs, a steering wheel, and a bell; add a gear panel if desired. Load the truck with tools and hoses before it speeds off to a fire.

The community fire department is an excellent prop source. It can often provide plastic fire hats, badges, and posters and other printed literature. It may even contribute old or worn equipment.

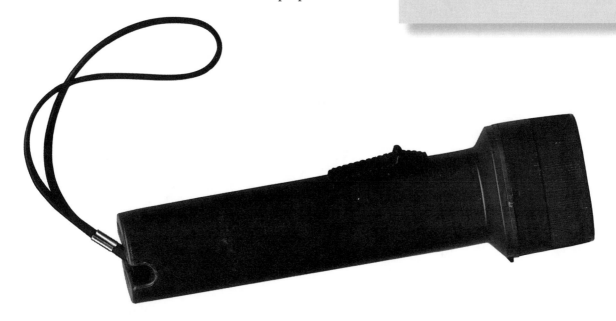

Florist Shop Center

Setting Up the Center

A Natural Boundary of classroom plants or a paper Tree Divider can help separate the Florist Shop from the rest of the classroom. Add shelves or counters for additional dividers.

Stock the shelves with baskets, plant pots, gardening tools, empty seed packets, seeds, and gardening gloves. On tables place foil and tissue paper, paper doilies, ribbons, and an assortment of artificial flowers and greens. Set aside an area where "customers" pay for their purchases. On a separate counter, add a phone, a cash register, and paper and pens.

Labeling the Center

Label furniture with Identification Labels and florist items with Tent Labels.

Signs in the Center

- ◆ Flower names: ROSES, DAFFODILS, TULIPS, DAISIES, MARIGOLDS, CARNATIONS, LILIES
- ◆ FLOWER SPECIAL TODAY
- ◆ PAY HERE
- ◆ THANK YOU

Florist Shop Center Props

- ◆ photographs of relatives and friends who may work in a florist shop or garden center and parents and children gardening
- ◆ pictures of florists, gardens, flowers, plants, bouquets, arrangements
- ◆ artificial flowers and greens

Scenario Props

♦ baskets
♦ cash register
♦ dried flowers
♦ empty seed packets
♦ garden tools
♦ hose (cut to short lengths)
♦ paper doilies
♦ tissue paper and foil
♦ plant pots
♦ plants: real and artificial
♦ ribbons and bows
♦ seeds
♦ spray bottles for misting plants
♦ telephone
♦ vases
♦ watering cans

Dress-up Props

♦ gardening gloves
♦ name tags
♦ smock or large shirts
♦ wallets and purses

Literacy Props

♦ books about flowers, flower arranging, gardens, growing things
♦ calendars
♦ home and garden magazines
♦ memo board
♦ money, checks, credit cards
♦ pads of paper
♦ price list
♦ seed catalogs
♦ seed packets
♦ small tags for gift cards
♦ telephone book
♦ writing utensils

Center Activity: Flower Arranging

Cut polystyrene foam into circles or blocks that fit plant pots and baskets. Place polystyrene foam, pots and baskets, artificial flowers, foil, and ribbons on a table in the area for flower arranging. Label the containers for all items. Supply a labeled chart to help guide "florists" in making flower arrangements.

If you set up the Florist Shop Center in the spring or summer, collect fresh flowers from classroom gardens or "wildflower walks." Hang bunches of flowers upside-down in the shop for drying and later use. Try pressing flowers and greens between pieces of white paper weighted with wooden blocks. Use pressed flowers to make a flower identification chart for the center.

A call or visit to neighborhood florist shops can help with the gathering of props. Contributions may include foil, pots, posters and pictures, gift cards, and artificial flowers. Some shops may even donate flowers that are no longer fresh enough to sell.

Grocery Store Center

Setting Up the Center

Shelves and counters of all kinds can separate the Grocery Store from the classroom.

Add a cashier window, cash register, and bags in one area. Stock shelves with plastic foods and empty food packaging of all kinds. Arrange foods together as they might be found in the grocery store: milk cartons, egg cartons, and juice bottles together; cereal boxes and other like foods together; and a produce section for fruits and vegetables. Also, include a magazine section, bakery, and frozen foods section. Provide baskets with handles for "shoppers," along with grocery store circulars and piles of expired coupons.

Labeling the Center

Tent Labels work best, because they are mobile and easily changed as foods are "bought," moved, and stocked. Try Paper Bag Labels in this center also.

Signs in the Center

- Areas of the store: MILK AND EGGS, CEREAL, BAKERY, FRUIT, VEGETABLES
- COME AGAIN
- COUPON DAY
- PAY HERE
- RECYCLE BAGS HERE
- SPECIAL TODAY
- THANK YOU

Grocery Store Center Props

- photographs of relatives and friends who may work in a grocery store, and community and neighborhood stores and workers
- pictures of stores and foods of all kinds

Scenario Props

- bags
- bakery boxes
- cash register
- empty cleaning products packaging (thoroughly rinsed and tightly capped)
- empty food packaging of all kinds
- empty milk cartons and egg cartons
- empty plastic water and juice bottles
- grocery store cartons
- plastic foods
- scale
- shopping baskets

156

Dress-up Props

♦ aprons
♦ name tags
♦ smocks or large shirts for "employees"
♦ wallets and purses

Literacy Props

♦ coupons
♦ grocery lists
♦ grocery store circulars
♦ money, checks, credit cards
♦ pads of paper
♦ receipts
♦ writing utensils

Center Activity: Coupon Sorting

Set up a coupon sorting activity at a table in the Grocery Store Center. Gather a large supply of expired coupons from old magazines, food packaging, newspapers, and store circulars. Fold a number of 9" x 12" pieces of paper in half and tape the sides closed. On each "envelope" print the name of a food type, such as CEREAL, CRACKERS, DETERGENT, and attach one coupon that belongs inside. Children sort the remaining coupons into the corresponding envelopes. Many of the products shown on the coupons will be familiar to them; others may need closer inspection. Make extra envelopes for on-the-spot labeling if needed. Keep the coupon envelopes for other storage when you disassemble the Grocery Store Center.

Involve parents in the collection of food packaging, receipts, and expired coupons. Seeing familiar packaging will help children identify with other props in the center; seeing unfamiliar packaging will help them develop an appreciation for differences among classmates.

Add to the collection as many ethnically and culturally diverse food packages as possible: for example, tacos, tortillas, egg rolls, chow mein noodles, rice, matzo, or pasta.

Grocery stores in the area may contribute displays, print signs, and packaging to add to the center.

Gym and Health Club Center

Setting Up the Center

Arrange shelves and counters as boundaries for the Gym. Turn shelves around so that the backs face toward the play area; because shelves are not necessary in this center, use the backs of the shelves as a picture display area. Try using a balance beam as a divider.

The needs of this center are minimal. Allow space for movement and supply props that can be used in the available space: jump ropes, balls, balance beams, and large wooden blocks. Include any classroom climbers and gross-motor equipment. Spread out large towels in one area for floor exercises. Encourage children to jump rope, step on and off large blocks, bounce balls, walk across balance beams, and exercise on towels. Add a cassette or CD player and music and/or exercises on tape. A bench for resting and putting on athletic shoes makes a nice addition.

Labeling the Center

Use large Free-standing Labels suggesting things to do in a different areas: EXERCISE, JUMP ROPE, BOUNCE, BALLS, BALANCE, CLIMB.

Signs in the Center

- BE HEALTHY
- BREATHE
- DRINK WATER
- EXERCISE
- GYM
- REST HERE
- TOWELS

Gym and Health Club Center Props

- photographs of parents and children exercising, biking, and running
- pictures of the following: people of all ages exercising, biking, and running; gyms and health clubs; healthy foods

Scenario Props

- balance beams
- balls
- bean bags
- classroom gross-motor equipment
- hula hoops
- jump ropes
- large blocks
- music selections
- tape recorders
- towels (large and small)

Dress-up Props

- ankle and wrist warmers
- athletic shoes
- T-shirts

Literacy Props

- books about health, bikes, games, exercising
- exercise books
- exercise charts
- instructions for equipment
- posters
- scales

Center Activity: Gym Jump

Trace several pairs of athletic shoes on heavy paper and cut them out. Tape the shoes to the floor in one area of the Gym, or place them around the outside edge of the Gym. Provide various colors of construction paper, pencils, scissors, and tape so children can follow your lead. Children will remove their shoes and trace around them on two different colors of paper. After writing their names on the paper shoes, they will cut them out and tape them in place on the floor, extending the pattern you started. (Provide rolled-up pieces of tape or let children roll their own.) Encourage children to use the shoe patterns for a step-and-jump workout around the Gym, stepping and jumping from shoe to shoe.

Make hand weights by filling small plastic shampoo or lotion bottles with sand. Fill completely and secure the cap tightly. Children may enjoy filling the bottles themselves, using a funnel. Add these "weights" to the Gym for children to hold and lift. Be sure to use bottles that are small enough for children's hands and not too heavy when filled. Vary sizes from a small bottle (sample or travel size) to a larger-sized bottle to provide different weights.

Make several kinds of streamers for Streamer Dancing in the Gym Center. Provide an assortment of music and set up a Streamer Dancing area, designated by a Free-standing Label, in the Gym.

- Tube Streamer: Glue ribbon diagonally on a paper towel tube. On one end tape crêpe-paper streamers of different lengths.

- Circle Streamer: Cut the center from a plastic coffee can lid, forming a plastic ring. Loop ribbons or crêpe paper around part of the ring.

- Baton Streamer: Tie one ribbon or piece of crêpe paper on a rhythm stick or pencil (unsharpened).

Hair Salon and Barber Shop Center

Setting Up the Center

Use shelves, chairs, and the sink from the Home and Family Center as boundaries for the center.

Divide the center into two separate sections: the Waiting Area and the Haircutting and Styling Area. In the Waiting Area, place a row of chairs and a supply of magazines and books. The cash register, telephone, and appointment book belong at a counter or table here. In the Haircutting and Stylist Area, stock shelves with empty shampoo, conditioner, and hair-care bottles and packaging. Include combs, brushes, hoses, curlers, plastic gloves, smocks, paper towels, and mirrors (large and handheld). Add an assortment of hair clips, barrettes, bows, and headbands. Remove cords from broken hair dryers, curling irons, and radios. These make fun props for the center.

Labeling the Center

Use Identification Labels and Tent Labels to name objects. Location Labels also work well for items in containers.

Signs in the Center

♦ PAY HERE
♦ PLEASE BE SEATED
♦ PRICE LIST
♦ SHAMPOO SALE
♦ THANK YOU
♦ WAITING AREA
♦ WASH AND CUT

Hair Salon/Barber Shop Center Props

♦ photographs of relatives and friends who may work in hair salons or barber shops, and children getting haircuts or shampoos
♦ pictures of barbers, hair stylists, hair styles

Scenario Props

♦ combs and brushes (labeled with children's names)
♦ curlers and clips
♦ dolls
♦ empty shampoo, conditioner, and other hair-care bottles (plastic)
♦ hair accessories: barrettes, bows, headbands
♦ hair dryers
♦ hot combs, curling irons
♦ kitchen sink
♦ mirrors
♦ paper towels
♦ plastic gloves
♦ radio
♦ towels

Dress-up Props

♦ name tags
♦ smocks or large shirts

Literacy Props

♦ appointment book and appointment cards
♦ books about barbers, hair, haircuts
♦ calendar
♦ magazines
♦ memo pads
♦ money, checks, credit cards
♦ telephone book
♦ writing utensils

Center Activity: Zany Wigs

Make wigs using yard-long strips of felt (2" wide) and yarn of all colors. Precut the yarn in long, medium, and short lengths. Curl some yarn pieces by making them wet and wrapping them around a pencil to dry. In the center of each felt strip, cut a long, lengthwise slit to within six inches of each end. Children attach yarn "hair" by placing one end of yarn at a time through the slit and tying a knot, filling the length of the slit with yarn pieces. The yarn hair can hang on either side of the strip; knots can be any size. The random way children tie the yarn only makes these wigs more fun. Wigs are worn by typing the felt strip around the forehead or at the back of the neck like a headband. Children can add bows or hair barrettes if they choose. Create blue, purple,

brown, or multi-color hair. Let children take wigs home or add them to the prop box. This is also "hair" that can really be cut! Add a "Wig Chart" showing four to six paper plate faces wearing different hairstyles from which children can choose. Label each paper plate–LONG HAIR, SHORT HAIR, CURLY HAIR, STRAIGHT HAIR, BLUE HAIR, PURPLE HAIR, for example.

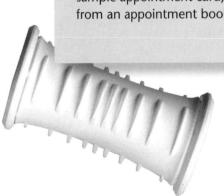

Tips

What's a Barber Shop without scissors? Make cardboard scissors for the center. Trace any pair of scissors and cut each of the two pieces separately. Use a hole punch to place a hole in the center of each piece. Fasten the scissors together loosely with a brass fastener. These "scissors" will move like real scissors but, most importantly, not cut hair.

Make Hair Salon and Barber Shop capes. Split pillowcases up one side and remove an oval from the bottom of the case. "Customers" wear these capes to protect their clothing from hair and water.

Local barbers or hair salons may contribute props such as posters, old hairstyle magazines, empty bottles, a sample appointment card, or a page from an appointment book to copy.

Home and Family Center

Setting Up the Center

Border the area with larger pieces of furniture, such as a stove, cupboard, or refrigerator. Arrange a table and chairs, rocking chairs, stools, clothing racks, and shelving units inside this area. Use rugs to designate space and set off "rooms." Use shelves, counters, and cupboards for smaller props, such as a telephone, dishes, clothing, accessories, cameras, and other items found in the home.

Hang pictures and photos on any wall surface or on the back and sides of large pieces of furniture. Set photos on shelves, counters, and tables in Stand-up Label structures or small Lucite Photo frames.

Labeling the Center

Place Identification Labels on shelf surfaces showing where things belong; Tent Labels also work well. In addition to providing print, labels will help children to tidy areas when they are finished playing. Label large pieces of furniture directly on the item with Identification Labels. Add Necklace Labels to dolls and animals in the Home and Family Center.

Signs in the Center

- Address (a label outside the center)
- BEWARE OF DOG
- NO TRESPASSING
- Room Identification: KITCHEN, BEDROOM, LIVING ROOM, and so on

Home and Family Center Props

- photographs of children's homes (exterior) and parents and children in the home
- pictures of houses, homes, families

Scenario Props

- cameras
- clocks
- dishes, cookware, cooking utensils
- dolls; clothes and beds for dolls
- empty food packaging
- furniture: tables and chairs, kitchen appliances
- play food
- pillows and blankets
- rocking chair
- rugs
- sponges, paper towels
- stuffed animals
- telephone

Dress-up Props

- clothing of all kinds
- hats
- jewelry
- shoes
- ties and scarves
- wallets and purses

Literacy Props

♦ books about home and families
♦ calendar
♦ cell phones, telephones
♦ computer
♦ cookbooks, recipe cards
♦ magazines, newspapers
♦ memo board
♦ writing utensils

Center Activity: Is It Safe?

In a large box, place empty food packaging, drink containers, and cleaning product packaging. Place two empty boxes nearby. Label one SAFE FOR YOU with a smiling face. Label the other one NOT SAFE FOR YOU with a frowning face. Children can sort through the packaging and place items in one box or the other. Use plain round stickers to make an assortment of "Happy" and "Unhappy" faces. Place these directly on products after all children have had an opportunity to sort the items.

Add multi-ethnic items to kitchen supplies, such as a wok, chopsticks, a pasta maker, a tortilla press, and empty packaging from ethnic foods—especially if the classroom population is ethnically diverse.

Consider the families in the classroom when stocking this area and include anything that may be representative of the things children see in their own homes.

Add a memo board to the Home and Family Center with a rebus schedule for a baby-sitter to follow. Begin with a picture of a telephone with several important phone numbers. Include other activities within a time frame. For example:

6:00 dinner (picture of a place setting)

7:00 homework (picture of a pencil and paper)

8:00 bath (picture of soap and a sponge)

9:00 story and bedtime (picture of a book and a bed or pillow)

Laundry Center
Setting Up the Center

Tie clotheslines around the center and use one or more clothes drying racks to separate the Laundry Center from the classroom. (A wooden or plastic clothes drying rack is an excellent classroom investment. Use it not only in Dramatic Play Centers, but also to dry paintings or hang wet mittens and hats.)

Set up four large boxes as washers and dryers. Leave the boxes as they are or let children help paint them white. Tape the ends closed. Cut a hole in the top of two of the boxes to be "washers" and a hole in the front of the other two boxes to be "dryers." Draw round knobs on the boxes or attach cardboard knobs with brass fasteners and label each. Stock shelves in the center with empty detergent boxes and fabric softener bottles. Add chairs, laundry baskets, and magazines. Hoses, clothespins, pillowcase laundry bags, and hangers round out the scene.

Labeling the Center

Use a combination of Identification Labels, Tent Labels, and Stand-up Labels. Make Tactile Labels using detergent.

Signs in the Center

- DETERGENT
- DRYERS
- FOLD LAUNDRY HERE
- OPEN; CLOSED
- WASHERS

Laundry Center Props

- photographs of relatives and friends who may work in laundry or dry-cleaning occupations
- pictures of families doing laundry; detergent ads

Scenario Props

♦ assortment of clothing to wash and dry
♦ assortment of towels, pillowcases, etc.
♦ baskets and tubs
♦ clotheslines
♦ clothespins
♦ detergent scoops
♦ empty detergent boxes
♦ empty fabric softener bottles and fabric softener sheet boxes
♦ hangers
♦ laundry bags

Dress-up Props

♦ aprons
♦ name tags
♦ smocks or large shirts

Literacy Props

♦ books about clothing, washing, cleaning
♦ magazines
♦ measuring cups
♦ newspapers
♦ paper for lists
♦ pencils
♦ tips about laundry

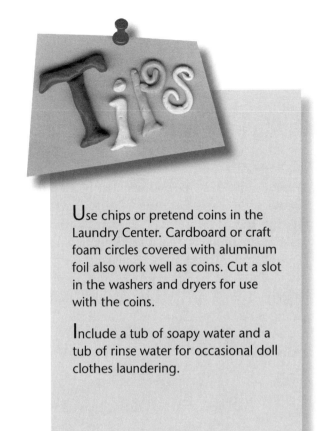

Use chips or pretend coins in the Laundry Center. Cardboard or craft foam circles covered with aluminum foil also work well as coins. Cut a slot in the washers and dryers for use with the coins.

Include a tub of soapy water and a tub of rinse water for occasional doll clothes laundering.

Center Activity: Sock Sorting

Cut pairs of socks from different colors of craft foam or construction paper. Print the color names on each sock. Use all lowercase letters on one sock and all uppercase letters on the other sock. Place the socks in a basket. Include clothespins. Hang a clothesline across a corner of the center. Children will sort the socks, hanging like-colored pairs together on the clothesline. For more fun, add several pairs cut from printed gift wrap or wallpaper. As socks are sorted, little fingers get lots of practice with manual dexterity and hand-eye coordination.

Museum Center

Setting Up the Center

Use a variety of shelves and boxes as boundaries for the Museum. Set boxes on their sides so they can be used for storage.

Stock shelves with divided boxes, egg cartons, small plastic sandwich bags, and trays of all sizes. Provide a table or two equipped with magnifying glasses, tongs, tweezers, mirrors, and flashlights for studying Museum materials. At another table area, set out blank labels and notebooks for labeling and documenting displays.

Decide on the theme of the Museum beforehand or create a theme as you and the children arrange the center. Add and make displays depending on the theme. Themes might include:

- art
- dinosaurs
- nature
- rocks
- seashells

Labeling the Center

Use Identification Labels to identify large pieces of furniture. Supply blank Tent Labels for on-the-spot labeling of "finds" and displays. Arrow Labels also work well in the Museum Center.

Signs in the Center

- DONATIONS
- DO NOT TOUCH
- OPEN; CLOSED
- PLEASE TOUCH
- QUIET PLEASE
- Signs relating to individual themes

Museum Center Props

- photographs of museum trips children may have made with their families, and of relatives and friends who may work in museums
- pictures of museums of all kinds; pictures that relate to the chosen Museum theme

Scenario Props

- cameras
- divided containers of all kinds
- flashlights
- frames
- magnifying glasses
- plastic gloves
- telephone
- trays
- tweezers and tongs

Dress-up Props

- gloves
- name tags
- smocks and large shirts

Literacy Props

- adhesive labels
- blank books
- calendar
- dictionaries
- identification books of all kinds: rocks, trees, leaves, shells
- money
- postcards
- telephone book
- writing utensils

Center Activity: Dinosaur Boxes

Use shoe boxes to make settings for dinosaur play and display. Paint the boxes inside and out. Children can help with this before the center is set up. Use colors such as brown, gray, and shades of green. Save lids, not needed for this project, for other activities. Place the painted shoe boxes in the Museum Center at a table set up with a variety of natural items—rocks, stones, pebbles, straw, leaves, sticks, wood chips, twigs, and small branches—in labeled containers. Provide white glue for children to use in attaching natural materials to the inside of the box as it sits on its side with the opening facing the child. Once children have created the natural environment in the box, let them choose several small plastic dinosaurs to include in the box. Provide a series of dinosaur name labels; have children choose the label that names the dinosaurs in their box. Provide a chart or book to help children match names to dinosaurs. Tape or glue the label on the top of the shoe box. Include the dinosaur boxes in a Dinosaur Museum display. Children will also enjoy interactive play with these boxes, in the process having many opportunities to match the dinosaurs to the labeled names.

Make a variety of sectioned and divided containers for sorting, classifying, categorizing, and displaying Museum "finds."

- Fill a shirt box lid, a shoe box lid, or a computer box lid with a number of smaller boxes by taping or gluing them in place.

- Use yarn to tie together a number of plastic berry baskets.

- Remove the thin end flap from the side of three egg cartons. Glue the cartons together by spreading glue on the inside of one egg carton lid and placing the egg cup section of another carton on the glue. Do the same to the lid of the second carton, attaching the egg cup section of the third egg carton to it. The result is three egg cup sections fastened together with one lid at the top. Use the lid to label or title the display.

If there is a museum nearby, visit it to collect brochures, postcards, and ideas for display.

Office Center

Setting Up the Center

Arrange bookcases, tables, and counters to set off the area and create boundaries. Set up tables, chairs, desks, shoe box filing cabinets, and shelf units. Stock shelves with paper, pens, and office supplies of all kinds. Fill tables and counters with computers, typewriters, calculators, telephones, calendars, desk sets, and clocks. Also use small bulletin boards, file folder systems, and briefcases in this center.

Labeling the Center

Use Identification Labels on furniture and supplies on shelves. Make use of Location Labels on closed containers, file folders, and file cabinet drawers. Add Cube Labels with the names of children working at various office tables. Remember, Cube Labels can contain four names each.

Signs in the Center

- IN MAIL/OUT MAIL
- OPEN; CLOSED
- PAY HERE
- THANK YOU
- WAIT HERE

Office Center Props

- photographs of relatives and friends who may work in an office, and any school personnel who work in the office
- pictures of office buildings, offices, office workers, office supplies (office supply catalogs are excellent sources)

Scenario Props

- desk set items
- hole punch
- shoe box file cabinets
- tape
- telephones

Dress-up Props

- briefcases
- glasses frames
- name tags

Literacy Props

- appointment book
- books about offices, buildings
- business cards
- calendar
- clipboards
- clock
- computer
- dictionary
- envelopes of all kinds
- file folders
- forms of all kinds
- index cards
- memo pads
- message pads
- paper of all kinds
- rubber stamps and ink pads
- telephone book
- typewriter
- writing utensils

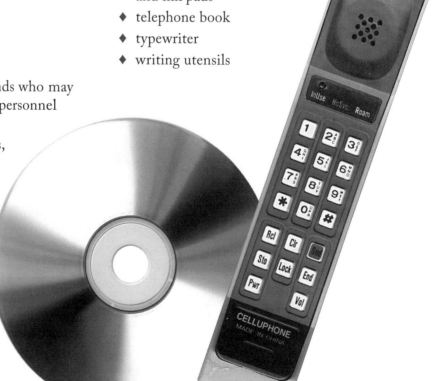

Center Activity: ABC Filing

Provide twenty-six ready-made file folders or make folders from brown paper grocery bags (see p. 127). Print a letter of the alphabet on each folder. Assemble a selection of pictures with the name of the pictured object printed in black marker directly on the picture. Children "file" the pictures in the folder by looking at the first letter of each word. Include cards with uppercase and lowercase letters for filing.

Make a telephone rotary card file with children's names and phone numbers. Write each child's name and telephone number on a separate index card. Place a hole in the upper left corner of each card and fasten the cards together with yarn or a metal ring.

Visit an office supply store or contact a number of offices in the neighborhood. Accept contributions of outdated forms, used envelopes, discarded paper, and old business cards. It is surprising how quickly literacy props for the Office Center will multiply.

Pet Store Center

Setting Up the Center

Arrange shelves, counters, and tables as boundaries for the area. Place boxes on the tables and counters. Position the boxes so that openings face upward, sideways, and downward. Cut the sides of downward-facing boxes to make "cages" for some pets. Use a utility knife to make a row of cuts in one or more sides of the box. Remove every other strip.

Place stuffed animals and animal puppets in the boxes and cages. Place small plastic animals in smaller containers. Stock shelves with empty pet food boxes and empty plastic water jugs. Include pet food dishes, small rugs, mats, towels, rubber balls, and pet toys. Cover a table with a towel or blanket and assemble a variety of brushes, combs, sponges, and spray bottles as a pet grooming area. Make collars and leashes with yarn and rope for the pet supplies area. Provide a cash register and a counter where customers can pay for pets and pet care items.

Labeling the Center

Label some animals with Identification Labels placed directly on boxes and cages; label others with Necklace Labels. Use Stand-up Labels to identify group of pets or list pet care tips.

Signs in the Center

- GROOMING AREA
- LOVE YOUR PET
- OPEN; CLOSED
- PAY HERE
- PET FOOD
- PET SALE

Pet Store Center Props

- photographs of children with family pets, and photographs of relatives and friends who may work in a pet store or with animals in some way
- pictures of families and pets, children and pets, pet stores, animals

Scenario Props

- animals: stuffed and plastic
- blankets and towels
- cash register
- empty pet food boxes
- empty plastic water jugs
- pet care items
- telephone

Dress-up Props

- gloves
- smocks or large shirts
- wallets or purses

Chapter 3: Dramatic Play

Literacy Props

♦ books about pets, pet care, families and pets
♦ calendar
♦ file folders
♦ memo pads
♦ money, checks, credit cards
♦ pet care brochures and pamphlets
♦ pet magazines
♦ posters
♦ receipts
♦ telephone book
♦ writing utensils

Center Activity: Classroom Aquarium

Turn a large box (a computer-paper box works well) on its side and place a number of holes in the top. The box lid is not needed for this project (save it for other uses). Glue light blue or green paper inside the box on all five surfaces. Children's finger paintings done with blue or green paint make an effective background inside the box.

Thread various lengths of blue and green yarn through the holes in the top of the box and knot. Let the yarn hang inside the box at different lengths. Cover the outside of the box with plain blue paper. Label the top AQUARIUM. Set the aquarium in the Pet Store Center, along with a box of fish stencils, white paper, scissors, glue, and markers. Have children make a fish for the aquarium by choosing a stencil to trace, cutting it out and decorating it on both sides. They should print their name on the fish and use a dab of glue to attach it to one of the pieces of yarn. Children can also make fish from craft foam. When the aquarium is full of fish, sprinkle some pebbles or seashells on the bottom of the box. Twist tissue paper on chenille stems to make aquarium plants. Cover the front of the aquarium with a piece of plastic wrap.

Make shoe box "cages" for the Pet Store Center. Cover each box with plain paper, tucking the ends to the inside. Place a blank square of white paper on each box for labeling pet names. Punch holes about 1" to 2" apart on the two long sides of the shoe box. Lace yarn through the top and bottom holes to make bars. Children can easily place and remove animals through the yarn bars.

Keep the aquarium and add it to other centers, such as the Waiting Room of the Veterinarian's, Doctor's, or Dentist's Offices; Home and Family Center, Museum (with a fish and shell display); or Restaurant Center (when a seafood theme is selected).

Contact local pet stores for contributions of pet care brochures, posters, and empty pet food packaging.

Pizza Shop Center

Setting Up the Center

Use shelves, counter, kitchen appliances, and tables from the Home and Family Center as borders. A cashier or food-serving window can also be used.

Divide the space into two areas: a kitchen area and a dining area. Place dishes, cups, cookware, kitchen gadgets, empty food packaging, towels, and napkins in the kitchen area. Choose food packaging that relates to pizza making: tomato sauce, crust mix, flour, eggs, oil, cheese, herbs, spices, and toppings.

Make a pizza oven with a large cardboard box placed upside-down with the opening on the bottom. Cut along the top and one side of the box to make an oven door that will open and close. If you choose, the "oven" can be painted with the help of the children. Fasten on cardboard knobs, using brass fasteners so that the knobs will turn. Label the knobs off and on. Make a pizza paddle for putting pizzas in and out of the oven. Cut a 12" square of corrugated cardboard with a 6" to 8" long, flat handle on one side (like a paddle). Cover with aluminum foil.

Add telephones, a cash register, and real pizza boxes to a counter near the cashier window separating the kitchen area from the dining area. In the dining area, place a tablecloth, menus, and napkins on the table or tables.

Labeling the Center

Use Identification Labels to label furnishings and other items. Use Arrow Labels to point out the dining area. Use Tent Labels on tables. Put Tactile Labels to use to identify spices and other ingredients in the kitchen.

Signs in the Center

- ◆ DINING
- ◆ DO NOT ENTER
- ◆ FREE DELIVERY
- ◆ OPEN; CLOSED
- ◆ PIZZA
- ◆ TAKE OUT
- ◆ TOPPINGS LIST

Pizza Shop Center

- ◆ photographs of relatives and friends who may work at a pizza shop, and families making or eating pizza together
- ◆ pictures of pizza shops, restaurants, food, families eating together

Scenario Props

- cash register
- cookware
- dishes, cups
- empty drink containers
- empty food packaging (pizza-related)
- grater
- kitchen utensils
- napkins
- placemats
- pizza boxes
- pizza cutters (check that they are not too sharp)
- potholders
- tablecloths
- telephone

Dress-up Props

- aprons
- wallets and purses

Literacy Props

- books about pizza, restaurants, families eating together
- calendars
- coupons
- menus
- money
- newspaper ads
- note pads for orders
- pizza recipes
- price list
- telephone book
- toppings list
- writing utensils

Center Activity: Design a Pizza

Cut 6" and 8" circle "pizza crusts" from brown cardboard, one for each child. Label several polystyrene foam food trays with the names of pizza ingredients and toppings. Cut paper shapes and fill each tray: red circles (1" smaller than cardboard crusts) for pizza sauce, thin-cut yellow strips for cheese, green curves for green peppers, brown mushroom shapes, small red or brown circles for pepperoni, small black and green circles for olives, and white spirals for onions. Make a chart guiding children through designing a pizza. Label everything step by step.

The chart might start with the crust and sauce, then tell children to choose three toppings (or four, depending on the number cut). Provide glue or paste and let children design their own pizzas. Children can bake their pizza using the cardboard pizza oven and the long-handled pizza paddle. Have children take pizzas home or include them in the Pizza Shop Center prop box.

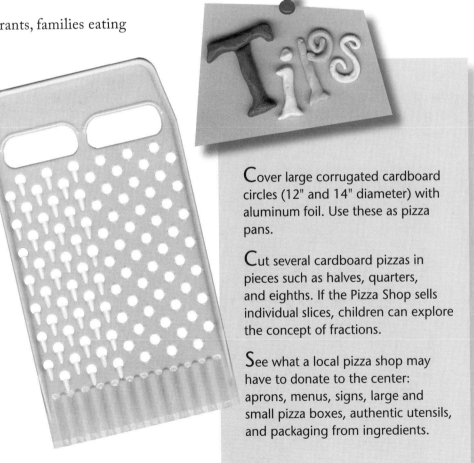

Tips

Cover large corrugated cardboard circles (12" and 14" diameter) with aluminum foil. Use these as pizza pans.

Cut several cardboard pizzas in pieces such as halves, quarters, and eighths. If the Pizza Shop sells individual slices, children can explore the concept of fractions.

See what a local pizza shop may have to donate to the center: aprons, menus, signs, large and small pizza boxes, authentic utensils, and packaging from ingredients.

Police Station Center

Setting Up the Center

Use a variety of counters and tables to separate the Police Station Center from the classroom.

Place a number of telephones, walkie-talkies, and radios throughout the area. Stock shelves with paper, folders, memo pads, envelopes, and writing utensils. Set up tables with calendars, desk sets, pencil holders, and telephone books. Use shoe box filing cabinets and milk carton mailboxes. Set up a "coffee" area with a pitcher and cups for coffee, tea, juice, or water. Hang up a map of the city; provide small bulletin boards and clipboards.

Labeling the Center

Label most of the center with Identification Labels. Use Stand-up Labels or Cube Labels to identify "police officers" at desks, important phone numbers, and working areas within the center.

Signs in the Center

- DIAL 911
- DRIVER'S LICENSE AREA
- EMERGENCY
- LOST AND FOUND
- PARKING TICKETS
- Road and traffic signs: STOP, SLOW, YIELD, SCHOOL ZONE, WAIT HERE

Police Station Center Props

- photographs of relatives and friends who may be police officers or who work at police stations
- pictures of police officers, police vehicles, safety practices

Scenario Props

- cameras
- car keys
- cell phones, telephones
- flashlights
- headphones
- pitcher and cups
- radios
- walkie-talkies

Dress-up Props

- badges
- hats
- wallets

Literacy Props

- books about police officers, police vehicles, safety, lost children and pets
- calculators
- calendars
- clipboards
- computers
- desk sets
- driver's licenses (expired)
- envelopes
- file folders
- forms of all kinds
- maps
- memo pads
- money
- "parking tickets"
- telephone books
- typewriter
- writing utensils

Center Activity: Steering Wheels and Driver's License

Include an area in the Police Station Center where drivers can get a license. Drivers can make a steering wheel to accompany the license and drive away! To make the license, cut manila folders or index cards to a 2" x 3" size. Divide the cards in half with a black marker; draw two horizontal lines on one side. Place the cards in a container on the table, along with a supply of pencils and markers. Include a camera and a chair where children can sit to have their "pictures" taken for the license. If possible, use real photos cut to fit the driver's license. If photos are not available, let children draw their faces in the squares on the licenses. Have them write their names on one line and their driver's license numbers (any numbers they choose) on the second line.

To make a steering wheel, children color the outer edge of a paper plate or cardboard circle. Next, they draw a letter "Y" that touches the rim at all three points. This letter can be widened as it is colored. Cut out the three sections made by the "Y." Children "drive" by holding and turning the steering wheel in front of them.

If space permits, "park" one or two bikes or "carton cars" in an area next to the Police Station. Label the area PARKING and POLICE CARS ONLY.

Make a Fingerprint File for the Police Station. Have each child write his or her name on an index card (or similar-sized paper). Use an ink pad so children can add their fingerprint to the card. Arrange the cards alphabetically in a box to complete the file. Set up a table with magnifying glasses to compare fingerprints. When the Police Station Center is dismantled, let children take home their own fingerprints.

Contact police stations for posters, rule books, signs, sample forms, safety brochures, and other authentic materials that may help to make the Police Station Center more realistic.

Post Office Center

Setting Up the Center

Make boundaries with shelves and counters. Add large cardboard cartons with slots in the tops for mail. Paint or cover boxes in blue and add a label: U.S. MAIL.

Stock shelves with envelopes of all sizes, paper, stamps, greeting cards, postcards, writing utensils, string, small unwrapped boxes, and boxes wrapped in brown craft paper. Set up two areas: an area where "customers" prepare and send mail and a Mail Room where "workers" sort, weigh, and stamp mail. Place a scale, stickers, rubber stamps, and ink pads here. Hang several maps in the Mail Room. Use a postal window through which "workers" sell stamps and help "customers."

Labeling the Center

Use Identification Labels to identify larger items. On desks and tables provide Cube Labels that identify postal workers. Use Stand-up or Tent Labels on counters and shelves.

Signs in the Center

- DO NOT ENTER
- LOCAL MAIL
- NEXT WINDOW PLEASE
- OPEN; CLOSED
- OUT OF TOWN MAIL
- PLEASE WAIT
- STAMPS
- THANK YOU
- U.S. MAIL
- ZIP CODES

Post Office Center Props

- photographs of relatives and friends who may work in the post office or at a mailing center
- pictures of post offices; mail trucks; mail boxes; and people writing, mailing, receiving, and reading letters

Scenario Props

- boxes of all sizes
- brown wrapping paper
- letter openers
- mail bags
- milk carton mailboxes
- scale
- stickers
- tape
- wet sponge for stamps

Dress-up Props

- badges or name tags
- blue smocks or large blue shirts
- hats

Literacy Props

♦ address labels
♦ adhesive labels
♦ books about mail, letters, the post office, mail carriers, stamps, packages
♦ envelopes of all sizes
♦ greeting cards
♦ paper
♦ postcards
♦ rubber stamps and ink pads
♦ stamps
♦ stationery
♦ writing utensils

Center Activity: Mail Sorting and Stamp Collecting

Collect mail for a few weeks before introducing the center and this activity. Ask parents, colleagues, and friends to save empty envelopes from mail they have received and unopened "junk mail." Set up a mail-sorting table in the Post Office Mail Room. Place a cloth bag full of the collected mail. Next to the bag, provide three labeled boxes: LETTERS, ENVELOPES, STAMPS. Attach an example of each to the front of the box. Add scissors, a letter opener, glue, and a stamp collection book. Prepare the collection book by fastening 9" x 12" paper together with binder rings or yarn. Title each page: STAMPS. Children sort through the mail in the cloth bag. They open the unopened mail and place the contents in the box labeled LETTERS. After cutting the stamps from the envelopes and placing them in the box labeled STAMPS, children place the envelopes in the box labeled ENVELOPES. When the stamps accumulate, they can be glued or taped in the stamp collection book. Stamp collection book pages can also be titled Animal Stamps, People Stamps, Art Stamps, Bird Stamps, Flower Stamps, USA Stamps, and Stamps from Other Countries. Recycle the mail and envelopes for art projects.

Open several sizes of envelopes and use them as patterns for making new envelopes in the center.

Let children make their own stamps with adhesive labels cut into 1" squares. They can decorate the squares with pencils, crayons, and markers.

A visit to the post office may yield a variety of props useful to the center: posters, pictures of stamps, labels, sample forms, change of address cards, sample mail envelopes, and stamp book covers.

Restaurant Center

Setting Up the Center

Shelves, counters, tables, and chairs form the boundaries for the center.

Further divide the center into two distinct sections: a kitchen and a dining area. Use rugs and mats to define these spaces. A row of chairs where "diners" can wait for a table also helps divide the center. Stock the kitchen with trays, dishes, cookware, baking supplies, cooking utensils, towels, sponges, empty food packaging, and a variety of kitchen appliances. Arrange tables and chairs in the dining area. Provide tablecloths, placemats, napkins, flower arrangements, plants (real and artificial), salt and pepper shakers, and menus. Add a telephone, a cash register, and note pads for taking orders.

Labeling the Center

Name objects in the center using hanging Identification Labels and Tent Labels placed on shelves and counters. Tactile Labels work well in the kitchen.

Signs in the Center

- ◆ DESSERT TRAY
- ◆ OPEN; CLOSED
- ◆ PAY HERE
- ◆ PLEASE WAIT TO BE SEATED
- ◆ RESERVED
- ◆ SALAD BAR
- ◆ THANK YOU
- ◆ TODAY'S SPECIAL

Restaurant Center Props

- ◆ photographs of relatives and friends who may work in a restaurant, parents cooking, children and parents eating out
- ◆ pictures of restaurants, chefs, families dining together, foods

Scenario Props

- baking supplies
- cash register
- cookware
- dishes and cups
- empty food packaging
- empty milk and juice containers
- flower arrangements
- napkins
- pitchers
- potholders
- salt and pepper shakers
- tablecloths and placemats
- telephone
- towels and sponges

Dress-up Props

- aprons
- chef hats
- dress-up clothes
- hats
- name tags
- wallets and purses

Literacy Props

- books about restaurants, food, cooks, chefs, families eating together
- cookbooks
- menus
- money, checks, credit cards
- note pads for writing orders
- recipes
- telephone book
- writing utensils

Center Activity: Restaurant Placemats

On a rectangular piece of paper or craft foam, draw the outline of a place setting: a spoon, fork, knife, plate, glass, and napkin. Label each item. Make copies of the "placemat" so that each child will have one. Add crayons and markers, scissors, glue, and magazines containing pictures of food.

Children should cut pictures of their favorite foods and glue them on the outline of the plate. Offer to print the name of each food on the plate at some time during center play. Use scissors to "fringe" two edges of the placement. Hang placements to decorate the restaurant, or pile them on a counter for use when serving.

Change some of the restaurant props to model different kinds of restaurants:

- Add lanterns, chopsticks, rice and related food packaging, fortune cookies, and a Chinese menu to create a Chinese Restaurant. Cover a shallow bowl with aluminum foil to use as a wok.

- Decorate the center with baskets, hats, and flowers to create a Southwestern Restaurant serving tacos, tortillas, and beans.

- An Italian Restaurant might have checkered tablecloths and breadbaskets on the table and serve a variety of pastas. Include empty pasta boxes with a variety of pasta shapes and egg cartons or muffin tins for sorting and investigation.

- Re-create a Diner by adding a chalkboard menu, short-order counter, and "jukebox." Place a cassette or CD player inside a colorful box to suggest a jukebox; a row of letters and numbers printed on the front of the box will help to make it more realistic.

Shoe Store Center

Setting Up the Center

Shelves and counters form the boundaries of the Shoe Store. Include a shoe tree or pile of shoe boxes with the boundary.

Stock the shelves with pairs of shoes, sandals, slippers, boots, and foot gear of all kinds. Include socks, belts, purses, and wallets. Prepare a checkout counter with a telephone, a cash register, bags, shoe boxes, memo pads, and writing utensils. Arrange a row of chairs where "customers" can sit to try on shoes. Place a full-length mirror and several small mirrors on the floor for customers' use in looking at shoes.

Labeling the Center

Use Identification Labels to identify furnishings and Tent or Paper Bag Labels to name socks and other items.

Signs in the Center

♦ PAY HERE
♦ PLEASE BE SEATED
♦ OPEN; CLOSED
♦ SALE TODAY
♦ SIZES 1–2, SIZES 3–4, etc.
♦ THANK YOU

Shoe Store Center Props

♦ photographs of relatives and friends who may work at a shoe store and children wearing new shoes
♦ pictures of shopping malls, shoes of all kinds

Scenario Props

♦ bags
♦ belts
♦ boots
♦ cash register
♦ empty shoe polish cans or bottles and cloths
♦ mirrors
♦ shoe boxes
♦ shoehorns
♦ shoelaces
♦ shoes of all kind
♦ socks
♦ telephone

Dress-up Props

♦ name tags
♦ wallets and purses

Literacy Props

♦ books about shoes, boots, shopping
♦ calendar
♦ catalogs
♦ money, checks, credit cards
♦ note pads
♦ order forms
♦ receipts
♦ shoe ads
♦ telephone book
♦ writing utensils

Center Activity: Foot Size Graph

Use a large piece of paper for this graph. Print the title of the graph across the top of the paper and list children's names down the left side. Provide several colors of yarn, scissors, and glue. Children will remove one shoe and use the yarn to measure their shoe or their foot. Children should hold the end of the yarn at their toe and cut off the yarn at the heel. They glue the yarn horizontally on the chart, next to their name. (Add a dot next to each child's name so they will all start at the same point.) Compare the sizes of children's feet by discussing the chart at a group time.

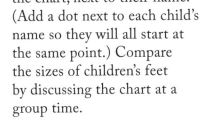

Use shoe boxes without lids to make a foot rest for "customers" to use when trying shoes. Set the box with the opening at the top and remove one of the ends of the box. Set the shoe box with the open end facing you. Cut both sides of the box diagonally from the lower back corners to the top front corners. Set the box upside-down with the opening next to the floor and the slant in front of the customer.

Make a foot measurement tool. Cut a 12" x 15" heavy piece of corrugated cardboard. Use a black marker to divide the cardboard into six 2" increments. Mark each increment with a number from 1 to 6. Cut two 7" slits (about 1" apart) lengthwise across a paper towel tube. Slip the cardboard through both slits on the tube; move the tube up and down on the cardboard to loosen it up. "Customers" place their foot on the cardboard, heel on the end, and the "shoe clerk" slides the tube down to meet the toe. The number closest to the tube is the "foot size."

Space Station Center

Setting Up the Center

Use shelves and cardboard boxes to create a boundary for the Space Station Center. Cut holes in the boxes and insert various sizes of gift wrap and paper towel tubes that have been covered with aluminum foil to make a Space Station. Draw knobs or buttons on the boxes or use brass fasteners to attach cardboard knobs that will really turn.

Arrange sections within the center to suggest a Lab, Experiment Stations, and a Launch Pad. Place the Lab near shelves and stock with tweezers, tongs, plastic containers, microscopes, magnifying glasses, large pieces of polystyrene foam, funnels, and measuring cups. Arrange Experiment Stations on tables or counters next to the Lab. Include items such as magnet sets, flashlights (with pieces of colored cellophane over the fronts), magnifying glasses, prisms, and scales. Set up the Launch Pad in the largest section of the center. Lay down a rug and set out a number of boxes, so children can build a spaceship. The boxes should be several sizes, including at least two that children can climb inside. Spray paint boxes before placing them in the center (silver is an especially good "space color"). Cut circular openings in two of the larger boxes to provide other climbing and crawling opportunities. Supply silver tape that children can use to connect the boxes, placing the two larger ones on the bottom and smaller ones on the sides and top. Try to include some cylinder-shaped boxes and some boxes cut diagonally in half, creating a triangular shape. After building the spaceship, equip it with a variety of tools, cameras, binoculars, telescopes, radios, kaleidoscopes, and walkie-talkies. Props such as backpacks, gloves, helmets, and goggles can also be added.

Labeling the Center

Make use of Arrow Labels and Tent Labels in the Space Station Center. Add large Free-standing Labels to identify the different sections of the center.

Signs in the Center

- ◆ CAUTION
- ◆ DO NOT ENTER
- ◆ EXPERIMENTS
- ◆ LAB
- ◆ LAUNCH PAD
- ◆ REPAIRS

Space Station Center Props

- ◆ photographs of relatives and friends who may work in astronomy labs
- ◆ pictures of planets, sun, moon, stars, space voyages, space vehicles, astronauts

Scenario Props

- ◆ backpacks
- ◆ binoculars
- ◆ boxes
- ◆ cameras
- ◆ clocks
- ◆ cloth bags
- ◆ flashlights
- ◆ kaleidoscopes
- ◆ magnets
- ◆ magnifying glasses
- ◆ microscopes
- ◆ plastic containers
- ◆ polystyrene foam
- ◆ prisms
- ◆ radio
- ◆ scales
- ◆ telescope
- ◆ tweezers and tongs
- ◆ walkie-talkies

Dress-up Props

- ◆ belts
- ◆ gloves
- ◆ helmets

Literacy Props

♦ books about space, astronauts, rockets, space travel, plants, sun, moon
♦ calendar
♦ clipboards
♦ constellation maps and charts
♦ dictionary
♦ graph paper
♦ maps
♦ paper and note pads
♦ science experiment books
♦ "space" maps
♦ telephone book
♦ writing utensils
♦ written formulas

Center Activity: Telescopes

Precut black construction paper squares 3" x 3"; using a straight pin, make a number of holes randomly in the center of each square. Trace the circular end of a paper towel tube onto the squares. Make cuts from the edges of the paper to the circle. Place black paper squares, paper towel tubes, tape, and markers in a box in the center. Include a flashlight and a book about the stars and constellations in the box. Hang up a chart of labeled stars and constellations. To make a telescope, children decorate a paper towel tube with markers and tape a black square over one end of the tube (the cuts previously made around the circle will make it easier for children to fit the paper over the end and tape it to the tube). After making their telescopes, children may look through it at any light source or take turns using a flashlight; one holds the flashlight and the other looks through the telescope. The light will shine through the pinpoints in the black paper and look like a night sky.

Make Space Helmets with one-gallon plastic water jugs. Cut the neck from the bottle so it will fit a child's head. Cut a square or oval from the handle section of the jug, removing the handle and creating an opening for the "astronaut's" face. Place colored tape over all cut edges for safety and comfort; add a few tape strips and stars to the helmet.

Create "Wonder Bottles" using clear plastic bottles, such as shampoo bottles, 1-liter soda bottles, and 8-ounce juice bottles. Fill each bottle about $1/3$ full of water and $1/3$ full of oil. Add a different food coloring or powered paint to each bottle. Place objects in the bottles: glitter in one, crayon shavings in another, and marbles in a third. Other items to add include sequins, scraps of foil, or Mylar. Place these "Wonder Bottles" in the Lab or Experiment Stations for shaking and watching. The motion of oil and water suggests the feeling of weightlessness.

Collect some stones and rocks (include a few fairly large ones) and display them on a tray in the Lab. Children can treat these "specimens" as "moon rocks," weighing them, examining them with magnifying glasses, and storing or displaying them.

Veterinarian Center

Setting Up the Center

Use shelves and various sizes of boxes as the boundaries. Large floor plants or paper Tree Dividers make interesting boundaries.

Divide the center into a Waiting Area and an Examining/Hospital Area. Place chairs, pet care information, magazines, and office supplies in the Waiting Area. Provide a number of tables and counters in the Hospital Area for pet examinations, care, and grooming. Use the shelves to assemble an assortment of empty pet food boxes and supplies, plastic water jugs, leashes, pet toys, towels, blankets, and pet food dishes. In the Examining Area, gather magnifying glasses, tweezers, eyedroppers, paper towels, empty pill and vitamin bottles, bandages, and other first-aid supplies. Set up a grooming table; provide sponges, towels, brushes, and other grooming tools. Use the boxes to create beds and waiting areas for sick pets.

Labeling the Center

Use Stand-up Labels to identify the various areas of the Center. Label other items with Identification, Tent, and Paper Bag Labels.

Signs in the Center

♦ OPEN; CLOSED
♦ PAY HERE
♦ PET SUPPLY SALE
♦ SICK PETS—QUIET PLEASE
♦ THANK YOU
♦ THE DOCTOR IS IN/OUT
♦ WAIT HERE

Veterinarian Center Props

♦ photographs of the following: relatives and friends who are veterinarians or who work at a veterinarian office, animal shelter, or other pet care facility; children and their pets
♦ pictures of veterinarians, animal hospitals, pets, families and their pets

Scenario Props

♦ blankets
♦ empty pet food packaging
♦ empty pill and vitamin bottles
♦ eyedroppers
♦ first-aid supplies
♦ leashes and collars
♦ magnifying glasses
♦ pet food dishes and mats
♦ pet toys
♦ plastic water jugs
♦ shoe box file cabinet
♦ stuffed animals, plastic animals
♦ telephone
♦ towels
♦ tweezers

Dress-up Props

♦ name tags
♦ smocks or large white shirts
♦ wallets and purses

Literacy Props

- appointment book and appointment cards
- books about pets, animal care, veterinarians
- calendar
- file folders
- identification tags
- paper and note pads
- pet care brochures and pamphlets
- pet care posters
- telephone book
- writing utensils

Center Activity: Pet Birds

Remove the label and cut the thick plastic bottom from several plastic 2-liter soda bottles. These will serve as bird cages for the pet birds children will be making. Place a strip of tape around the cut bottom to cover any rough edges. Print BIRD on several adhesive labels, one for each bottle. Cut a 2" circle of cardboard and use the point of scissors to place a hole in the center. Thread a 16" piece of yarn through the hole. Pull the yarn through the hole in the circle until 4" is on one side and 12" is on the other. Knot the yarn on each side of the circle, close to the hole. Holding the 4" piece of yarn, lower the circle into the bottle until the 12" piece of yarn comes out the pour top. Pull on the 12" yarn until the circle catches tightly in the neck of the bottle. Tie a loop in the end for hanging the bird cage. Place these "bottle cages" in the Veterinarian Office. Children can make a felt or craft foam bird for the cage. Provide precut felt or craft foam bird shapes, glue, small felt triangles and ovals, and feathers. Children can glue felt or foam scraps and feathers on the bird. Glue the bird to the 4" piece of yarn in the bottle. The plastic bottle makes a cage for the bird. Make additional labels available if children would like to name their birds. Let children take birds and bird cages home, or they can hang the cages in the Veterinarian Office or the Home and Family Center. To do so, use hooks, a clothes dryer rack, or a rope attached between two corners. Another fun way to hang bird cages is to attach a hula hoop to three or four pieces of string hanging from the ceiling. The hoop will hang horizontally. Hang the bird cages at different lengths around the hoop.

Make an animal examination chart similar to the chart of the human body used in the Doctor's Office Center (p. 148). On different sheets of paper, drawer several common pets. Print the name of the animal on the top or bottom of the paper and label the parts of the animal's body. Make a number of copies of each animal "chart." Attach several of each to a clipboard. The "veterinarian" can use the charts when examining pets and talking with pet owners. He or she places an X on the part of the animal that hurts or is injured.

Make pet leashes and collars out of a variety of items, depending on the sizes of the stuffed animals in the center:

- cuffs removed from sweatshirts (these slip over the heads of stuffed animals easily and stay on well)
- the outer rim cut from plastic margarine container lids or coffee can lids in various sizes
- elastic hair bands

Tie yarn or rope leashes onto these collars. Braid several strands of yarn for a thicker, sturdier leash. Add a name tag to the collar, as desired.

Keep the Pet Birds in class, including them in other centers such as the Home and Family Center and the Pet Store Center.

The Role of the Teacher

How to Facilitate Your New Print-Rich Environment

Now that the environment is well defined and rich in print, the interest areas and Dramatic Play Centers are stocked with literacy props, and the curriculum is full of informal literacy references, what is your role as the teacher in the emergent literacy classroom? As designer of the classroom and manipulator of the environment, you assume a role of extreme importance. Adult participation in the classroom must be subtle, yet nurturing. With a keen awareness of what is occurring in the many interest and play areas of the classroom, the observant teacher takes cues from the children and acts accordingly. The introduction of literacy props, including suggestions for the use of these materials, is essential.

Extending Play through Group Time

Once the literacy props have been introduced, the teacher moves in and out of play scenarios, extended play by reacting and responding to initiations made by children. Suggesting and modeling appropriate behaviors and uses of literacy props will guide and encourage children in their own usage of the props. Examples of these techniques, as well as of the art of open-ended questioning and effective assessment of centers in the emergent literacy classroom, follow.

The most effective use of time in the literacy-friendly classroom is a pattern of alternating brief teacher-directed times with longer child-initiated times. Teacher-directed times generally take the form of circle times or group times that involve you and the whole class. (The terms *circle time* and *group time* are used interchangeably in this resource.) During whole-group interactions, you can connect literacy to the many distinct areas of the curriculum.

It is also the time when the teacher can introduce the various literacy props and print inclusions through the classroom. Visual examples and a few brief comments work best. For example:

♦ "In the Sand Table this week, you will find some new signs with our trucks and digging toys. There are also some signs without words, in case you can think of another sign we need."

♦ "In the Block Area, look for some boxes I have cut to look like bridges, tunnels, and garages. Think of what we can write on the front of the boxes."

♦ "Look for something new on the Book Tray in the Library."

♦ "The book we read last week is in the Art Area. You may want to paint or color a new cover picture for the book. We can write the new title on your picture when it's finished. Markers and paints are in a drawer this week. Look for the picture and the word to find them."

♦ "Help finish our classroom animal book this week in the Book-making Center. Or, there are some new Bag Books to use if you would like to make your own book."

♦ "Investigate the new mixtures on the Science Table and tell me what you think of them. I will write your words to share with everyone at group time."

After this group time introduction to the week's activities, give children a long period (at least an hour) to explore, investigate, and play. As the week progresses, use the group time to share things going on in the classroom: dictated words from the Science and Music Area, new child-made books and title illustrations, a review of how the classroom book is progressing, children's ideas for Sand Table signs and car structures, and final preparations for the parent letter. Sharing child-generated print, books, and ideas serves as a recognition of children's efforts and interactions with literacy and an incentive to other children to become more involved with the materials.

Let the interests and needs of the children dictate possible introduction of other activities and projects throughout the week or adaptation and enhancement of those already available. If the classroom follows a weekly or monthly theme, introduce and implement print-rich experiences the same way, designing the activities and various interest areas in the classroom to reflect the theme.

Effectively Assessing Centers

Having prepared the environment, gathered materials for the activities and introduced them, and piqued children's curiosity, your role becomes one of spectator, advisor, resource person, and scribe.

As **spectator,** the teacher moves in and out of interest areas, observing how children are incorporating print into play. The goal here is to see what children are doing with the props and plans. What do they seem to like best and least? What materials do they utilize and how? What kind of literacy connections are being made? This serves an important assessment function as well. You are assessing how literacy inclusions are accepted, what forms are most interesting to children, and what the next step might be.

As **advisor,** the classroom teacher may suggest and question.

- "Why is this Sand Table sign here? What does it say?
- "Why did you sort these objects into this bag? Yes, you are right. The word on the bag does say STONES." Or, "Well, this word starts with an S like STONES, but look at the rest of the word. Is there something else on your tray that starts with an S, but ends this way? Yes, I think you have found it. The shells go in this bag."
- "After you sign our letter, you may draw some pictures. Here are the words telling our parents what we are collecting. Can you draw a shoe box or a milk carton?

As **resource person,** the teacher is available to help find, locate, and add to materials.

♦ "You can't find the markers and paint in the Art Area? Well, let's look for the words together."

♦ "I see you are making a book about pets. You want to know what I think you should include? Well, I'm not sure. Let's look in the library. I think there are some pet books to give us some ideas."

♦ "You have signed the NO column. You don't like this music today? Let's look through the tapes in the Music Corner to see if you want to suggest something for tomorrow."

As **scribe,** the teacher is available to print children's dictated words in any center. Let children know that you will be writing their responses. Offer to record a child's words or ask if a child would like to see his or her words in print. Offers and suggestions such as these should be informal and conversational, never intrusive or directive. If a child chooses not to take advantage of the offer or suggestion, move on, issuing an invitation: "Okay, let me know if you change your mind." Children may initiate the process themselves, requesting that you record their words, especially if such practices have been reinforced. Write children's words as they dictate them and make every effort to read words back immediately. This supports the connection between words and print and allows children to correct any inaccuracies. Each classroom center or interest area offers many opportunities for the written recording of words. Here are some examples of appropriate open-ended questioning:

♦ "How would you like to title your drawing? Should we write it on the picture or on a label that you can place on the picture?"

♦ "What kind of garage is this? Does the garage have a name? Let's write it on a label and put it on the box."

♦ "What other signs should we write for the Sand Table today?"

♦ "Should we write the names of the pets in your book? Do you want to write them or should I?"

♦ "Our animal book is getting very full. Tell me what to write on the pages."

♦ "How does this mixture on the Science Table feel? What do you think it is? I will write your words and we will share them at group time."

♦ "Is there anything else we need in this letter to parents? What should we include?"

♦ "I like what you brought for the Sharing Table. Can you write your name to let everyone know you brought it? What should we write about it?"

Implementing the Dramatic Play Center and Introducing Props

Implement Dramatic Play Centers in much the same way you do curriculum-related interest centers. As before, use a circle time to introduce the theme of the center as well as the literacy props that children will find in the center. If you have involved children in the planning of the center, review the group-made list of needs and follow it as props are introduced. Introductions here, as for interest center activities, should be visual and brief. Tell children about the Dramatic Play Center(s) at the same time you present the Building Area, Art Area, and other curriculum-related activities areas. When you let children know that the classroom activities will be available all week, tell them that the Dramatic Play Centers will be set up for several weeks. This helps children understand that everyone will have many turns to engage in activities and play in centers. Opportunities in Dramatic Play Centers, like those in classroom interest centers, should never be rushed. Set aside enough time for children to choose and exchange roles, set up scenarios, and become involved with literacy props. Do not allow time limits to intrude on children's tendencies to lose themselves in play.

Inform children of the center theme and suggest how the props might be used.

♦ "We have a new center in the classroom: a Shoe Store. You will find lots of shoes to try on and mirrors to use. You will need to decide who will sell shoes and who will buy shoes. Here are some things to use when you try on shoes." (Show the foot measurement device, foot rest, and sales slips.) "The salesperson can measure feet, write an order, and use the telephone, computer, and the cash register. The customer can pay for shoes with money, a check, or a credit card; order shoes from a catalog; and call the Shoe Store. There is a chart for everyone's foot measurement, too. Look for your name and show us the size of your foot or shoe."

♦ "We will begin a Veterinarian Office in one of our Dramatic Play Areas. The office has cages and beds for the animals, an examination area, and a place to groom pets. One or two children at a time can be veterinarians; other children can be their assistants or people bringing their pets to the office. Here are some of the things you will find to use in the center: charts for examining the animals; files to keep records; appointment cards; paper for writing prescriptions; pet magazines to read while you wait for a doctor; and money, checks, or credit cards to use for paying the bill. Make a Pet Bird in the center if you like."

After setting up play centers and introducing materials, the teacher's role is again that of spectator and advisor. Visiting the centers and gently nudging children toward the literacy materials is all that is necessary. Too much directed play and too much teacher involvement in play settings unnecessarily limits children's inclination to discover and explore on their own and find their own uses and purposes for literacy props. Whereas literacy modeling is effective in many areas of the classroom, such as the Library, Book-Making Center, and Cooking Area, too much adult intervention in Dramatic Play Centers is distracting and should be avoided.

In particular, the adult must take care not to become the center of attention, the "writer" in the center and the "leader" of play. Children often look to an adult presence for direction and leadership. But the proper role models in a dramatic play setting should be the children themselves. Those children who choose to use the literacy materials model literacy behaviors for their peers, whether they "write" prescriptions, take orders on a note pad, pay by check or credit card, make a grocery list, "read" a magazine in the Waiting Room, or consult a repair manual. Children who are not using literacy props in these ways find a need to interact with the props as they interact with their peers—that is, their interactions in the center and their communications with peers who are more literacy involved encourage them to make use of literacy props themselves.

Dramatic Play is the one area in the classroom where teachers do not offer to record children's words unless this is part of the center activity. Children should use the literacy materials as independently as possible, filling out forms, orders, and checks in their own "writing." Do attend to "how do you spell" questions, because here the child is initiating the writing. Ask "What does it say?" questions to give children an opportunity to interpret their own invented writing and begin to understand the function of print. Teachers' interventions in Dramatic Play Centers take the form of encouragement and suggestions to child players:

♦ "I like the shoes you chose. Are you paying with cash or a check?"

♦ "Where are you traveling? Did you buy a ticket? Did you get a map to follow?"

♦ "Doctor, what's wrong with your patient? Will you be writing a prescription for some medicine?"

♦ "You are buying some pretty flowers. Are they a present for someone? Maybe you should fill out a gift card."

Following these brief interactions, the teacher moves away, perhaps observing how the suggestions are taken, but making sure the adult presence does not interrupt the play. Observations of Dramatic Play Centers also serve an assessment purpose, giving teachers an opportunity to evaluate literacy props and their use in the center. What is being used and how? How much "reading and writing" is occurring and what is encouraging these actions? This will be a great help in planning ideas for making upcoming centers even more literacy-rich.

Make the Home and Family Center a permanent classroom center. Add at least two or three new centers every two or three weeks. Try staggering centers, setting up one for three weeks and one for two. This lets you introduce a new center weekly. Centers may or may not be related in some way. If the centers are related, encourage play between centers. Children in the Home and Family Center can shop at the Grocery Store Center, or children in the Archaeology Center can take their "finds" to the Museum Center.

When preparing and setting up Dramatic Play Centers, start slowly and build comprehensive collections. Keep in close communication with parents, informing them of each upcoming center and related classroom needs. Use parents' jobs as a reference and as a resource, and incorporate any photographs parents may contribute. These will be most significant in building play centers that have meaning for children.

In summary, pick and choose the Interest and Dramatic Play Centers that best meet the needs of the classroom and the available materials. Use this resource as a guide to working with the school community and the parent population, and, especially, as the inspiration for centers and activities relating to the children in meaningful and recognized ways. Add literacy props and materials to the classroom at every opportunity, and then stand back and "let it happen." Linking literacy inclusions with teacher support, encouragement, suggestions, and modeling is sure to yield a classroom full of children who accept print as a meaningful form of communication. Children's familiarity with print as it touches every part of their play will help them understand its value and appreciate their need to know it. A classroom bursting with the many forms and tools of literacy is sure to spark the interest of every child in some way. It is the challenge of every teacher to recognize this spark and respond to it encouraging, accepting ways.

Try thinking of the classroom as one big recipe. Like making a cake, if the ingredients are right, the cake will turn out fine. If not, all the extra mixing and stirring in the world will not help. In fact, it may even hurt. Add literacy props and activities in the same way. "Sprinkle" them into the classroom, stir them around a little, and just "let it bake." The result will be a batch of motivated, enthusiastic learners and future lifelong readers!

Appendices

Appendix 1

Other books to use for title, word, and illustration changes (change the word in parentheses):

- *(Daddy) Makes the Best (Spaghetti)*—Anna Grossnickle Hines
- *If You Give a (Mouse) a (Cookie)*—Laura Joffe Numeroff
- *Make Way for (Ducklings)*—Robert McCloskey
- *(Mary) Wore Her (Red) Dress and (Henry) Wore His (Green) Sneakers*—Merle Peek
- *(Red) Is Best*—Kathy Stinson
- *Silly (Sally)*—Audrey Wood
- *Wake Up Mr. (B)*—Penny Dale
- *Why (Worms)?*—Gillian Davies
- *(Everything) Grows*—Bruce McMillan
- *Guess Whose (Shadow)?*—Stephen Swinburne
- *(Brown Bear), (Brown Bear), What Do You (See)?*—Bill Martin, Jr.
- *(Panda Bear), (Panda Bear), What Do You (See)?*—Bill Martin, Jr.

Appendix 2

Parent Letter Sample for Cooking Activities

Dear Parents,

Cooking is an activity that provides children with valuable experiences in many different areas of the preschool curriculum:

- language skills: "reading" and following the recipe; communicating with others
- following directions: step-by-step procedures
- fine-motor coordination: pouring, stirring, cutting, slicing
- math: counting, measuring, dividing, separating
- science: observing changes and reactions in mixtures

We are putting together a collection of cooking and kitchen items for our classroom cooking activities. Perhaps you can help by providing some of the items listed below. They need not be brand new, just in good working order. Duplicates are also fine: we often have more than one "cook" stirring, measuring, and scooping.

Thank you for your help.

Items needed:

- cookie sheets
- baking pans: cake, pie, bread, muffin, and cupcake
- measuring sets: spoons, cups
- spoons, ladles, whisks, spatulas
- graters
- knives: plastic or butter knives
- rolling pins
- cutting boards
- mixing bowls: all sizes
- potholders
- timers: all kinds
- blenders
- electric mixers

Appendix 3

Sample for a Traveling Teddy Journal Entry

Date: _____

Hi! My name is Traveling Teddy and I belong to all the children in (teacher's name) classroom or at (school name).

I am called Traveling Teddy because I love to travel. My home is in the classroom, where children come to play each day. On Friday, I visit someone's home, but I always return to school on Monday.

My first visit was to (teacher's name) house. (Include some personal tidbits about your weekend. Children will enjoy hearing a little about your life outside of the classroom.)

Example: I watched (teacher's name) chop vegetables for soup. We also made apple pie. It was so delicious!

(Teacher's name) cat really like me. He sniffed my ears. We played together and he fell asleep right on my tummy.

I played with (teacher's name) children, (name) and (name). We built a playground out of blocks and read my book.

I went to a neighbor's birthday party with (teacher's name) daughter, (name). I ate a lot of cake and sat with another Teddy Bear. I had great fun!

(Teacher's name) brushed my fur and got me ready to go back to school.

Who will I visit next? I can't wait to find out and write about it here in my journal.

Appendix 4

Traveling Teddy's Introduction Letter

Hi! My name is Traveling Teddy.

I came to your house for the weekend. I can take part in any of your family activities. There are only a few things I can't do. I can't take a bath with you, so please don't get me wet. I like to sleep on a soft chair in your bedroom or on the rug beside your bed, but not in bed with you. Mostly I need lots of love and care.

I brought my blanket, brush, and book along in my backpack. Don't forget to read my journal to see what I've been up to. And please remember to take me and my backpack back to school with you on Monday. Everyone will be waiting to hear about our fun. It's so nice to visit with you.

Love,
Traveling Teddy

Appendix 5

Stories That Work Well with Tokens

Buttons:
   "A Lost Button" from *Frog and Toad Are Friends*—
      Arnold Lobel
   Buster Loves Buttons—Fran Manushkin
   Button Box—Margaretta S. Reid
   Corduroy—Don Freeman

Seeds:
   Alison's Zinnia—Anita Lobel
   The Carrot Seed—Ruth Krauss
   Rosey's Garden—Satomi Ichikawa
   Vegetable Garden—Douglas Florian

Pebbles:
   Rock Finds a Friend—Randall Wiethorn
   Some Frogs Have Their Own Rocks—Robert Wiest
   Stone Soup—retold by a variety of authors
   Sylvester and the Magic Pebble—William Stieg

A Sprinkle of Sand:
   Big Bird Can Share—Dina Anastasio
   Moe the Dog in Tropical Paradise—Diane Stanley
   The Quicksand Book—Tomie dePaola

Peanuts:
   Curious George Goes to the Circus—H. A. Rey
   *Make Me a Peanut Butter Sandwich and a Glass of
      Milk*—Ken Robbins
   Peanut Butter Rhino—Vincent Andriani

Acorns:
   A Tree Is Nice—Janice May Udry
   Nuts to You!—Lois Ehlert
   Squirrels—Brian Wildsmith

Paintbrushes:
   The Art Lesson—Tomie dePaola
   Mouse Paint—Ellen Stoll Walsh
   Why Worms?—Gillian Davis

Beans:
   Jack and the Beanstalk—numerous versions
   Oh Beans!—Ellen Weiss
   Vegetable Garden—Douglas Florian
   The Lima Bean Monster—Dan Yaccarino

Coins/Pennies:
   A Pickle for a Nickel—Lilian Moore
   Joey on His Own—Eleanor Schick
   26 Letters and 99 Cents—Tana Hoban
   Bunny Money—Rosemary Wells

A Sprinkle of Powder:
   Curious George—H.A. Rey
   Jolly Snow—Jane Hissey
   Magic Growing Powder—Janet Quin-Harkin

Plastic Eggs:
   Two Eggs, Please—Sarah Weeks
   The Egg—M. P. Robertson

Paper Shapes:
   Yoko's Paper Cranes—Rosemary Wells
   Max's Starry Night—Ken Wilson-Max

Appendix 6

More Choral Participation Books

A Dark, Dark Tale—Ruth Brown
Barn Dance—Bill Martin, Jr.
Caps for Sale—Esphyr Slobodkina
Goldilocks and the Three Bears—Lucy Kincaid
Have You Seen My Car?—Eric Carle
Have You Seen My Duckling?—Nancy Tafuri
I Know an Old Lady—Glen Rounds
Jesse Bear, What Will You Wear?—Nancy White Carlstrom
Roll Over!—Merle Peek
The Dress I'll Wear to the Party—Shirley Neitzel
The Hokey Pokey—Larry La Prise, Charles P. Macak,
   and Tafft Baker
This Old Man—Carol Jones
Three Little Pigs—James Marshall
We're Going on a Bear Hunt—Michael Rosen

Appendix 7

More Sound Effect Books

Achoo! Bang! Crash! The Noisy Alphabet—Ross MacDonald
Animal Lingo—Pam Conrad
Chicka Chicka Boom Boom—Bill Martin, Jr.
Crash! Bang! Boom!—Peter Spier
Fiddle-I-Fee—Melissa Sweet
Inside a Barn in the Country—Alyssa Smith Capucilli
Jonathan Cleaned Up, Then He Heard a Sound—Robert
   Munsch
Knock! Knock!—Jackie Carter
Mortimer—Robert Munsch
Once: A Lullaby—Anita Lobel
SHHHH!—Suzy Kline

Sounds My Feet Make—Arlene Blanchard
Thump, Thump, Rat-a-Tat-Tat—Gene Baker
Tikki Tikki Tembo—Arlene Mosel
Yuck!—Mick Manning

Appendix 8
More Add-on Story Ideas

All I Am—Ellen Roe
Goodnight Moon—Margaret Wise Brown
Here We Go 'Round the Mulberry Bush—Will
    Hillenbrand
If You're Happy and You Know It—Jane Cabrera
Old MacDonald—Amy Schwartz
Over in the Meadow—David Carter
Quick as a Cricket—Audrey Wood
Rooster's Off to See the World—Eric Carle
Row, Row, Row Your Boat—Iza Trapani
Shake My Sillies Out—Davia Allender
Spider on the Floor—True Kelley
The Very Busy Spider—Eric Carle
The Very Hungry Caterpillar—Eric Carle
This Is the Way—Anne Dalton
Time to . . .—Bruce McMillan
We Are Alike . . . We Are Different—Cheltenham
    Elementary School

Appendix 9
Sample Letters to Guest Readers (To Friends)

Dear Friend,

Being read to is one of the pleasures of childhood. In our classroom, we read every day.

It is almost as fun to read a story to children as it is for them to listen to one! We are looking for Guest Readers to visit our classroom and read us a book. We will have a short and easy-to-read book ready for our Guest Reader, and we will set aside a few minutes for him or her to look it over before reading. The visit will take no longer than 30 minutes.

The goal is to add some variety to our daily Story Times and to help children realize that everyone reads. So often, young children associate books solely with school and teachers. What a wonderful experience it will be for them to see a variety of people whom they associate with other jobs in a new role—Reader! We think it will be as rewarding for you as it will be for us.

If you would like to be one of our Guest Readers, please get in touch with us by phone to set up a time. We hope to hear from you.

Your friends at _____

Sample Letters to Guest Readers (To Parents)

Dear Parent,

Being read to is one of the pleasures of childhood. In our classroom, we read every day.

It is almost as fun to read to children as it is for them to listen! We are looking for Guest Readers to visit our classroom and read us a book. We will have a short and easy-to-read book ready for our Guest Reader, and we will set aside a few minutes for him or her to look it over before reading. You are also welcome to read one of your child's favorite books from home. The visit will take no longer than 30 minutes.

The goal is to add some variety to our daily Story Times and to help children realize that everyone reads. So often, young children associate books solely with school and teachers. What a wonderful experience it will be for them to have a variety of parents, grandparents, or older brothers and sisters read to them in the classroom! What's more, your child will take much pleasure in sharing his or her family with us in this way. We think it will be as rewarding for you as it will be for us.

If you would like to be one of our Guest Readers, please let us know so we can set up a time for you to visit. We hope to hear from you soon.

Your friends at _____

Appendix 10
Book Suggestions for Guest Readers

Bus Driver:
    Gus the Bus—Olga Cossi
    School Bus—Donald Crews
    Wheels on the Bus—illustrated by Sylvie Kantorovitz
        Wickstrom
    The Little School Bus—Carol Roth
    The Bus for Us—Suzanne Bloom
    The Seals on the Bus—Lenny Hort
Musician:
    Clap Your Hands—Lorinda Bryan Cauley
    I See a Song—Eric Carle
    Music, Music for Everyone—Vera B. Williams
    Daddy Played Music for the Cows—Maryann Weidt
    Little Lil and the Swing-Singing Sax—Libba Moore
        Gray
    Sweet Music in Harlem—Debbie A. Taylor
Dentist:
    Dr. DeSoto—William Stieg
    Loose Tooth—Steven Kroll
    My Tooth Is About to Fall Out—Grace Maccarone
    Arthur's Tooth—Marc Brown
    Albert's Impossible Toothache—Barbara Williams
    Have You Ever Seen a Moose Brushing His Teeth?—
        Jamie McClaine

Farmer:
  Inside a Barn in the Country—Alyssa Smith Capucilli
  Let's Go to the Farm—Pat Whitehead
  The Tiny Seed—Eric Carle
  Arthur's Tractor: A Fairy Tale with Mechanical Parts—
    Pippa Goodhart
  A Packet of Seeds—Debra Hopkinson
  A Farm of Her Own—Natalie Kinsey-Warnock

Police Officer:
  Emergency—Gail Gibbons
  I Read Signs—Tana Hoban
  Red Light Green Light—Margaret Wise Brown
  Keeping You Safe: A Book About Police Officers—Ann
    Owen and Eric Thomas
  Officer Buckle and Gloria—Peggy Rathmann
  Preschool to the Rescue—Judy Sierra

Weather Forecaster:
  Cloudy with a Chance of Meatballs—Judi Barrett
  One Sun—Bruce McMillan
  The Snowy Day—Ezra Jack Keats
  Elmer's Weather—David McKee
  *The Story of Punxsutawney Phil, "The Fearless
    Forecaster"*—Julia Spencer Moutran
  Raindrop, Plop!—Wendy Cheyette Lewison

Librarian:
  Franklin's Magical Reading World—Paulette Bourgeois
  I Can Read with My Eyes Shut—Dr. Seuss
  I Took My Frog to the Library—Eric A. Kimmel
  *My Librarian Is a Camel: How Books Are Brought to
    Children Around the World*—Margriet Ruurs
  Please Bury Me in the Library—J. Patrick Lewis and
    Kyle M. Stone
  Library Lil—Suzanne Williams

Waitress:
  Pass the Fritters, Critters—Cheryl Chapman
  Pizza Party—Grace Maccarone
  Wednesday Is Spaghetti Day—Maryann Cocca-Leffler
  Fast Food! Gulp! Gulp!—Bernard Waber
  Pancakes, Pancakes!—Eric Carle
  The Greatest Potatoes—Penelope Stowell

Mail Carrier:
  A Letter to Amy—Ezra Jack Keats
  The Jolly Postman—Janet and Allan Ahlberg
  One Monster After Another—Mercer Mayer
  Mailing May—Michael O. Tunnell
  Hail to Mail—Samuel Marshak
  Dear Mr. Blueberry—Simon James

Construction Worker:
  Building the New School—Ann Martin
  The Clever Carpenter—R. W. Alley
  Hammers, Nails, Planks and Paint—Thomas Campbell
    Jackson
  Construction Countdown—K. C. Olson
  Fix-It—David McPhail
  B Is for Bulldozer: A Construction ABC—June Sobel

Baker:
  The Gingerbread Man—Lucy Kincaid
  If You Give a Moose a Muffin—Laura Joffe Numeroff
  In the Night Kitchen—Maurice Sendak
  Ella Takes the Cake—Carmela and Steven D'Amico
  Jake Baked the Cake—B. G. Hennessy
  No More Cookies!—Paeony Lewis

Firefighter:
  The Fire Cat—Esther Averill
  Firefighters—Robert Maas
  I Want to be a Firefighter—Edith Kunhardt
  New York's Bravest—Mary Pope Osborne
  Firefighters to the Rescue—Kersten Hamilton
  Even Firefighters Hug Their Moms—Christine Kole
    MacLean

Appendix 11
Sample Parent Letter Requesting Stories Taped by Parents

Dear Parents,

We are always looking for new ways to bring stories and books into our classroom.

Stories recorded on tape are particularly helpful to us. We use taped stories in a number of ways in the classroom; they make especially good independent "reading" activities for children.

We make use of pre-recorded books-on-tape that are purchased or borrowed from the library. We also tape our own stories, either teacher-read or made with children's own sound effects.

We would like to extend our taped story collection by adding stories recorded by parents. Children will delight in hearing their own parents' voices reading some of their favorite books and in sharing their parents in this way with friends.

We are looking for family volunteers (mothers, fathers, siblings, and grandparents) to record a story for us. We will choose and provide the book, or you are welcome to record a story of your own choice. We will provide a blank tape and a short list of guidelines to use when recording. If you do not have a tape recorder, we will lend you ours overnight.

We hope you would like to be one of our Readers. If you are willing, please return the bottom portion of this letter. Thank You.

— — — — — — — — — — — — — — —

Yes, I would enjoy reading a story for my child and his or her classmates.

_____ Please choose a book for me to record.
_____ I have chosen a book.

Title of book chosen:

_____

Parent's name:

_____

Appendix 12

Guidelines for Recording a Story

1. Choose a quiet room and time of the day.
2. Record the story as you read it to your child. Or, if you prefer, record it out of your child's presence— he or she will enjoy hearing it for the first time in the classroom.
3. Test the recorder and your voice level first by taping a few words. Rewind and listen to what you have recorded. If it sounds good, rewind and begin again. If not, adjust your voice level, record, and listen again.
4. State your name first, whose mother, father, or relative you are, and then the title and author of the book. Example: "This is _____ _____'s _____. I am reading _____ by _____."
5. Read the story slowly and clearly, turning pages quietly as you go.
6. Have fun reading. Add expression to the story, just as you would if you were reading the book to your own child.
7. When you have finished, listen to the whole story. Imagine your child and her or his classmates enjoying your story over and over again. Smile.

Thank you for a new story. If you would like to do another one, please let me know.

Appendix 13

More "Rewrite a Favorite Story Book" Ideas

- *Pretend You're a Cat* by Jean Marzollo becomes "Pretend You're a Dog (or Fish or other animal)"
- *Harold and the Purple Crayon* by Crockett Johnson becomes "Harold and the Blue Marker" or "Harold and the Red Pencil"
- *The Wheels on the Bus* by Maryann Kovalski becomes "The Wings on the Plane" or "The Pedals on the Bike"
- *Jump, Frog, Jump!* By Robert Kalan becomes "Swim, Fish, Swim!" or "Fly, Bird, Fly"
- *Draw Me a Star* by Eric Carle becomes "Draw Me a Moon" or "Draw Me a Sun"
- *A Walk in the Rain* by Ursel Scheffler becomes "A Walk in the Snow"
- *Goodnight Moon* by Margaret Wise Brown becomes "Good Morning Sun"
- *Snapshots from the Wedding* by Gary Soto becomes "Snapshots from the Picnic" or "Snapshots from the Vacation (or other family event)"
- *Little Blue and Little Yellow* by Leo Lionni becomes "Little Red and Little Yellow," "Little Red and Little White (or two other colors to mix and create a new color)"
- *All You Need for a Beach* by Alice Schertle becomes "All You Need for a Farm" or "All You Need for an Amusement Park (a Restaurant, a School, or any place)"

Appendix 14

More Rhymes and Poems

Around and About—Marchette Chute
A Zooful of Animals—William Cole
Cat Poems—Myra Cohn Livingston
Color—Christine Rosetti
Custard and Company—Ogden Nash
Dear Children of the Earth: A Letter from Home— Schim Schimmel
Dogs, Dragons, Dreams—Karla Kuskin
Dragons, Dragons—Eric Carle
Father Fox's Pennyrhymes—Clyde Watson
Fold Me a Poem—Kristine O'Connell George
Hailstones and Halibut Bones—Mary O'Neil
Have You Seen Trees?—Joanne Uppenheim
I'm Like Me—Siv Widerberg
In a Spring Garden—Richard Lewis
Out and About—Shirley Hughes
Pieces: A Year in Poems & Quilts—Anna Grossnickle Hines
Pudding is Nice—Dorothy Kunhardt
Rainy Day: Stories and Poems—Caroline Feller Bauer
Rainy Rainy Saturday—Jack Prelutsky
Read Aloud Rhymes for the Very Young—Jack Prelutsky
Ring of Earth—Jane Yolen
Ring Out, Wild Bells—Lee Bennett Hopkins
Sing to the Sun—Ashley Bryan
Snowy Day—Caroline Feller Bauer
Someone I Like: Poems About People—Judith Nicholls
The Sun in Me: Poems About the Planet—Judith Nicholls and Beth Krommes
Tickle Toe Rhymes—Joan Knight
Turtle in July—Marilyn Singer
Tyrannosaurus Rex Was a Beast—Jack Prelutsky
Under Your Feet—Joanne Ryder
Voices on the Wind—selected by David Booth
Welcome and Other Poems—Geoffrey Summerfield
Where the Sidewalk Ends—Shel Silverstein

Appendix 15

Books for All Areas of the Classroom

Art Area: Books about color, artists, drawing, painting, sewing, making things:

A Child's Book of Art—Lucy Micklethwait
Anno's Alphabet—Mitsumas Anno
Art Dog—Thacher Hurd
The Art Lesson—Tomi dePaolo
Black Is Beautiful—Ann McGovern
Black on White and White on Black—Tana Hoban
Brown Bear, Brown Bear, What Do You See?—Bill Martin, Jr.
Cleversticks—Bernard Ashley
Drawing with Letters and Numbers—Syd Hoff
Draw Me a Star—Eric Carle

Getting to Know the World's Greatest Artists series—
   Mike Venezia (DaVinci, Monet, Picasso, Rembrandt,
   Van Gogh)
Glorious ABC—Eden Cooper
I Spy: An Alphabet in Art—Lucy Micklethwait
Little Blue and Little Yellow—Leo Lionni
Look What I Did with a Leaf—Morteza E. Sohl
Make a World—Ed Emberley
Mouse Paint—Ellen Stoll Walsh
Picasso and Minou—P. I. Maltbie
Purple, Green, and Yellow—Robert Munsch
Red, Blue, Yellow Shoe—Tana Hoban
Seen Art?—Jon Scieszka
Who Said Red?—Mary Serfozo
Why Worms?—Gillian Davies
The Wonderful Pigs of Jillian Jiggs—Phoebe Gilman
You Can't Take a Balloon into the Metropolitan Museum—
   Jacqueline Preiss Weitzman

Beads, Peg Boards, Mosaic Tiles Area: Books about
dress-up, jewelry, maps, counting, design, color:

Angelina and the Princess—Katherine Holabird
At the Mall—Christine Loomis
Babar Loses His Crown—Laurent DeBrunhoff
Bears in Paris—Niki Yektai
Bing: Get Dressed—Ted Dewan
The Birthday Thing—SuAnn Kiser and Kevin Kiser
The Bora-Bora Dress—Carole Lexa Schaefer
A Cache of Jewels and Other Collective Nouns—Ruth Heller
Cinderella's Dress—Nancy Willard
The Color Box—Dayle Ann Dodds
Dandelion—Don Freeman
The Dress I Wore to the Party—Shirley Neitzel
Flower Girl—Kathy Furgang
Handtalk Birthday—Remy Charlip
Happy Birthday Moe Dog—Nicholas Heller
Is It Red? Is It Yellow? Is It Blue?—Tana Hoban
Jewels for Josephine—Amye Rosenberg
Maebelle's Suitcase—Tricia Tusa
The Paper Bag Princess—Robert Munsch
The Quilt Story—Tomi dePaola

Block and Building Area: Books about construction,
buildings, travel, houses, castles. Add books about
animals, vehicles, and various people if you make these
toys available with blocks:

ABC USA—Martin Jarrie
A House Is a House for Me—Mary Ann Hoberman
And So They Build—Bert Kitchen
Architects Make Zigzags—Roxie Munro
As the Crow Flies: A First Book of Maps—Gail Hartman
Big Rigs—Hope Irvin Marston
Building the New School—Ann Martin
The Clever Carpenter—R. W. Alley
Dig, Drill, Dump, Fill—Tana Hoban
Earth Movers—Tony Potter
Flying—Donald Crews

Hard Hat Area—Susan L. Roth
How Many Trucks Can a Tow Truck Tow?—Charlotte
   Pomerantz
The Little House—Virginia Lee Burton
Mike Mulligan and His Steam Shovel—Virginia Lee
   Burton
Raise the Roof!—Anastasia Suen
The Toolbox—Anne and Harlow Rockwell
Truck—Donald Crews
A Truck Goes Rattley-Bumpa—Jonathan London
Underground Train—Mary Quattlebaum

Cooking Area: Books with food, cooking, party, and
picnic themes:

A Was Once an Apple Pie—Edward Lear
Blueberries for Sal—Robert McCloskey
Bread, Bread, Bread—Ann Morris
Dim Sum for Everyone!—Grace Lin
Eating the Alphabet—Lois Ehlert
Food for Thought—Joost Elffers and Saxton Freymann
How My Parents Learned to Eat—Ina R. Friedman
Hot Fudge—James Howe
In the Night Kitchen—Maurice Sendak
Pancakes, Pancakes!—Eric Carle
Pizza Party—Grace Maccarone
The Princess and the Pizza—Mary Jane and Herm Auch
Showdown at the Food Pyramid—Rex Barron
Stone Soup—Marilyn Sapienza
The Story of Noodles—Ying Chang Compestine
The Teddy Bears' Picnic—Jimmy Kennedy
Thunder Cake—Patricia Polacco
Today Is Monday—Eric Carle
Too Many Tamales—Gary Soto
What Food Is This?—Rosemarie Hausherr

Dramatic Play Area (Home and Family): Home, family,
and occupation books:

Arthur's First Sleepover—Marc Brown
The Doorbell Rings—Pat Hutchins
Five Minutes Peace—Jill Murphy
Goodnight Moon—Margaret Wise Brown
Home to Me, Home to You—Jennifer A. Ericsson
A House Is a House for Me—Mary Ann Hoberman
I Am a Chef—Dick Swayne
I Love My Family—Wade Hudson
In a People House—Theo LeSeig
More More More Said the Baby—Vera B. Williams
Moving—Fred Rogers
My Dad Is Awesome—Nick Butterworth
My Mom Is Excellent—Nick Butterworth
A Picnic in October—Eve Bunting
Sounds of Home—Bill Martin, Jr.
Tar Beach—Faith Ringgold
Time To—Bruce McMillan
To Market, To Market—Anne Miranda
What Does My Teddy Bear Do All Day?—Bruno Hächler
William's Doll—Charlotte Zolotow

Math Area: Books about numbers, counting, money, comparison. Cooking and recipe books also have a place in the math area. If a cooking center is not a regular part of the classroom, incorporate recipe books in the math area:

100 Days of School—Trudy Harris
Best Counting Book (1 to 100)—Amye Rosenberg
Count and See—Tana Hoban
A Dozen Dogs: A Read-and-Count Story—Harriet Ziefert
Fish Eyes: A Book You Can Count On—Lois Ehlert
Five Little Monkeys Jumping on the Bed—Eileen Christelow
How Much Is a Million?—David M. Schwartz
Math Curse—Jon Scieszka
One Cow Moo Moo—David Bennett
One Crow: A Counting Rhyme—Jim Aylesworth
One Gorilla—Atsuko Morozumi
One Hungry Monster—Susan Heyboer O'Keefe
1,2,3's—Brian Wildsmith
The Right Number of Elephants—Jeff Sheppard
Rooster's Off to See the World—Eric Carle
Ten Black Dots—Donald Crews
This Old Man—Carol Jones
What Comes in 2's, 3's, and 4's?—Suzanne Aker
Who's Counting?—Nancy Tafori

Music Area: Books featuring music, dance, parades, bands, instruments, movement, musicians:

The Alphabet Symphony—Bruce McMillan
Berlioz the Bear—Jan Brett
Clap Hands—Helen Oxenbury
Clap Your Hands—Lorinda Bryan Cauley
Color Dance—Ann Jones
Crash! Bang! Boom!—Peter Spier
Dance, Tanya—Patricia Lee Gauch
Dancing Boy—Ronald Himler
I See a Song—Eric Carle
Music, Music for Everyone—Vera B. Williams
Nicholas Cricket—Joyce Maxner
Old MacDonald—Amy Schwartz
Once: A Lullaby—Anita Lobel
Parade—Donald Crews
Ragtime Tumpie—Alan Schroeder
Row, Row, Row Your Boat—Iza Trapani
Rum Pum Pum—Maggie Duff
Shake My Sillies Out—illustrated by David Allender
She'll Be Comin' Round the Mountain—Philemon Sturge
Spider on the Floor—True Kelley

Science Area: Books about all phases of nature, growth, weather, the solar system, experiments, and discovery:

A B C E D A R: An Alphabet of Trees—George Ella Lyon
All About Magnifying Glasses—Melvin Berger
All About Seeds—Melvin Berger
Bugs—Nancy Winslow Parker and Joan Richards Wright
The Carrot Seed—Ruth Krauss
Flower Alphabet Book—Jerry Pallotta
Fresh Fall Leaves—Betsy Franco

Icky Bug Alphabet—Jerry Pallotta
"Magic School Bus" series—Joanna Cole, Bruce Degen
Nicky the Nature Detective—Lena Anderson
Red Leaf, Yellow Leaf—Lois Ehlert
Rocks in His Head—Carol Otis Hurst
Science Verse—Jon Scieszka,
Spiders—Gail Gibbons
The Tiny Seed—Ruth Krauss
Under the Sea from A to Z—Ann Doubilet
What's Inside Insects?—Angela Royston
The Yucky Reptile Alphabet Book—Jerry Pallotta

Water/Sand Table or Sensory Area: Books about construction, water, the beach, seasons, and the weather. Add sensory-themed books to various materials in the table:

A Beach Day—Douglas Florian
A Fish Out of Water—Helen Palmer
Building the New School—Ann Martin
Come Away from the Water, Shirley—John Birningham
A Cool Drop of Water—Lynne Cherry
Dig, Drill, Dump, Fill—Tana Hoban
Earth Movers—Tony Potter
Little Beaver and the Echo—Amy MacDonald
The Marvelous Mud Washing Machine—Patty Wolcott
Mud—Wendy Cheyette Lewison
Muddigush—Kimberly Knutson
Mud Puddle—Robert Munsch
Pepper's Muddy Day—Michael Sullivan
Ruth's Bake Shop—Kate Spohn
This Year's Garden—Cynthia Rylant
Three Days on the River in a Canoe—Vera B. Williams
Tunnels—Gail Gibbons
Yellow Submarine/The Beatles—story adapted by Charlie Gardner

Outside Play Areas: Don't forget outdoor play areas when distributing books throughout the environment. Use baskets, bins, and bags for outdoor books and put out just three or four books at a time. A blanket or other sitting area where children can go to look at the books when they are not climbing and running is helpful. Remember, books placed outdoors may become more worn:

ABC of Cars and Trucks—Anne Alexander
ABC's of Ecology—Isaac Asimov
The Dandelion Wish—Sandra Ann Horn
A Garden Alphabet—Isabel Wilner
All Butterflies—Marcia Brown
Andy and the Tire—Craig Lov
A Tree Can Be—Judy Nayer
A Tree is Nice—Janice May Udry
Have You Seen Trees?—Helen Oppenheim
Henry Bear's Park—David McPhail
How to Dig a Hole to the Other Side of the World—Faith McNulty
If You Find a Rock—Peggy Christian
Life in the Meadow—Eileen Curran
Play Ball, Amelia Bedelia—Peggy Parish

Playground Fun—Sharon Gordon
A Pocketful of Cricket—Rebecca Caudill
Push-Pull, Empty-Full—Tana Hoban
Roxaboxen—Alice McLerran
Tacky and the Winter Games—Helen Lester
Thomas' Snowsuit—Robert Munsch
Tree House Fun—Rose Greydanus

Appendix 16
More Book-making Ideas

Traditional Book: The usual format, wherein pages are bound together by some means on the left-hand side.

Shape Book: Try a variety of shapes following the traditional book format. Cut the cover and all the pages the same size and shape. Fasten together on the left side. Often, the shape can fit the topic—for example, a round Ball Book, a square House Book, a semicircular Turtle Book, or a fish-shaped Fish Book.

Tiny Book: A traditional book made with very small paper (3" x 5" or smaller). Children are fascinated by small things and enjoy creating these fit-in-your-pocket books.

Giant Book: A traditional book made with very large paper (12" x 18" or larger). This makes a fun book to share at circle time. Initiate a giant classroom book to which everyone may contribute.

Accordion Book: Fanfold paper to create a book that opens into one long piece of paper. Children enjoy using this format to make books showing objects or creatures that grow or continue in length, such as a Snake Book, Road Book, or Garden Book. (Fasteners are not required.)

Partner Book: The Plastic Bag Books described on page 83 offer a wonderful opportunity for teacher and child to make a book together. For a Partner Book, however, the paper cut to fit the bags will not be plain, but will have shapes, objects, people, or animals drawn on it. Your own drawings should occupy a small area of the paper, so that the child can draw and add to the picture. Assist the child in adding story words as needed. Alternatively, two children can work on a Partner Book, drawing and exchanging as they choose. Most other types of books adapt well to Partner Books.

Envelope Book: Prepare a traditional paper book, and glue an envelope on every other or every third page. Children can draw and/or print the story on the pages, then include a surprise drawing in the envelope. This format is well suited to a Guessing Game Book. Older children may be able to print the story on the pages themselves, saving the story illustrations for the envelopes. They then remove the drawing to look at it as they read each page. Try making a Counting Book this way. On a page illustrated with balls, write the words HOW MANY BALLS? Put the numeral answer in the envelope. A Color Game Book also works well. A page might contain a black-and-white illustration of the sun and the words WHAT COLOR IS THE SUN? The envelope holds the answer: a yellow sun picture with word YELLOW written across it.

Folded Paper Book: Similar in size to an Envelope Book or a Paper Bag Book, a Folded Paper Book works effectively for Guessing Game and Finish-the-Picture Books. In lieu of the paper bag or envelope "pages," simply fold the bottom or side of traditional pages over so that the answer or part of the picture is concealed. When preparing these books, cut paper about 3" larger, either by length or width, and fold over.

Small to Large Book: Make a book of any size using felt pages instead of paper. Place holes in the left side of each piece of felt and attach the pages together with yarn. Out of smaller scraps of felt, cut an assortment of shapes, objects, people, and animals. Children can use these to create pictures directly on the felt pages of the book, telling the story as they go. Record or write stories as children dictate them. Remove felt shapes when the story is finished and the book is ready to use again. To make a permanent book, glue the felt shapes directly on the felt pages.

Appendix 17
More Songs That Are Easy to Re-create

- *"Are You Sleeping"*: Change sleeping to any action word and substitute children's names for Brother John. For example, Are You Dancing?/Our Friend Steve or Are You Running?/Our Friend Jill. Keep the last part of the song as it is. Children may also enjoy adding movement to this song.
- *"Eensy Weensy Spider"*: Change the title words to Dotted Spotted Ladybug or Slinky Squirmy Worm.
- *"Farmer in the Dell"*: Change the title words to Mother/Father in the House, choosing different family members for each verse. Or, change the title words to Animals in the Zoo, choosing different animals each time, such as Tiger picks a monkey, monkey picks an elephant.
- *"Row, Row, Row Your Boat"*: Change the words in the title to Ride, Ride, Ride Your Bike (change the words in the second line to Quickly down the lane). Or, try Drive, Drive, Drive Your Car or Pull, Pull, Pull Your Wagon.
- *"If You're Happy and You Know It"*: Change the word *happy* to words describing a variety of emotions and feelings; vary the actions in the rest of the song to match the feeling: If You're Shy and You Know It, Hide Your Eyes or If You're Angry and You Know It, Stomp Your Feet.
- *"Wheels on the Bus"*: Change the first and last word to include all types of vehicles—for example, Wings on the Plane, Pedals on the Bike, Horn on the Truck.

Appendix 18

More "What Will Happen" Curiosities

- ♦ Float a dry sponge in a bowl of water.
- ♦ Put the end of a strip of cotton fabric in a bowl of water, letting six inches or so hang out of the bowl onto the tray.
- ♦ Display a jar of snow.
- ♦ Place a cup of wet sand on the tray. (The top of the sand will begin to dry.)
- ♦ Place one white carnation in plain water, one in red colored water, and one in blue colored water.
- ♦ Set two small green plants on a tray, one in a closed paper bag.

Appendix 19

Prop Collection Introductory Letter to Parents

Dear Parents,

We will be collecting a variety of items to use as props in the various interest areas of our classroom. We are all involved in the collection of these props. Some we will be making: others can be found around the house. Many props can be found at your workplaces. The items we will be looking for are often discarded, outdated, or available in large quantities. Every workplace will be of value to us because we will be re-creating many of these settings for pretend play in our classroom. We will be collecting all types of props, particularly those that involve any type of reading and writing that is required for the job.

Our purpose in collecting these items it to make our interest areas as lifelike and realistic as possible and to give children a variety of opportunities to use reading and writing materials during pretend play.

Children take pride in sharing things from their home and family. Contributing items from your workplace will give children this opportunity as well as allow them the experience of using materials from parents' workplaces in their own workplace . . . our classroom.

It will be helpful for us to know what kind of workplaces may be available to us as possible prop sources. Please take a minute and list your place of work and those of other family members who may be willing to contribute. We are most interested in the type of workplace rather than the name of your workplace. We would only want items you and your supervisor are comfortable donating. Thank you.

— — — — — — — — — — — — — — — — —

Please return

Name _____

Yes, I might be able to help with your prop collection.

Our family's workplaces include:

Name of Workplace

_____
_____
_____

Type of Business

_____
_____
_____

Appendix 20

Prop Collection Request Letter to Parents

Dear Parents,

We are collecting items to use as props for the various interest areas of our classroom. This week, we are looking for props for the areas listed below. We have suggested a variety of items we could use as props, but you may think of others relating to our themes. All contributions are welcome.

Look for a collection box in the following location of our classroom: _____.

Thank you for your help. You can be certain your donations will be a valuable contribution to our fun and learning in these areas.

Area 1: Props we can use:

_____
_____
_____

Area 2: Props we can use:

_____
_____
_____

Appendix 21

Early Childhood Literacy Web Sites For Teachers and Parents

Carol Hurst's Children's Literature Site
- ♦ Reviews of books for kids, ideas for integrating books in the classroom curriculum, and thematic book/activity collections
- ♦ http://www.carolhurst.com

ABC Teach
- ♦ Literature theme units, making books, writing activities, and more
- ♦ http://www.abcteach.com/contents/literaturetoc.htm

American Library Association Authors and Illustrators
- ♦ Sites for children's authors and illustrators, books listed by theme, and many fun and informative sites for kids
- ♦ http://www.ala.org/parentspage/greatsites/lit.html#c

Association for Library Service to Children (ALSC)
- ♦ Literary and Related Awards
- ♦ http://www.ala.org/ala/alsc/awardsscholarships/literaryawds/literaryrelated.htm

A to Z Teacher Stuff—Children's Literature Activities Index
- ♦ A variety of children's literature links
- ♦ http://atozteacherstuff.com/stuff/literatu.shtml

Caldecott Medal Home Page
- ♦ http://www.ala.org/ala/alsc/awardsscholarships/literaryawds/caldecottmedal/caldecottmedal.htm

Get Ready to Read
- ♦ Early Literacy information and ideas for teachers and parents, plus activities for children
- ♦ http://www.getreadytoread.org/

Literacy Center.Net (The Early Childhood Education Network)
- ♦ Monthly Play and Learn literacy lessons for children in 160 countries
- ♦ http://www.literacycenter.net/

Mr. Rogers' Neighborhood
- ♦ A variety of early learning activities
- ♦ http://pbskids.org/rogers/R_house/

Multicultural Children's Literature
- ♦ Lists sites for children's books with multicultural themes and positive role models
- ♦ http://www.lib.msu.edu/corby/education/multicultural.htm

National Education Association's Read Across America
- ♦ Ideas for celebrating Read Across America day, which is Dr. Seuss's birthday
- ♦ http://www.nea.org/readacross

PBS Between the Lions Get Wild About Reading
- ♦ Online stories with related games, songs, and print-outs
- ♦ http://pbskids.org/lions/

Early Childhood Literacy Web Sites For Kids

Books to read online:
- ♦ http://www.ipl.org/div/kidspace/storyhour/
- ♦ http://www.magickeys.com/books/
- ♦ http://wiredforbooks.org/kids.htm
- ♦ http://www.alfy.com/teachers/teach/thematic_units/Fairy_Tales/Fairy_1.asp
- ♦ http://www.starfall.com/
- ♦ http://www.sunshine.co.nz/nz/kia/books/index.html

Listen to stories online:
- ♦ http://www.storylineonline.net/
- ♦ http://www.kennedy-center.org/multimedia/storytimeonline/

Appendix 22
Classroom Arrangements

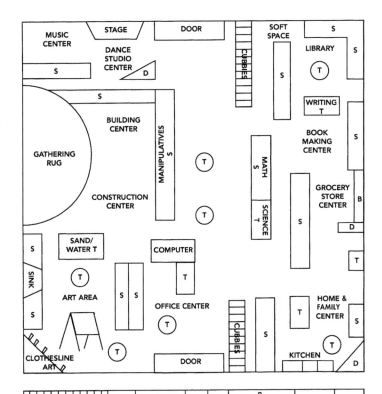

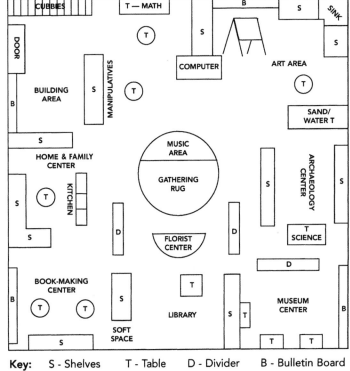

Key: S - Shelves   T - Table   D - Divider   B - Bulletin Board

(continued on next page)

Classroom Arrangements *(continued from page 203)*

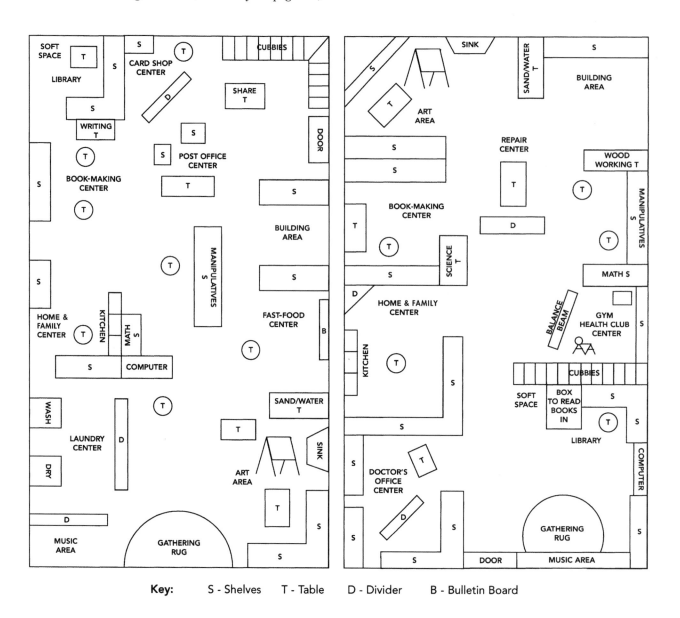

Key: S - Shelves   T - Table   D - Divider   B - Bulletin Board